INDIAN FISHING

EARLY METHODS ON THE NORTHWEST COAST

Hilary Stewart

Douglas & McIntyre
Vancouver / Toronto

University of Washington Press
Seattle

98 99 00 01 02 8 7 6 5 4

First paperbound edition, 1982

Published in Canada by Douglas & McIntyre Ltd.
1615 Venables Street, Vancouver, British Columbia
ISBN 0-88894-332-6

Canadian Cataloguing in Publication Data
Stewart, Hilary, 1924-
Indian Fishing

Includes bibliography and index.

1. Indians of North America — Northwest coast of North America — Fishing. 2. Indians of North America — Northwest coast of North America — Implements. I. Title
E98.F4S84 639'.2'009701 C77-002037-2

Published in the United States of America by
The University of Washington Press, Seattle, Washington
ISBN 0-295-95803-0

Library of Congress Cataloging in Publication Data
Stewart, Hilary.
Indian Fishing.

Bibliography: p.
1. Indians of North America — Northwest coast of North America — Fishing. I. Title.
E78.N78S763 639'.2'09795 77-950
ISBN 0-295-95803-0

Cover design by Jim Skipp
Text design by Nancy Legue and Mike Yazzolino
Typesetting by Vancouver Typesetting Co. Ltd.
Printed and bound in Canada by Best Gagné Book Manufacturers Inc.

This book was produced with Canada Council assistance to the author.

The motif accompanying chapter titles is the dog salmon design federally commissioned from Haida artist Bill Reid for the 1974 International Law of the Sea conference presentation portfolio. It is reproduced here with the kind permission of the artist.

Acknowledgments

It has taken a lot of energy and enthusiasm on the part of a great many people in libraries, archives, museums, universities and research institutes, and in Indian Band Councils and government departments, to make this book possible.

To the many people, unnamed here, who gave of their time and knowledge to enrich the pages of this book, my deepest thanks.

In particular, I would like to thank Paul Bragstad, Dr. Erna Gunther, Anthony Pomoroy, Patricia Severs, and Dr. Michael Kew of U.B.C. for the valuable contributions drawn from their own special studies; Dr. Wayne Suttles, Portland State University and Dr. Nancy Turner, B.C. Provincial Museum, for their information on nettle fibre and other plant uses in fishing technology; Don McQuarry at the Pacific Environment Institute, West Vancouver, for his patient co-operation in my fishing experiments; Dorothy Kennedy and Randy Bouchard of the B.C. Indian Language Project, Victoria, B.C. for permission to use material from their unpublished manuscript "Utilization of Fishes, Beach Foods and Marine Animals by the Tl'ŭhus Indian People of British Columbia," also Simon Birch for permission to quote from Sir Arthur Birch's letter.

For special research assistance I would like to thank Bill Holm, curator of the Thomas Burke Memorial Washington State Museum, Seattle; Ron Weber of the Field Museum of Natural History, Chicago; and U. Vincent Wilcox, curator of the Museum of the American Indian Research Annex. Their help and personal interest have been a great asset.

My thanks to Tricia and Nick Gessler at the Haida Museum, Masset, the Masset Band Council and Frieda Unsworth of Port Clements for various kinds of support during my research on the Queen Charlotte Islands. Thanks also to Augustus Wilson, who at the Yakoun River fish camp readily shared his knowledge, his boat and his salalberry jam with me; and to Robert Davidson, encamped at the river with his family, for letting me invade his privacy with my camera.

To Chief Charles Jones of the Pachenaht Band, Port Renfrew, special thanks for sharing with me the wealth of his knowledge and the richness of his wisdom.

I am very much indebted to Dr. Charles E. Borden, professor emeritus, Department of Anthropology and Sociology, U.B.C., for the time he has generously given to conscientiously checking this work and for suggested revisions. His kindness and continued friendship remain invaluable to me.

My warm thanks and appreciation go to Bill Ellis of Canadian Native Prints, Vancouver, B.C., whose close, personal interest and constant support on many levels during my work on this book have meant a great deal to me. In addition, the use of early engravings from his extensive collection of original antique prints has enhanced the illustrations for this work.

Museums in Canada and the United States have been the main source for most of the visual material in this book. I have greatly apppreciated the opportunity to go through the collections in order to photograph and make drawings of the many items of fishing gear, and for permission to reproduce them.

I extend my thanks to the Directors, Curators and staff of the following museums: The National Museum of Man, Ottawa, Ont., British Columbia Provincial Museum, Victoria, B.C.; Museum of Anthropology, University of British Columbia, Vancouver, B.C.; Centennial Museum, Vancouver, B.C.; Museum of Archaeology and Anthropology, Simon Fraser University, Burnaby, B.C.; Hastings Mill Museum, Vancouver, B.C.; Thomas Burke Memorial Washington State Museum, Seattle, Wash.; Washington State Historical Society, Tacoma, Wash.; Portland Art Museum, Portland, Ore.; National Museum of Natural History, Washington, D.C.; American Museum of Natural History, New York, N.Y.; Museum of the American Indian, New York, N.Y. and the Alaska State Museum, Juneau, Alas.

Over the years I have been greatly appreciative of the valuable help of the late Wilson Duff, formerly professor of Anthropology, University of British Columbia. Internationally renowned in the field of Northwest Coast art and other native studies, he gave significant help and guidance in many areas of this work.

For the interest and encouragement Wilson Duff gave to the various facets of my work, for the contributions of his time and knowledge, I can only remain deeply indebted.

DEDICATED TO THE MEMORY OF WILSON DUFF.

Foreword

For many years Northwest Coast cultures have exerted a magic appeal to layman and specialist alike. We have been swept off our feet by the potlatch, dazzled by dance and sculpture, lured into searching out the rules and meanings of mythology and art. Because there is such richness in accounts of these cultures, we have been easily distracted from examining workaday routines of daily living. Technology has been neglected. Hilary Stewart's work on fishing is a welcome contribution that will do much to achieve a more balanced understanding of Northwest Coast life.

Technology is fundamental to all cultures, although we sometimes forget this in the face of such natural abundance as characterizes the northwest. The coast was home for a variety of land and sea mammals, great flocks of waterfowl, and above all, teeming hordes of fish. These were the foundations upon which Northwest Coast cultures were built. But nowhere were riches of nature always abundant or entirely free for the taking. Some of them, on the contrary, were exceptionally hard to get at, as you will see. It was technology, plus the knowledge of its application, which provided the vital links — means for tapping the resources.

What we see revealed in this book is an incredibly varied and highly refined assemblage of tools, techniques and knowledge, the culmination of thousands of years of evolutionary development. These tools and techniques were not imported ready made, nor did they suddenly spring into being. They developed slowly and painstakingly as more effective variations were invented or introduced and applied to achieve more rewarding ends. The final result adds up to one of the most elaborate and productive fishing technologies achieved by any non-industrial society.

Out of the total range of technology, that is the arts and industries of material things, Hilary Stewart has chosen to tell us about *fishing*. Taken thus, her topic cuts across other categories conventionally used when dealing with material culture. It touches upon the work of men and women, upon things made of stone, wood, and the full range of materials available, but it doesn't attempt to cover such categories. Appropriately it sticks to fishing and the use of fish, themes at the heart of Northwest Coast cultures.

The artistry of Hilary Stewart's work is undeniable, but I take that as an added bonus. The meat and substance reside in its descriptive accuracy. Each of the illustrations of artifacts was made from an actual specimen and identifying information is provided. Illustrations of the working use of various devices could not, for the most part, be made from actual observation, and so they are necessarily reconstructions of how it was. But in this the author has used every clue available — descriptions by anthropologists, explorers and Indian informants, information from old photographs, and her own experience.

It is in this last respect that Hilary Stewart has her own unique strength. Artistry and descriptive accuracy are enhanced by her practical ability. Refusing to be mystified by deficient descriptions of long forgotten processes, or to be stymied by absence of data, she has set about experiencing the "hows" of doing, by teaching herself. I have before me on my desk a three-foot length of twisted cedar bark twine. It's smooth, shiny and strong — just the sort of thing to use for cod-line, just the sort of material made in great skeins by Northwest Coast women for just that purpose. Hilary

Stewart made it from red cedar bark, split, dried, softened, then twisted on her thigh, as she describes in the book — in order to "see how it was done." She has also made nettle fibre twine, kelp line, several styles of fish hooks and a host of other objects. All of them are workable and tested.

It is such concern for detail and process, above all else, which marks this book apart. Drawings of the application of hooks, nets and the like, are meant to show how the objects worked, and the drawings do more, in this respect, than any photograph or description could hope to do. One finds the working of such familiar things as halibut hooks and harpoons more clearly shown here than in any other available work, and we find here, for the first time, understandable illustrations of such nearly forgotten devices as the Salish reef nets, trawl nets, sturgeon harpoons and how they were actually used.

There are, of course, questions which the work does not answer. It is not meant to be a definitive study nor a book for scientists, although they will be informed by it. The Northwest Coast culture area extended from Yakutat Bay in Alaska to Northern California. This book looks at the cultures ranging from Alaska south to Washington. The distribution and frequency of use of artifacts from tribe to tribe is not discussed. Rather, the coastal area is treated as a whole. One must not conclude however that every device or process was equally popular with all the tribes.The author has been honest and practical in the face of the considerable difficulty of sorting out tribal styles and tendencies. She has identified each piece and each process, as best she can, with recorded occurrences. When she tells us that a particular hook was made, or a specific fishing process was used, by a particular tribe, we may depend upon her accuracy. Hilary Stewart tells us what she knows, she does not jump to conclusions or generalize. Readers will be well advised to follow her example.

Finally, it should be made clear at the outset that this book is more than a bare account of the technology of fishing. It is about fish and fishing in the total lives of Northwest Coast people, and that is as it should be. Indians did not separate material and spiritual realms of experience as we tend to do. Fish were holy. Fishing was a connection between humans and the spirit world, never simply a matter of creating tools out of wood and bone, then putting them to work.

Fittingly this book opens with a myth and concludes with Indian prayers and poetry. In between are "practical" considerations. But separateness of these parts is an illusion. The reality of fishing, for the Indians, was in the whole. We will gain in our understanding of the Indians' world, and of our own, if we follow Hilary Stewart's lead and attempt to see the interdependence of myth, tool and prayer. In such unity resides the genius of Northwest Coast culture.

Michael Kew
Associate Prof. of Anthropology
Department of Anthropology and Sociology
University of British Columbia

Introduction

For the past 20 years my home has been on the Pacific Northwest Coast, and over the years I have explored at leisure and with unending curiosity the islands and inlets, the bays and beaches of this intricate and rugged shoreline. Inland, I have been drawn to the lakes and streams, and to the rivers that flow to the sea.

It was during the three years' research for my previous book *Artifacts of the Northwest Coast Indians* that I became aware of the amazing resourcefulness of the coast Indians in harvesting the wealth of the river and sea. In the past, the availability and abundance of fish accounted for the large populations of native peoples along the coast, and its importance was reflected in almost every aspect of their lives from pre-birth to after death.

Being involved in outdoor education, including survival in the wilderness, I realized that there was much to be learned from a people who had "survived" on the coast for over 9,000 years; survived, flourished and established a complex and rich culture. My practical interests widened from wild edible plants and the resources of the intertidal zone to the fishing technology of the coastal peoples.

Thus the idea for this book was born, and over the next three years I researched the various fishing gear and techniques employed by coast Indians in catching, processing, preserving and cooking fish. I marveled at the years of accumulated knowledge and experience required to produce a hook, spear, net or trap that was exactly right for the fish and the environment in which it was taken, and I was impressed by the skill of the fisherman in using his gear.

My research has ranged from talking with elderly Indian people to making and using a wooden halibut hook; from browsing through early journals and unpublished manuscripts to reading recent reports of current archaeological field work. In spite of research that was far from exhaustive, I found there were more ways of catching, preserving and cooking fish than could possibly be included in a book such as this.

Many of the illustrations showing the use of some type of fishing gear are based on descriptions recorded over the years by explorers, traders, ethnologists and missionaries. While every effort has been made to render the subject exactly as described, it is possible that I have visualized some aspect incorrectly. Sometimes an otherwise thorough description has lacked one or two details and I have had to complete the drawing with an educated guess.

Almost all the fishing gear and associated materials have been illustrated from my photographs and drawings of articles in museum collections; a few are taken from photos in archives, or in catalogues or other books. Certain items, although with little or no documentation, were too interesting to be excluded.

Because of the wide variety of types of fishing gear and the ways in which they were used by different Indian groups and sub-groups, there are bound to be differences of opinion over the use of this or that fish hook or trap, or one way or another of preserving salmon eggs or of rendering eulachon oil. Inevitably, I suppose, errors will be discovered, despite the considerable checking, cross checking and experimenting that has been carried out.

While the time period covered is up to and including contact by visitors from other lands, I have included old photographs to give a thread of continuity with the practices of today's native fishermen. Contemporary photos show that there are still Indians who catch and preserve fish by methods little changed in hundreds — probably thousands — of years. The traditions still serve; the major changes are the materials used. A nylon net replaces one of nettle fibre, and a butchering knife is made of metal instead of ground slate or shell. Too resourceful to ignore new materials, the Indian people started early with their substitutions: a nail as a fish hook barb; sail-maker's thread, strong and fine, to lash the barb to the hook; hemp rope for fish line.

For the purpose of this book I have categorized the types of fishing gear not by their cultural use but by the methods used: hook and line, nets, traps, and so on. By eliminating repetition where one type of hook or net was used by more than one cultural group, this arrangement gives greater cohesion to the subject.

Fish, and the salmon in particular, was not only a vital food for sustenance but also a major influence on the lifestyle and well being of the Indian people; indeed, it played an important role in shaping and strengthening the cultures of the entire Northwest Coast.

I hope this book will give a better understanding of the importance of fish for the indigenous peoples of the coast and its rivers, and an appreciation for the skill, knowledge and great effort that went into its harvest. I hope, also, this understanding will lead to a greater respect for the fisherman and his aboriginal rights.

Author's Note, 1994

First published in 1977 by J. J. Douglas in Canada, and by the University of Washington Press in the United States, *Indian Fishing: Early Methods on the Northwest Coast* interested a wider range of people than I had expected. These included leisure and commercial fishers, a woodcarver who worked with yew and a woman with a passion for drying foods. Also children, one of whom came to my door seeking help with a replica fish hook he was making. That pleased me a lot.

In 1978, *Indian Fishing* won a British Columbia Book Award (the forerunner to the B.C. Book Prizes), and the government presented a copy to every school in the province. An elegantly bound Japanese-language edition was published in 1987.

After several years of being out of print, *Indian Fishing* is available again. Readers should know that the word "Indian" (a misnomer initiated by Columbus, who mistakenly thought he had arrived in India), is now largely being replaced by the more appropriate First Nations.

Indian Fishing was first published seventeen years ago, and because this is a reprint and not a revised edition, it seems expedient to inform readers of the following updated name changes which more accurately reflect the coastal cultures. In the cultural Key on page 11, and in the book wherever they are mentioned: Bella Coola is now Nuxalk; Kwakiutl is now Kwakwa̱ka̱'wakw, except for the people of Fort Rupert, for whom Kwakiutl (also spelled Kwa-gulth) is correct; Nootka, which was changed in the 1970s to West Coast, is now Nuu-chah-nulth.

Reference Keys

Each specimen illustrated is accompanied by a measurement, together with a number-letter combination. The measurement, in centimetres, represents the maximum length or height of the item; the number represents the source, and the letters refer to the linguistic or cultural group who used that item. This number-letter system is also used within the text.

Thus, by referring to the indexes, the reader may determine that a fish hook notated 10-HA is in the Museum of Man, Ottawa, and was collected from or used by the Haida people. The cultural designation refers to that particular specimen and does not necessarily imply that no other group used that type of hook.

Specimens having two numbers will show both the reference from which they were drawn and the collection where they are housed.

Drawings that reconstruct a fishing method, such as a fence weir, or show the use of fishing tackle or gear, such as a herring rake, carry a number that refers to the source of this information.

Some items of fishing gear do not have any known provenience, but if they are from the Northwest Coast area and of sufficient interest, I have chosen to include them anyway.

Cultural Key

BC Bella Coola
CS Coast Salish
HA Haida
KW Kwagiutl
MK Makah
NK Nootka
TL Tlingit
TS Tsimshian
X Provenience not known

Reference Index

10 National Museum of Man, Ottawa, Ont.
11 British Columbia Provincial Museum, Victoria, B.C.
12 Museum of Anthropology, University of British Columbia, Vancouver, B.C.
13 Vancouver Centennial Museum, Vancouver, B.C.
Museum of Archaeology and Ethnology, Simon Fraser University, Burnaby, B.C.
15 Hastings Mill Museum, Vancouver, B.C.
16 Thomas Burke Memorial Washington State Museum, Seattle, Wash.
17 Washington State Historical Society, Tacoma, Wash.
18 Gerber Collection, Seattle, Wash.
19 Portland Art Museum, Portland, Ore.
20 Museum of Primitive Art, New York, N.Y.
21 National Museum of Natural History, Washington, D.C.
22 American Museum of Natural History, New York, N.Y.
23 Museum of the American Indian, New York, N.Y.
24 Alaska State Museum, Juneau, Alas.
25 Field Museum of Natural History, Chicago, Ill.
25a British Museum, London, England.
26 City Archives, Vancouver, B.C.
27 Vancouver Public Library, Photo Archives, Vancouver, B.C.
28 The Kwakiutl of Vancouver Island. Franz Boas
29 The Northern and Central Nootkan Tribes. Philip Drucker
30 Indians of the Northwest Coast. Philip Drucker
31 Indian Life on the Northwest Coast of North America. Erna Gunther
32 The Coast Salish of British Columbia. Homer Barnett
33 The Tlingit Indians. Krause and Gunther
34 Indians of the Northwest Coast. P.E. Goddard
35 Coast Indians of Southern Alaska and Northern British Columbia. A. Niblack
Indians of Puget Sound. Haeberlin and Gunther
37 The Upper Stalo Indians. Wilson Duff
38 B.C. Studies. Nos. 6 and 7. U.B.C.
39 Current Archaeological Research of the Northwest Coast. G. McDonald
40 Utilization of Fishes, Beach Foods and Marine Animals by the Tl'ûhus People of B.C. Dorothy Kennedy and Randy Bouchard

41 Indian Food. Health and Welfare, Canada
42 Indians of the Pacific Northwest. Ruth Underhill
43 Art of the Kwakiutl Indians. Audrey Hawthorn
44 Art of the Northwest Coast Indians. Bruce Inverarity
45 Images: Stone: BC. Wilson Duff and Hilary Stewart
46 Form and Freedom. Bill Holm and William Reid
47 Art in the Life of the Northwest Coast Indians. Erna Gunther
48 People of the Potlatch. Vancouver Art Gallery/University of British Columbia
49 Art of the Northwest Coast. Lowie Museum of Anthropology, University of California
50 Arts of a Vanishing Era. Whatcom Museum of History and Art
51 Indian Primitive. Ralph Andrews
52 Coast Salish. B.C. Heritage Series Volume 2
53 Haida. B.C. Heritage Series Volume 4
54 Stone Fish Traps of the Bella Bella. Anthony Pomoroy. Current Research Reports, Simon Fraser University
55 Augustus Wilson of the Masset Band, Masset, Queen Charlotte Islands, B.C.
56 Chief Charles Jones of the Pachenaht Band, Port Renfrew, Vancouver Island, B.C.
57 The Indian Voice. April, 1976
58 The Adventures and Sufferings of John R. Jewitt. John R. Jewitt
59 Some Common Marine Fishes of British Columbia. G.C. Carl
60 Photo by the author
61 Primitive Art. Franz Boas
62 Canadian Native Indian Prints Ltd., Vancouver, B.C.
63 Photo by Pat Severs, archaeologist. Director, Blue Jackets Creek dig, Queen Charlotte Islands, B.C.
64 American Antiquarian and Oriental Journal. Vol. 12. James Dean
65 Feasting with Cannibals. Stanley Walens. Northwest Coast Conference, Simon Fraser University, 1976.
66 The Religion of the Kwakiutl Indians. Part 2. F. Boas
67 Ethnology of the Kwakiutl. F. Boas. 1921
68 Tsimshian Mythology. F. Boas. 1925
69 Analysis of the First Salmon Ceremony. E. Gunther
70 Katzie Ethnographic Notes. Wayne Suttles. Anthropology in B.C. 1955
71 The Salmon. Roderick Haig-Brown. 1974
72 Reminiscences of the West Coast of Vancouver Island. Rev. C. Moser
73 Eulachon — Salvation. Scott Lawrance. Raincoast Chronicles. No. 5
74 Dr. Nancy Turner, Botany Division, B.C. Provincial Museum, Victoria
75 **The Economic Life of the Coast Salish of Haro and Rosario Straits. Wayne Suttles**
76 David, Young Chief of the Quileutes. Ruth Kirk
77 Artifacts of the Northwest Coast Indians. Hilary Stewart
78 The Tsimshian — Their Arts and Their Music. Barbeau, Wingert, Garfield
79 Indian Petroglyphs of the Pacific Northwest. Ray and Beth Hill.
80 The Bella Coola Indians. T.F. McIlwraith
81 The Excavation of Water Saturated Archaeological Sites (wet sites) on the Northwest Coast of North America. Edited by Dale Croes
82 Notes on the Ethnology of the Indians of Puget Sound. T.T. Waterman

How the Fish Came Into the Sea

A Tlingit Myth.

"After Raven bring daylight to all the people he keep walkin' north, lookin' around, he keep going up, up north. And he see something big, big just like a scow way out on the sea, like a floating box, and he ask:
" 'What is it out there?'

" 'That's a tank. All different kinds of fish in there. They try to keep them in there so there's no fish going around this ocean.'

"Well, he's thinkin' about it, how he's gonna get it. Raven send that black and white bird with the long tail — the magpie — to go up and cut a cane for him, and he fix it like octopus finger, he carve it like two tentacles of the octopus. He's gonna try to drag in that big scow with it, no matter how far off a thing is, that octopus finger cane will always reach it.

"In the evening Raven got all the peoples together and they beat drums. He hold the cane in his hands and move it around, going up, going down, going around, testing it. All right. That woman said she's satisfied with it. Then he get all the peoples down on the beach and they begin to sing, and he start to hook it, he tried to pull that thing ashore. And he tried again.
"OOOH, OOOH, OOOH, OH, OH!
"Saying to the people 'Sing stronger all the time' and he tried again.

"And he begin to draw it in to shore little by little. Finally he pull it onto the beach and he jump inside, and he open each door. He open the doors for smelts (fish, small fish) and the smelts comes out from that tank. After that herrings, and oolichons, and out of the other sides, king salmon first, and humpies, and coho, and later on the one they call the fall fish, dog salmon, and last comes the ones that stop, the halibut and flounders and cod, and he pushed them out.

"See, just the way he opened the doors, is just the way they come every year. No mistake on it. And Raven is satisfied, he released all that fish to go around this world."

The late Billy Wilson Senior, of Hoonah, Alaska, recalling legends of the Tlingit. Photo: Paul Bragstad.

This Tlingit legend was told to Paul Bragstad, a California teacher, photographer, and fisherman, by Billy Wilson, Senior, in Hoonah, Alaska, in 1974. Billy Wilson, a fisherman and silversmith all his life, died the following year at the age of 85 .

The legend not only tells how all these fish came into the world, but also accurately defines, with the sequence in which the doors are opened, the order of their annual migration. The ones that "stop," or stay, are those that do not migrate.

The original transcript has been edited by this author and a few details added from a variation of this legend in *Tlingit Myths and Texts* by John Swanton, 1909.

(Original recording and transcript by kind permission of Paul Bragstad.)

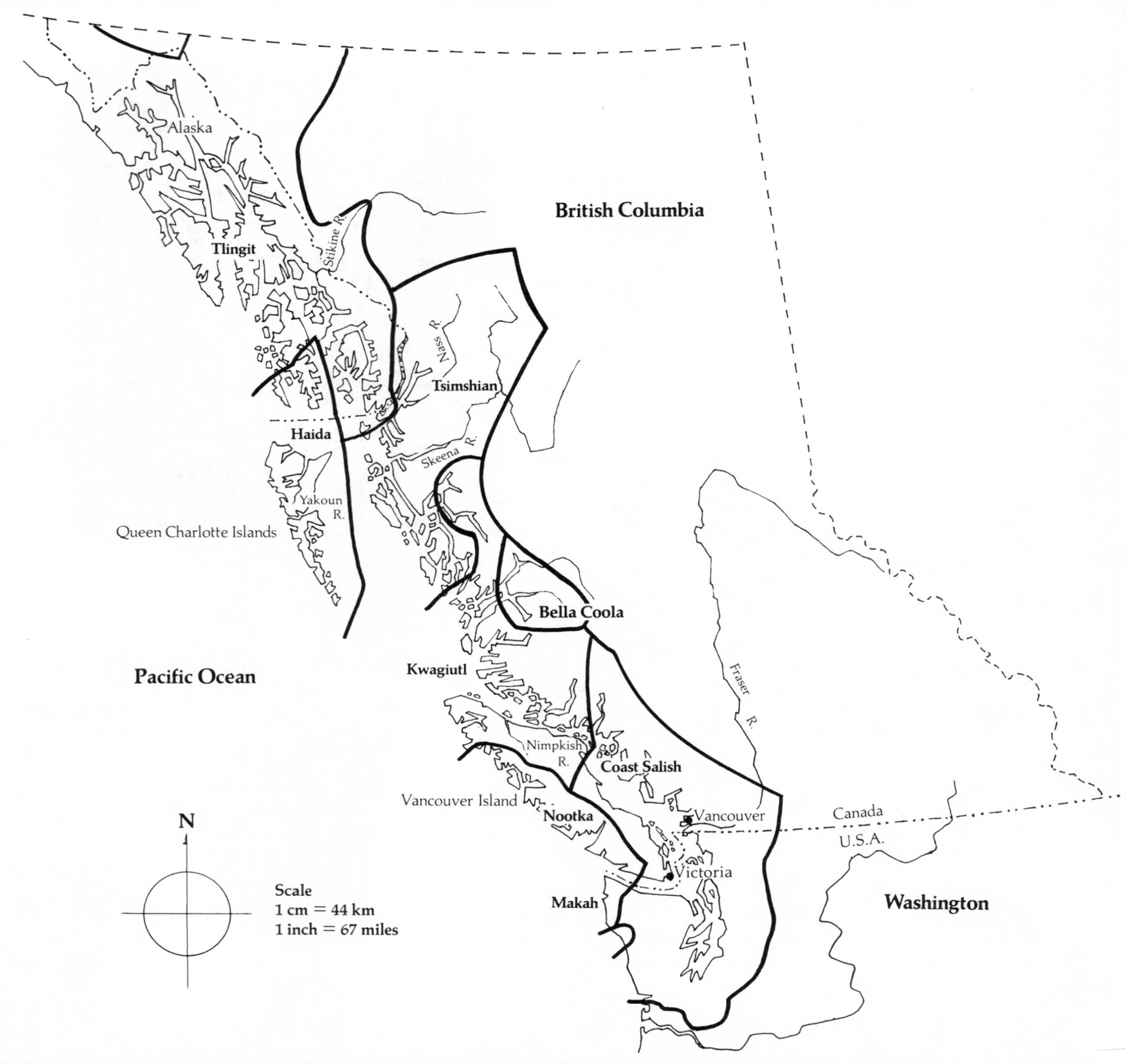

Alaska
British Columbia
Stikine R.
Tlingit
Nass R.
Tsimshian
Haida
Skeena R.
Yakoun R.
Queen Charlotte Islands
Bella Coola
Pacific Ocean
Kwagiutl
Fraser R.
Nimpkish R.
Coast Salish
Vancouver Island
Nootka
Vancouver
Canada
U.S.A.
Victoria
Makah
Washington
N
Scale
1 cm = 44 km
1 inch = 67 miles

Contents

The People of the Sea

At the mouth of a river a sleek canoe is being paddled by a thickset youth, his eyes watching the surface of the water, his spear at the ready. Seeing a salmon jump, he at once speaks to it in prayer:

"Haya! Haya! Come up again, Swimmer,
that I may say 'Haya,' according to your wishes,
for you wish us to say so, when you jump,
Swimmer, as you are speaking kindly to me
when you jump, Swimmer."

The salmon hears the prayer and jumps again. *"Haya! Haya!"* And the spear flashes toward the silver swimmer.

On a warm day late in summer, when the stinging nettles have grown tall from moist air and rich earth, a small group of women cut the slender stems that tower over their heads. From the split and dried stalks their experienced hands prepare long fibres, spin the fibres into twine, and knot the twine into fish netting so strong it can lift a load of herring from the water into a canoe.

With gnarled hands an old man pulls a piece of hollow kelp stem from the ashes of a fire. From it he draws a slender stick cut and shaped from a hemlock branch, and deftly bends the steamed wood into a curving U shape. He is making a set of fish hooks for catching halibut.

A baby's constant crying fills a crowded plank house on the edge of a village, and a young mother soothes her child by rubbing rat fish oil on its small naked body.

Using a piece of rough dog fish skin as sandpaper, a carver smooths the inside of a wooden bowl he has made in the shape of a frog. It is to hold eulachon oil for a coming feast. He inlays the rim with sea-snail opercula, securing them with fish glue.

An old woman tends a smouldering fire as smoke curls its way through the rafters of a smoke house, curing and drying great quantities of butchered fish hanging from the poles. Then she goes outside to the drying racks and checks on the rows of half dried fish.

A man brings his canoe loaded with halibut and black cod through twelve miles of rough water back to the beach of his village. Though hungry and tired, he unfastens, cleans and puts away all his fishing gear before eating a meal.

At one time scenes like these were reflections of everyday life along the thousands of miles of Pacific Northwest Coast and the rivers that flowed to it. The terrain, profuse with islands, channels, inlets and bays, sheltered many hundreds of villages housing many thousands of Indian peoples of several different cultures. They spoke different languages, and many of their beliefs,

"Habitations in Nootka Sound, North America," popular engraving from Captain Cook's Third Voyage Around the World, *published in 1784. Noticeable to the early explorers were the many fish drying racks to be found at the summer villages of the coast.* 62.NK

their ways of doing things, their ceremonies and their design styles differed one from another, but the one thing they all had in common was the sea and their dependency upon it.

All villages hugged the water's very edge; all houses faced towards the water. To the Indians of the Northwest Coast, the sea and the rivers were not just a way of life but life itself. In some areas there were inland trails for hunting, berrying, trading and other activities, but the waterways were the main highways. These were traveled swiftly by dugout canoes of various sizes and styles developed to meet different needs. The long, straggling row of canoes on the beach in front of the village was evidence of the people's marine mobility. The same scene was repeated in villages on those rivers which flowed into the sea.

The people traveled to socialize, to attend a feast in another village, or to trade, exchanging goods they had in plenty for those not available in their area. They traveled to make war, to revenge a wrong, or to capture slaves for a chief's household; they traveled to hunt sea mammals, to reach a good berrying place, to collect basketry materials or slate for tools. And they traveled to fish.

The beaches of the sea produced an abundance of shellfish, edible invertebrates and seaweeds. The long kelp stems of the rocky coast were made into strong fishing lines and storage bottles for eulachon oil. Sea shells were made into tools, implements, and ornaments. Many myths, songs, dances, and ceremonies were based on some aspect of the sea or the river, its spirits, the underwater world or the characteristics of the fish. Creatures of the sea became family crests or spirit helpers, and were carved into bowls, painted on possessions, tattooed on the body, woven into baskets, and everywhere incorporated into the patterns of life.

Indeed, mankind itself was born on the edge of the sea. It was Raven, according to the Haida, alone and lonely in an empty world, who wandered down to the beach. From the wet sand at his feet came a bubble and a small sound. He saw a half buried, partially open clam shell and looked closer, bending his head to listen. He heard a soft sigh and the two halves of the shell began to open. A small face peered out then shyly withdrew again, afraid. Raven called to the face in a whisper and it slowly reappeared, stretched its neck, looked up at him and quickly withdrew again.

Once more Raven whispered "Come out, come out!" Another sigh came from the shell and another face peered from between the valves. Soon there were more sighing sounds and more small faces until a whole row of them appeared from the edge of the shell. Little arms came out, pushing the clam shell open wider. Unfolding, stretching and emerging, hordes of little people released themselves from the open shell and went

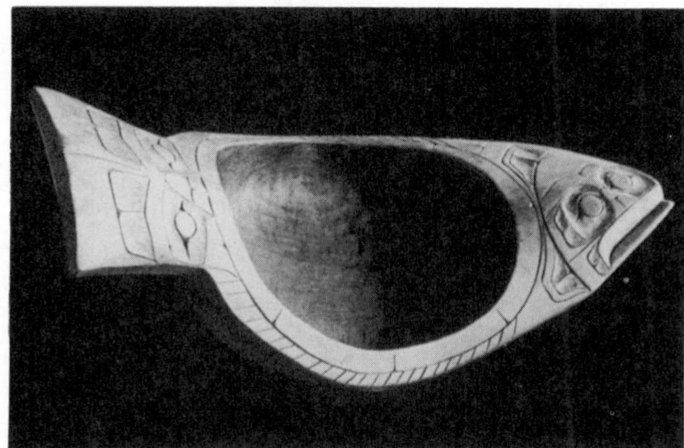

Halibut bowl carved by Jerry Smith of Alert Bay, owned by the author. 60.KW

Fish is part of design on large, finely woven basket. 60.24.TL

off to populate the land. They were the first people, and born of the shore they still lived by the shore.

A part of the vast system of life-support for the sea is the rivers that drain into it; among those of the Northwest Coast are the Stikine, the Nass and the Skeena to the north; centrally the Bella Coola and the Nimpkish; to the south the Squamish and

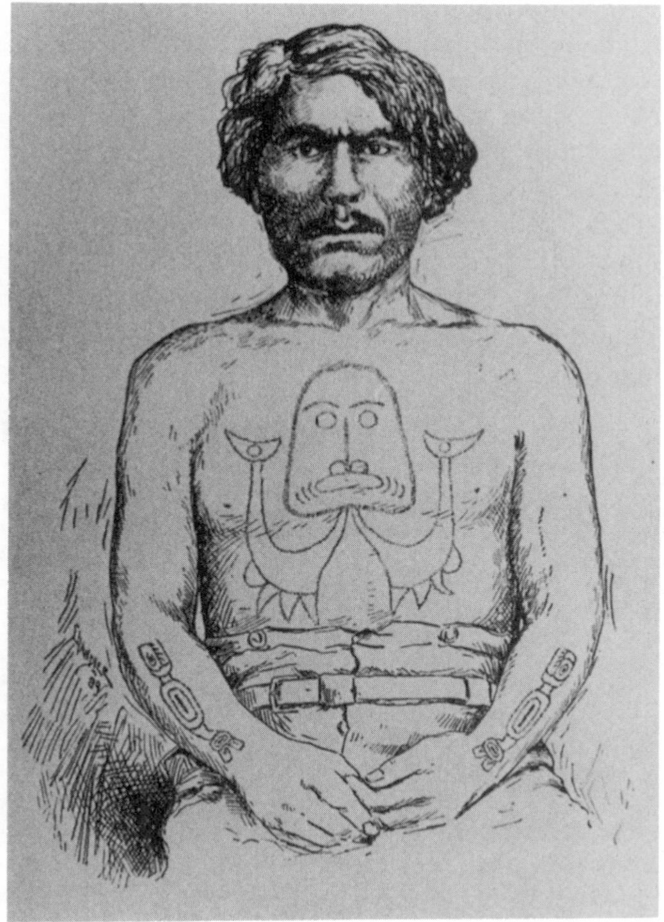

Tattoo designs on chief represent codfish on chest and salmon on arms. Circa 1878. 35.HA

the great Fraser River. Into these and countless other waterways swarmed the teeming millions of fish on the annual migrations, and along these valleys and inlets, and the nearby islands, thousands of people made their homes.

Villagers without nearby access to fishing runs made the often long journey by dugout canoe to reach their traditional fishing grounds. In the spring, the summer or the fall, depending on the locale and species of fish running, entire families moved out from their villages, glad of the change of activity and happy to have the chance of meeting friends and relatives who also gathered at the fishing grounds. They set up temporary camps and spent many weeks by the river, the men catching the fish, the women butchering and preserving them. Preserving the catch ensured a supply of food throughout the winter when the salmon were not readily available and when conditions for catching other fish were not as favorable.

Poling a canoe upriver on the Skeena. 11.TS

During the establishment of Fort Langley on the Fraser River, July and August entries from an 1827-28 journal (author unknown) make numerous references to the constant flow of canoes heading up the river for the salmon fishing. It names tribes, some from as far afield as Vancouver Island, and describes how the canoes moved two and three abreast lashed with planks between them to form a kind of barge that carried a whole family with its household goods. From mid-July to late August frequent journal entries note "Indians passing up in hundreds" . . . "Families from the Saanch [sic] village at Point Roberts have been passing in continued succession during the day all bound for the Salmon Fishery" . . . "Indians in swarms proceeding to the fishery above."

The September entries kept tabs on the number of canoes returning with their load of dried fish, many of which stopped at the fort to trade some of the catch. "Sept. 22nd, 1828 . . . 150 Cowichans families stopped at the wharf . . . there are now 345 canoes of Cowichans already passed." The following day saw "100 canoes" go down the river, the next day "60 more canoes" and the day after "200 canoes of Whooms stopped alongside the wharf, they are on their way to Burrards Canal for the winter." (This probably refers to Burrard Inlet, where there were winter villages.)

Families owned specific places at the fishing grounds and these were known and respected by others. A man might invite a relative to fish with him, or someone might request permission to use another's fishing spot, and if he needed the food he was not refused. A good fishing place could even be leased out to someone for payment. The rights and privileges to fishing places were inherited from one generation to the next, or sometimes gained through marriage. Year after year families exercised the rights they had owned for hundreds of years, taking the fish they needed to feed their families and others of the village, to give feasts, to trade, and to keep going through the winter. It is no wonder Indian peoples today consider unjust the laws that deprive them of those long-held rights.

While the five species of salmon were the favorite catch, they did not migrate in such large numbers in the north, so that the Haida and Tlingit were far more dependent on the halibut, a large fish plentiful in that area. Caught in quantity by highly specialized gear, halibut could be preserved well by drying and smoking, and provided good reserves of food for winter.

Eulachon, caught in tremendous quantities in the rivers, were most valued for the rich oil they contained. In addition, the sea provided herring, various species of cod, kelpfish, red snapper, dogfish, flounder, smelt, devil fish (octopus), and many others. The rivers yielded sturgeon, trout, steelhead, and more.

The Northwest Coast Indian was totally adapted to living with the fickle ocean, its inlets, channels and straits, and the rivers that flowed to the sea. He knew the ebb and flow of the tides, the currents, the changing winds that turned the water from a gentle ally to a violent, cruel enemy. He understood and respected the sea, its creatures and the entire coastal environment in a way the white man cannot. He loved the coast with a deep reverence, and in return the coast was good to him, providing him with wealth and nourishment for both body and spirit.

Because he was so completely in tune with the ways of the sea and river and all that was in it, the Indian was able to devise many methods for reaping its harvest. Differences in geography, climate, tides, species of fish and variations in culture led to different procedures in catching fish and different ways of making the gear required. But among all people dwelt the deeply inherent tradition of gathering the bounty of sea and river.

Fisherman returns with canoe load of halibut, circa 1900. 17.MK

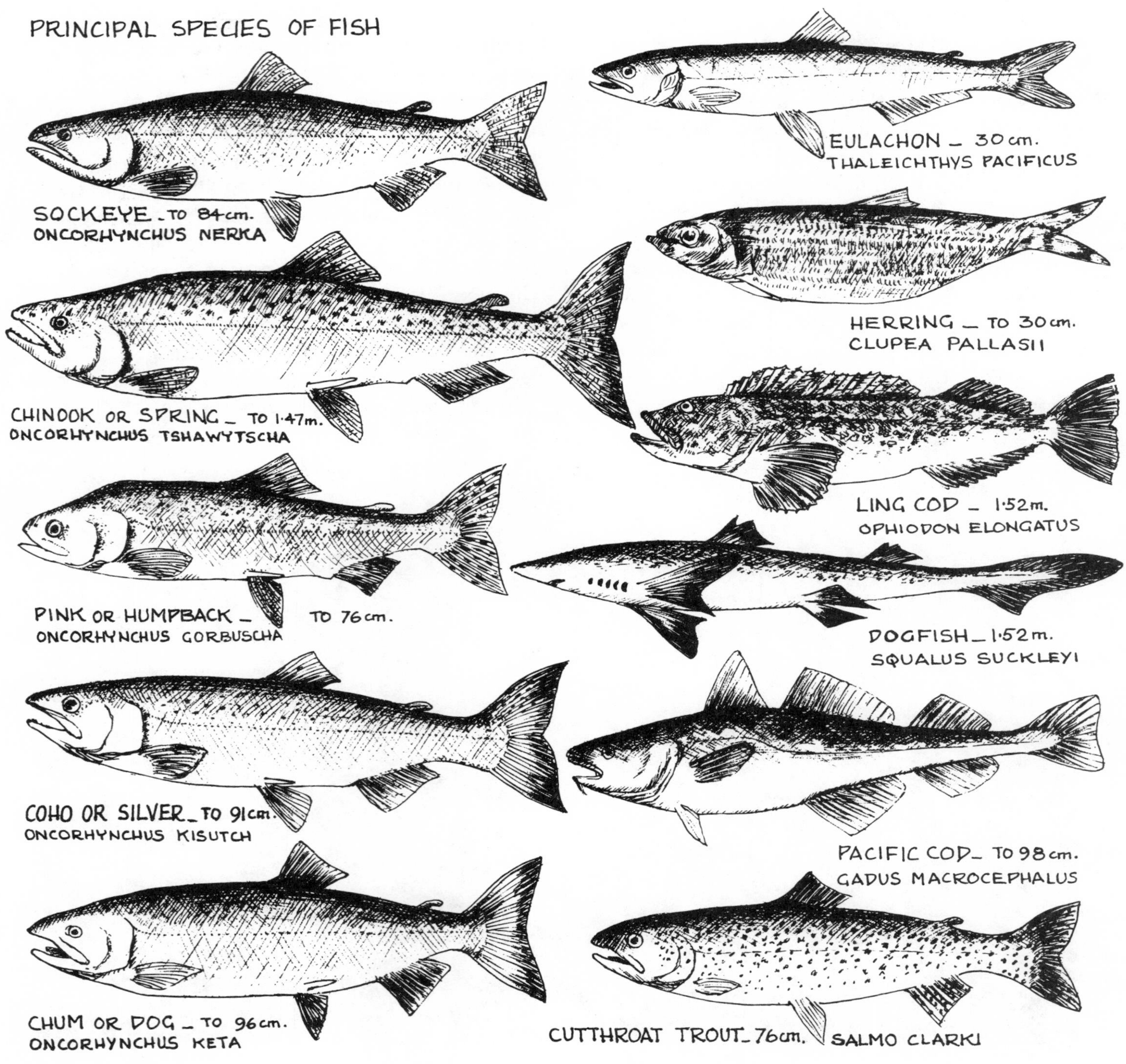
PRINCIPAL SPECIES OF FISH
SOCKEYE _ TO 84 cm.
ONCORHYNCHUS NERKA
CHINOOK OR SPRING _ TO 1·47 m.
ONCORHYNCHUS TSHAWYTSCHA
PINK OR HUMPBACK _ TO 76 cm.
ONCORHYNCHUS GORBUSCHA
COHO OR SILVER _ TO 91 cm.
ONCORHYNCHUS KISUTCH
CHUM OR DOG _ TO 96 cm.
ONCORHYNCHUS KETA
EULACHON _ 30 cm.
THALEICHTHYS PACIFICUS
HERRING _ TO 30 cm.
CLUPEA PALLASII
LING COD _ 1·52 m.
OPHIODON ELONGATUS
DOGFISH _ 1·52 m.
SQUALUS SUCKLEYI
PACIFIC COD _ TO 98 cm.
GADUS MACROCEPHALUS
CUTTHROAT TROUT _ 76 cm.
SALMO CLARKI

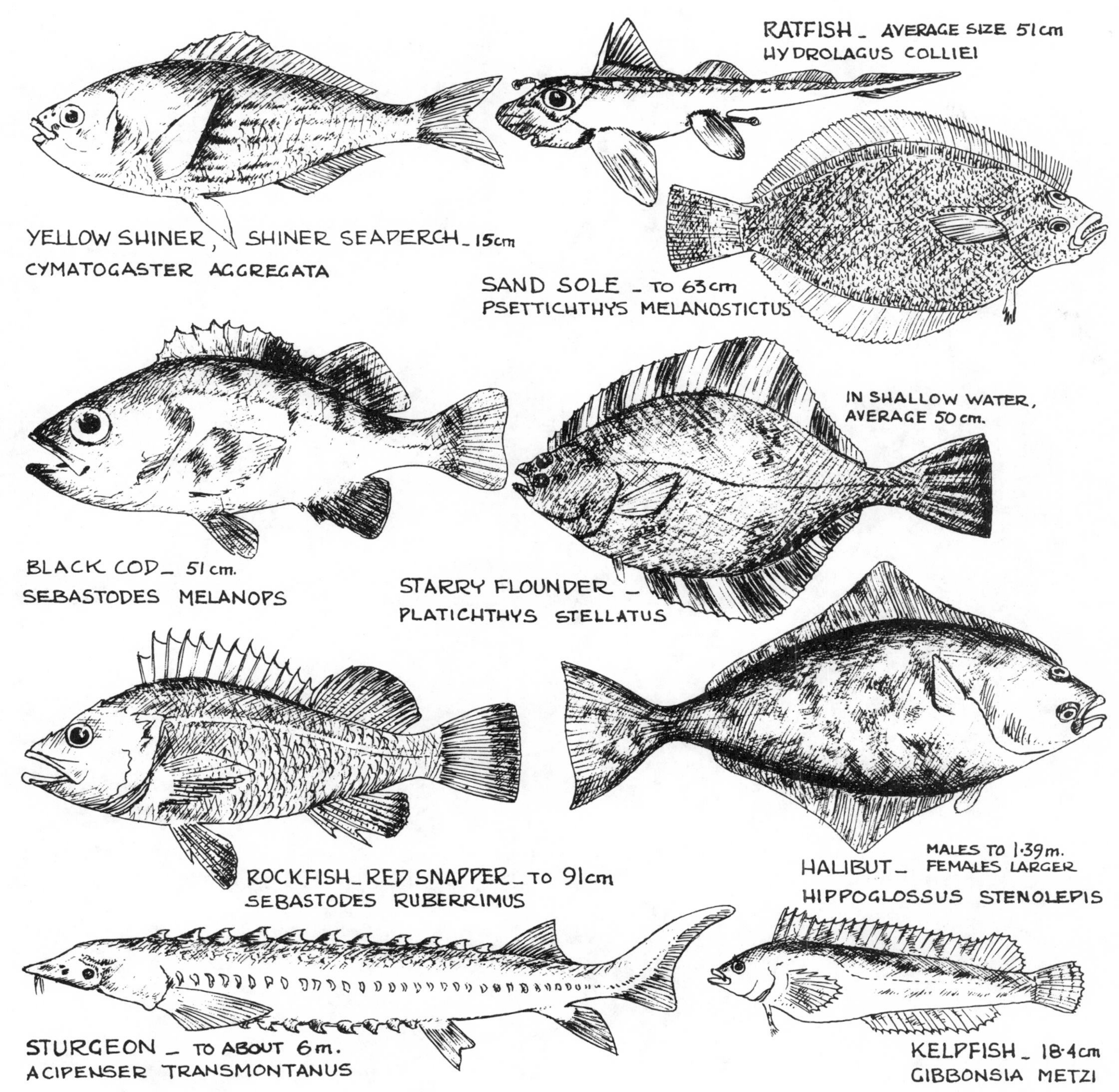
RATFISH _ AVERAGE SIZE 51cm
HYDROLAGUS COLLIEI
YELLOW SHINER, SHINER SEAPERCH _ 15cm
CYMATOGASTER AGGREGATA
SAND SOLE _ TO 63cm
PSETTICHTHYS MELANOSTICTUS
IN SHALLOW WATER, AVERAGE 50cm.
BLACK COD _ 51cm.
SEBASTODES MELANOPS
STARRY FLOUNDER _
PLATICHTHYS STELLATUS
ROCKFISH _ RED SNAPPER _ TO 91cm
SEBASTODES RUBERRIMUS
HALIBUT _ MALES TO 1·39m. FEMALES LARGER
HIPPOGLOSSUS STENOLEPIS
STURGEON _ TO ABOUT 6m.
ACIPENSER TRANSMONTANUS
KELPFISH _ 18·4cm
GIBBONSIA METZI

25.HA

Hook, Line and Sinker

Of all fishing gear, the most familiar is the fish hook. Over thousands of years the Indian peoples of the Northwest Coast designed and perfected hooks and their accessories — baits, lures, sinkers, floats, and lines — for fish of various sizes, habitats, characteristics, and behaviour. Their fishing gear was so well suited to the environment, and their skill so practised, that they saw no need to change when white men sailed into their waters and introduced other kinds of hooks. The bone barb was eventually replaced with one of iron; linen thread or hemp string took over from spruce root, and rope replaced the kelp line, but the hook remained essentially the same.

In 1885 Albert Niblack, on a survey of northern British Columbia and Alaska, wrote in his report published by the U.S. National Museum: "The apparently clumsy hooks of this region have been found to possess so many advantages over the type used by Europeans that they are retained to this day." He wistfully adds, "There is little in the art of fishing we can teach these Indians."

In truth, there is much in the art of fishing that the natives could have taught the newcomers, particularly in the early years. Captain Dixon and his crew, for example, anchored their square-rigged ship in a sheltered bay in 1787 and lowered a boat so that the crew, hungry for fresh food, could catch fish. The results of using European fishing gear and fishing methods on this coast must have been less than encouraging, judging from an entry in Dixon's journal. He describes the Indians' successful method of catching halibut with their baited hooks, lines, and floats, then remarks:

"Thus we were fairly beat at our own weapons, and the natives constantly bringing us plenty of fish, our boat was never sent on this business afterwards."

In Captain Vancouver's journal is another instance of Indians' supplying fish to white men whose fishing attempts have failed. Of the canoemen who followed him up what is now Burrard Inlet, he reports:

"Our Indian visitors remained with us until, by signs, we gave them to understand we were going to rest, and, after receiving some acceptable articles, they retired, and, by means of the same language, promised an abundant supply of fish the next day, our seine having been tried in their presence with very little success."

A great many journals and diaries recounting the early days of the white man's visits tell of quantities of fish being brought to the ships, either as gifts or for trade. Many a ship's crew was indebted to the skill of native fishermen. And to the native's fish hook.

The size, shape, material, and manufacture of

hooks show a wide range of ideas and techniques. Baited hooks were used in trolling for salmon and for catching cod, dogfish, kelpfish, and other species. Undoubtedly some worked better than others and some lasted longer.

Tiny fish hooks of wood tipped with slender bone barbs have been unearthed in archaeological excavations, while many museums house large, elaborately carved wooden halibut hooks complete with line and float. Also found archaeologically are fish hook shanks of stone and bone. These shanks are not frequently found, yet interestingly the bone ones excavated in the Queen Charlotte Islands (Haida) are similar to those of slate from Yuquot (Nootka) and from Sooke (Coast Salish), both on Vancouver Island. Neatly carved and shaped to receive the barb at the correct angle, often with a heel to prevent the barb lashing from slipping, they are also grooved to secure the leader. As well as being durable, such hooks also acted as their own sinker.

Fishing Lines

Excellent lines for the fisherman came from many materials. Perhaps the most ideally suited was the bull kelp *(Nereocystis luetkeana)*, a seaweed found in rocky areas along the whole coast in the upper subtidal zone and to a depth of several fathoms. From its holdfast, a rootlike structure tenaciously clinging to the rock, the seaweed sends out a long stipe, like a stem, for up to 25 metres (about 81 feet). The stipe, about one centimetre (3⁄8 inch) in diameter at the base, is cylindrical and solid, gradually increasing in thickness to become a hollow tube terminating in a bulb which serves as a float to hold the seaweed up. The solid part of the stem was used for fish lines after being soaked in fresh water, stretched, and twisted for extra strength. Lengths of these were joined together with a special knot to give the fisherman a long line of great strength.

I handled one of these coiled-up lengths of kelp line in the American Museum of Natural History, in New York, and became interested in the type of knot used in joining the many lengths of kelp. Using my shoe laces I studiously followed the intricacies of the tied kelp ends and finally succeeded in learning to make the knot. Back on the west coast of Vancouver Island that summer and involved in a survival course, I showed my achievement to a knot-tying friend instructing in outdoor education and mountain climbing. "That," he observed, "is called a fisherman's knot!"

The following year I found some medium length kelp stipes freshly washed up on the beach after a wild wind and rain storm that had howled down the coast all day, making August seem like December. Sheltered by a stand of spruce our camp had withstood a taste of the unleashed temper of the outer coast, though my sleeping bag took a soaking, and I thought again of the big planked houses of the early Indian people. How comforting it must have been when the wind blew to have a fire burning, food in the cooking box, and dozens of people adding to the warmth.

From the kelp stipes I made, by soaking, stretching, twisting and knotting together, a 14-metre length of fish line. The 0.7-centimetre (1⁄4-inch) thick kelp stipe blackened and shrank to a thin line. Tough and wire-like, it was unrecognizable as kelp, but when immersed in water again it reverted to its original thickness within the hour, maintaining the twist.

Whale sinew was utilized for lines, as was nettle fibre. Fishing lines of inner cedar bark were

Seventy-four year-old Hanna Parnell of Masset, Queen Charlotte Islands, making halibut line from inner cedar bark, 1975. 60.HA

Braided sinew 7 cm thick (1/2 inch), probably for harpoon lanyard. 19.X

Reel of inner cedar bark twine, suitable for making fish net. 21.X

Halibut line of inner cedar bark. 16.TL

Long halibut line of inner cedar bark, 1.0cm thick (3/8 inch). Vancouver Island. 21

Twine made from nettle fibre. 21.X

Lengths of kelp line knotted together to make single halibut line approximately 60 metres (66 feet) long. 21.NK

common along the entire Northwest Coast, and were used particularly where a heavy line was needed. In Old Masset, also called Haida, in the Queen Charlotte Islands, I watched the gnarled but deft hands of 74-year-old Hanna Parnell twisting lengths of split inner cedar bark into a three-strand rope, "for halibut line" she said in her native tongue. Hanna had already completed about 18 metres (60 feet) of the strong pliable rope, and I felt a deep admiration and respect for a woman who still maintained the knowledge and skill, and indeed the enjoyment, of making a useful item from the materials of her environment. Her grandchildren, accustomed to diesel-powered, electronically equipped fishing vessels with sonar depth sounders, were more familiar with nylon lines and steel hooks mechanically winched in over the side of the boat to bring in halibut for the fish packing plants.

Hanna Parnell knew that her cedar bark line would never feel the pull of Great-One-Coming-Up-Against-the-Current, but her experienced hands prepared the cedar bark and made the rope anyway, and it seemed to me that it was serving another purpose, in another era, with just as much meaning.

Sinkers

Sinkers varied in size from a small pebble to a hefty rock either grooved or perforated for attaching to a rope. The larger sinkers functioned as anchors to maintain the position of an item of fishing gear underwater; a cluster of these stones provided anchorage for a dugout and its crew. Small and medium-sized sinkers were used with a hook and line.

Similar stones weighted the bottom edge of a net to hold it taut. Many of these weights were smooth, unmodified river cobbles secured to the net in various ways with pliable twigs and lashings. Now that techniques exist for preserving materials from archaeological "wet sites" (water-saturated digs), excavation is going ahead in sites where these net weights, complete with lashings, are being found in a good state of preservation as a result of their waterlogging.

When a large sturgeon tried to escape the hook by heading out to sea, pulling the canoe after it, a kind of sea anchor was used. A heavy stone on a length of rope was tossed over the side to slow down the progress of the fish.

Heavy and suitably shaped rocks, lashed with rope and wire, still function as sinkers and weights.

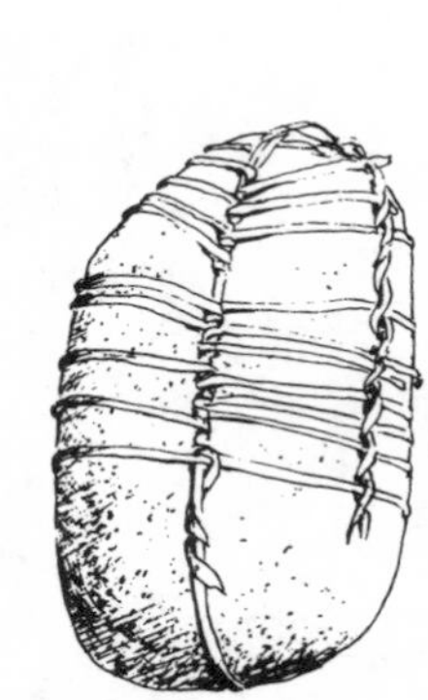

STONE WRAPPED IN STRANDS OF SPLIT CEDAR WITHE. 14·6cm 81·12·CS

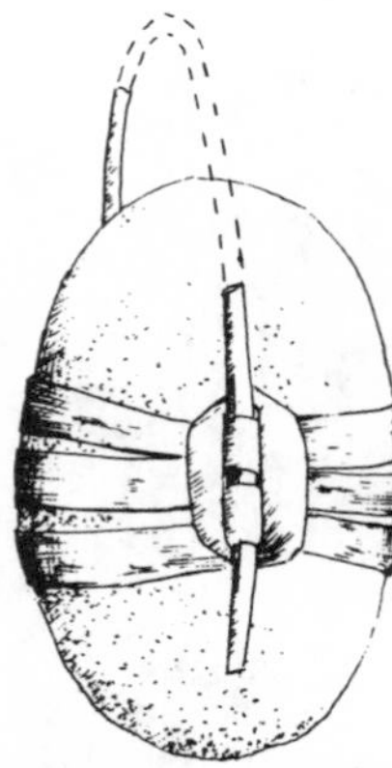

NATURAL RIVER COBBLE WITH CHERRY BARK BINDING. 9·2cm 81·CS

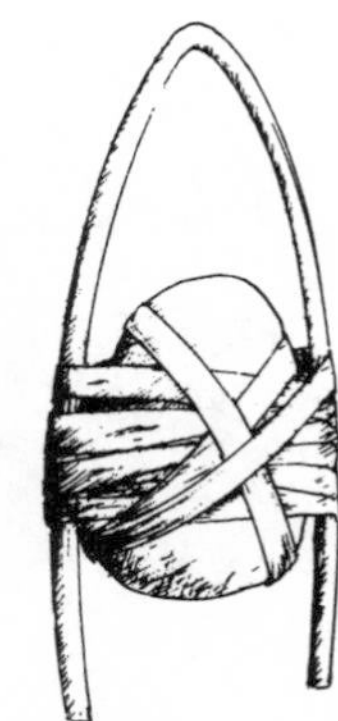

STONE HELD IN BENT TWIG WITH CHERRY BARK - 81·CS

SINKERS

CHERRY BARK WRAPPED STONE, PROBABLY A SINKER
9·0cm. 16·32·CS (?)

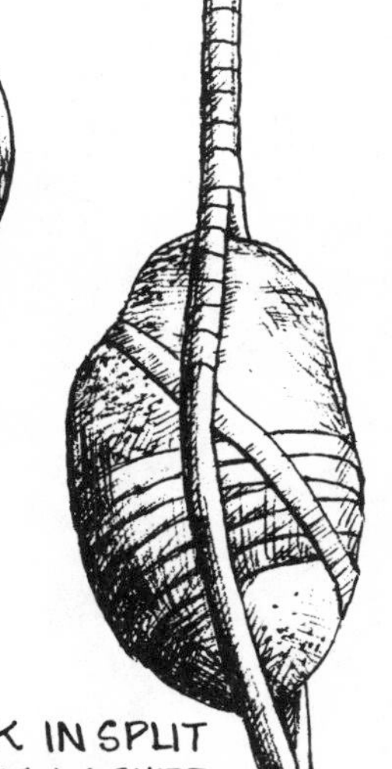

ROCK IN SPLIT STICK LASHED WITH CHERRY BARK
28·0cm. 11·X

SMALL PERFORATED SINKER, USED WITH SMALL FISH HOOK.
4·4cm. 12·X

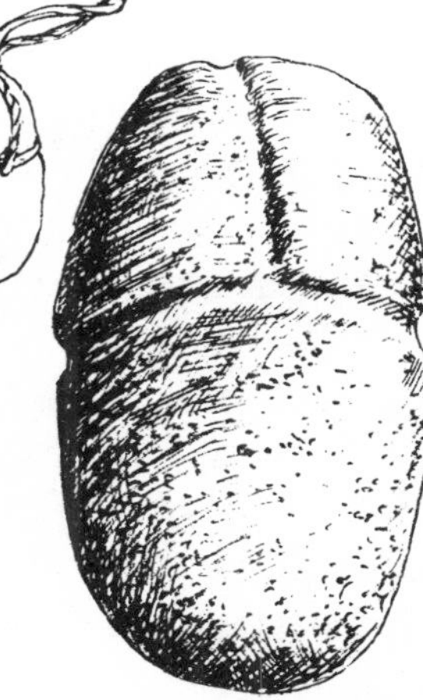

GROOVED SINKER FOR HALIBUT LINE
17cm 77·X

GROOVED SINKER FOR HALIBUT LINE
12cm. MK

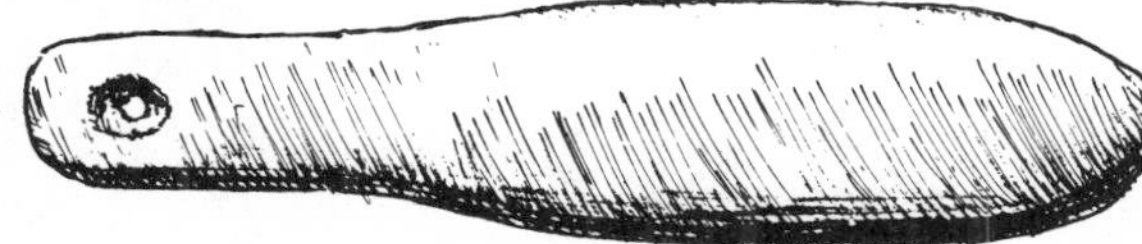

USUALLY THOUGHT OF AS A CLUB, BUT MAY BE SINKER FOR STURGEON NET. 32cm. 37·12·CS

11cm 77·MK

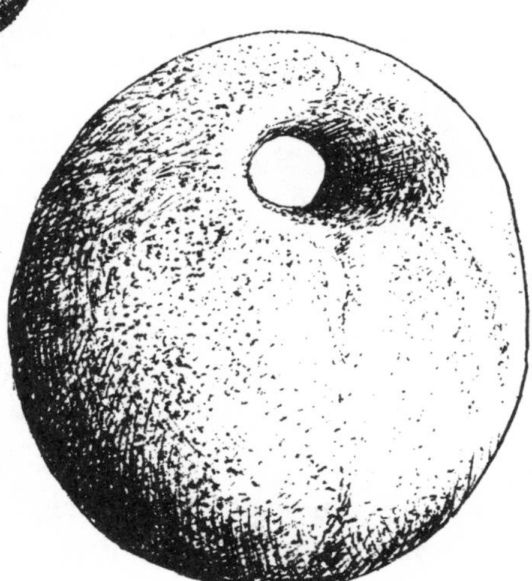

CEDAR WITHE ROPE FOR ATTACHMENT 16·0cm. 23·X

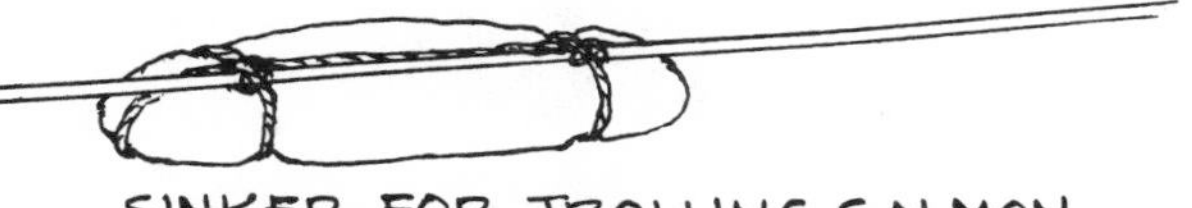

SINKER FOR TROLLING SALMON.

ANCHOR STONE; COULD BE USED TO ANCHOR DOWN FISH TRAP, END OF NET, FISH LINE ETC. 29·5cm 13·X

Steam-Bent Hooks

The U-shaped, steam-bent hook was the characteristic halibut hook of the southern and central peoples, although this type of hook would also catch cod and dogfish and its smallest version took kelpfish.

The Makah, great halibut fishermen, frequently made their hooks out of yew wood; others used fir, balsam, spruce or hemlock knotwood. The flaring, curved back tip of the hook ensured that the fish only took the baited part carrying the barb, since it could not open its mouth wide enough to include the curved tip.

During my research on fishing gear, I heard about a very old Indian man living in Port Renfrew, on the west coast of Vancouver Island, who used to make and use steam-bent hooks. The better part of a day's journey, by ferry and a winding, rocky, washboard road that clung high up the mountain side as it followed the coast, eventually brought me to the village, the reservation, and Chief Charles Jones of the Pachenaht Band.

Although Chief Charles was busy in his workshop, a small tidy shed by the river's edge, he bade me enter and pulled up a stool for me. He had used the U-shaped hooks for fishing up until 1950 or so; he said he still made them for sale to anyone who cared to buy them. He spoke of going into the forest to find the right wood, and shaping it. As he described the steam-bending process, his powerful, gnarled hands mimed the careful bending of the wood to the U-shape. I felt the sensitivity of fingers that told him when the wood had steamed long enough to begin the bending. "Gotta be *just limber,*" he said, "when it's just *limber* then it bends right."

I asked the chief a lot of questions about the old ways of fishing, and showed him photos I had taken of different hooks from various museums. With each photo he either nodded, as if in recognition of an old friend, and described how

Chief Charles Jones of the Pachenaht Band, Port Renfrew. 60. NK

the hook was used, or denied it for his area, Southern Nootka. "That's a Haida hook, we never used that . . . . Kwagiutl, they made that kind of hook . . . ."

Of the curved back arm of the steam-bent hook, he told me that this prevented the fish from fighting. If the arm were straight, it would cause more discomfort by lying on the cheek of the fish, and "he'll fight all the way up to the top." He also said the curve prevented the hook from being swallowed by too small a fish; it could only be snagged by the lip, from which the hook could be removed and the fish returned to the water unharmed.

I felt privileged to share a small part of the great storehouse of Chief Charles's knowledge, but also I felt somewhat inadequate in the shadow of his experience and wisdom. Eventually we parted. I thanked the Chief and offered him a lift back to his house, but no, he preferred to walk. With upright back and cane in hand he went off down the road and I went to my car.

As I caught up with him I felt a compulsion to satisfy my curiosity about his age, and pulled up beside him. "Chief Charles, may I ask you one more question?"

"Sure!" he nodded, his voice booming.

"How old are you?"

"I'll be a hundred years old in July*!" he said, and his eyes sparked with the joy of that thought. And I shared his joy.

For a considerable time there had been some dispute concerning the behaviour of the bentwood hook underwater. Did it float up from the point of attachment, or did it hang down? To try to find out, I made a halibut hook by steam-bending a quarter section of wood cut from a yew branch. I lashed on a bone barb with split cedar root, baited it with octopus and lowered the hook, with its stone sinker, into a tub of water. The hook floated up from the sinker.

I should have been satisfied, but there were still some doubts. I raised the question with Donald Abbott, Curator of Archaeology at the B.C. Provincial Museum in Victoria. He admitted that the answer had never been settled to everyone's satisfaction, although he had heard of an old timer who had lost several hooks overboard that sank. I felt that these might have been the more recent iron-barbed hooks, not the earlier bone-barbed hooks such as the one I had made.

To settle the matter once and for all, Abbott obtained permission to take a classic bentwood bone-pointed halibut hook out of the museum's ethnology collection for testing. That particular hook, from Barkley Sound, had been checked by Jan Freidman, an expert in wood identification known for her work at the famous Ozette archaeological site at Cape Alava, Washington. She had said that it was made from fir.

Abbott secured octopus bait to the hook, donned his diving gear, and in the chilly ocean waters of a January day went down to a depth of 40 feet, taking the hook with him. The result was that the hook sank.

I was convinced of the hook's behaviour but had to discover why fir wood should sink when yew, a more dense wood, floated. The answer lay in which part of the wood was used for making the hook. The wood from a knot, where the branch grows through the trunk, is extremely hard and dense. Even when a fallen tree has rotted, the spike of the knot is still sound, and it was this wood, from fir and other trees, which was used to make the tough bentwood halibut hooks.

* July 1976.

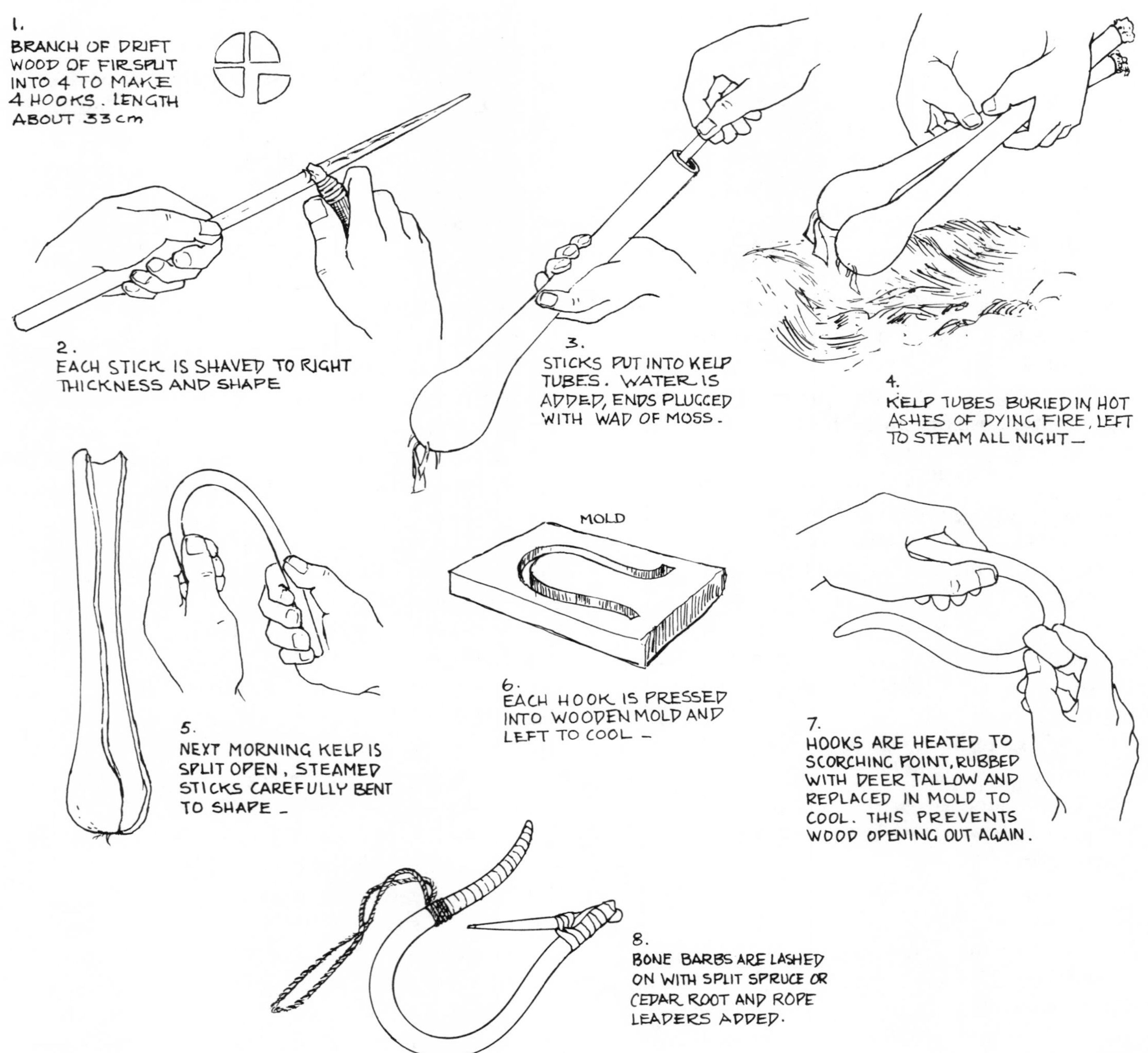
MAKING LARGE BENTWOOD HOOKS
1.
BRANCH OF DRIFT WOOD OF FIR SPLIT INTO 4 TO MAKE 4 HOOKS. LENGTH ABOUT 33 cm
2.
EACH STICK IS SHAVED TO RIGHT THICKNESS AND SHAPE
3.
STICKS PUT INTO KELP TUBES. WATER IS ADDED, ENDS PLUGGED WITH WAD OF MOSS.
4.
KELP TUBES BURIED IN HOT ASHES OF DYING FIRE, LEFT TO STEAM ALL NIGHT –
5.
NEXT MORNING KELP IS SPLIT OPEN, STEAMED STICKS CAREFULLY BENT TO SHAPE –
MOLD
6.
EACH HOOK IS PRESSED INTO WOODEN MOLD AND LEFT TO COOL –
7.
HOOKS ARE HEATED TO SCORCHING POINT, RUBBED WITH DEER TALLOW AND REPLACED IN MOLD TO COOL. THIS PREVENTS WOOD OPENING OUT AGAIN.
8.
BONE BARBS ARE LASHED ON WITH SPLIT SPRUCE OR CEDAR ROOT AND ROPE LEADERS ADDED.
28-KW

MAKING SMALL BENTWOOD HOOKS

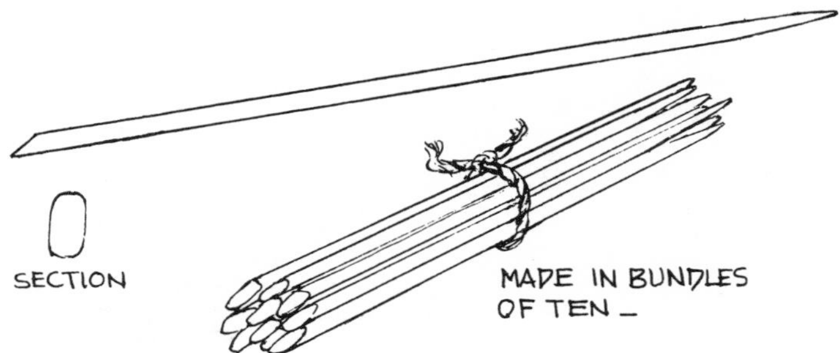

1.
LENGTH IS ONE HAND WIDTH, EACH STICK WHITTLED TO A SQUARED OVAL SHAPE. ONE END IS POINTED, THE OTHER HAS A FLATTENED SIDE TO TAKE BARB.

2.
STICKS ARE SOAKED IN SMALL BOX OF FRESH WATER PRIOR TO STEAMING.

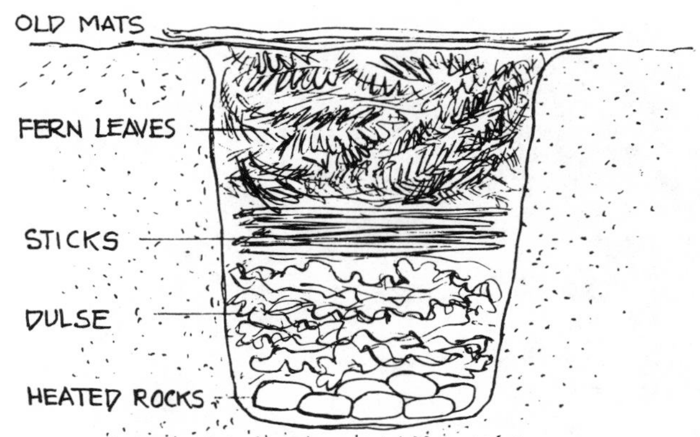

3.
PIT DUG IN CORNER OF THE HOUSE AND FILLED UP AS ABOVE _ WATER IS ADDED, CREATING STEAM BUILD-UP WITHIN PIT _

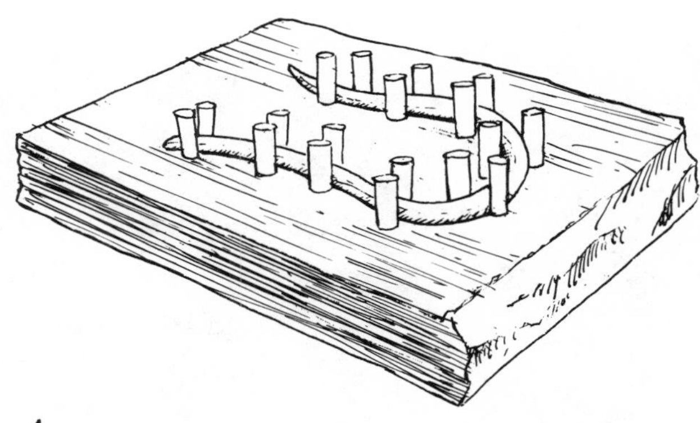

4.
AFTER STEAMING FOR 15 MINS. STICKS ARE REMOVED, BENT TO SHAPE AND PRESSED INTO MOLD, WHICH IS MADE OF 7 TO 10 PAIRS OF HARDWOOD PEGS DRIVEN INTO CEDAR BOARD IN SHAPE OF HOOK.

5.
AS WITH LARGE HOOKS, EACH IS REHEATED AND GREASED WITH TALLOW. BONE POINT IS LASHED TO FLAT SIDE WITH SPLIT SPRUCE ROOT AND LEADER ADDED.

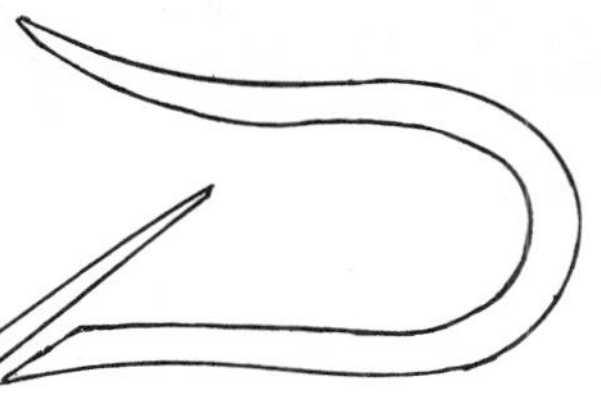

28-KW

MAKING A FISH HOOK BARB OF BONE

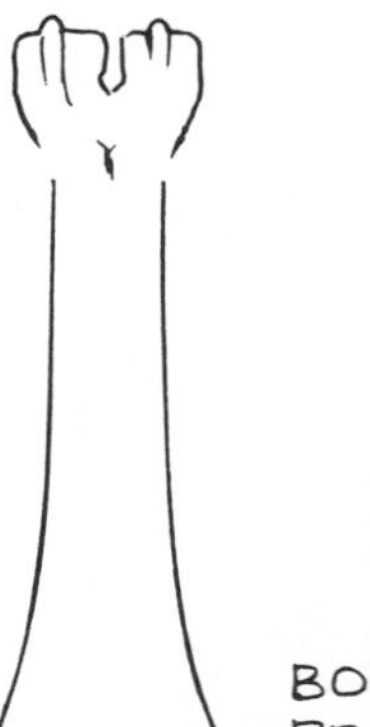

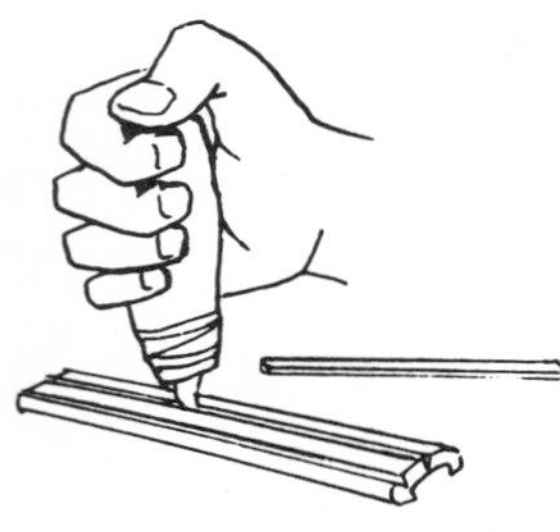

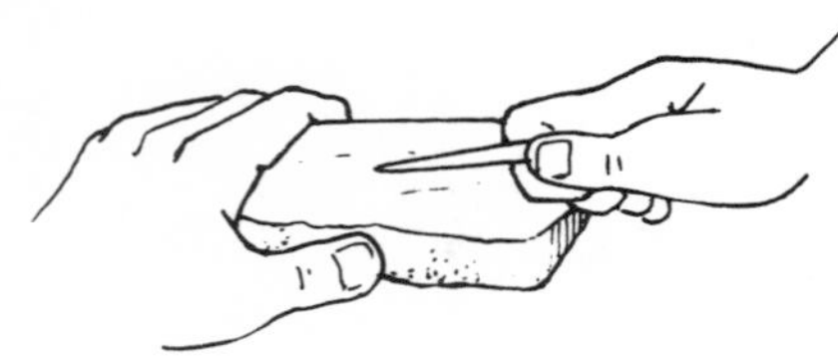

Argillite dish depicting halibut, with abalone shell inlay. 15cm (6 inches)
60.13.HA

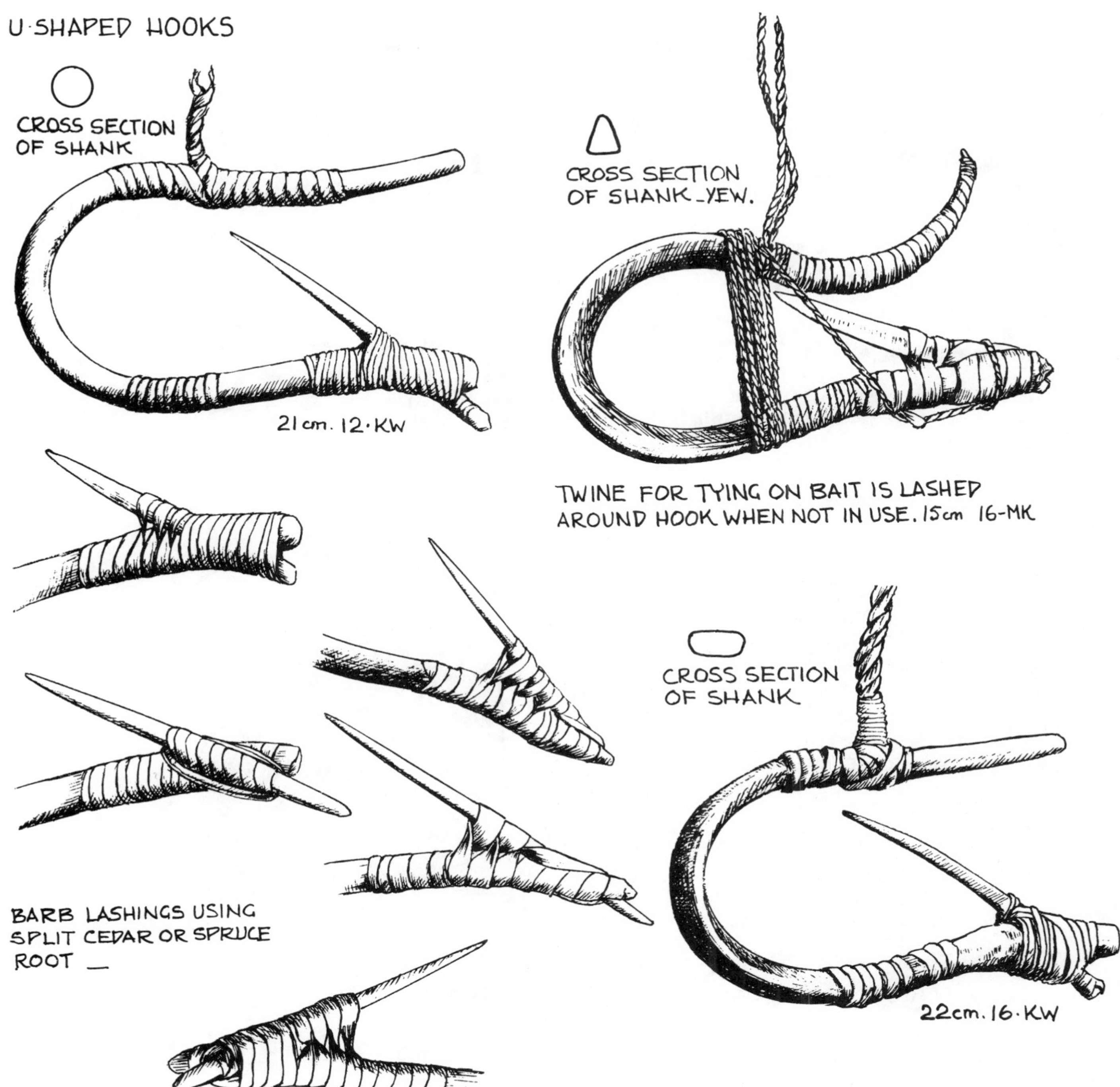
U·SHAPED HOOKS
CROSS SECTION
OF SHANK
21cm. 12·KW
CROSS SECTION
OF SHANK_YEW.
TWINE FOR TYING ON BAIT IS LASHED
AROUND HOOK WHEN NOT IN USE. 15cm 16-MK
CROSS SECTION
OF SHANK
BARB LASHINGS USING
SPLIT CEDAR OR SPRUCE
ROOT _
22cm. 16·KW

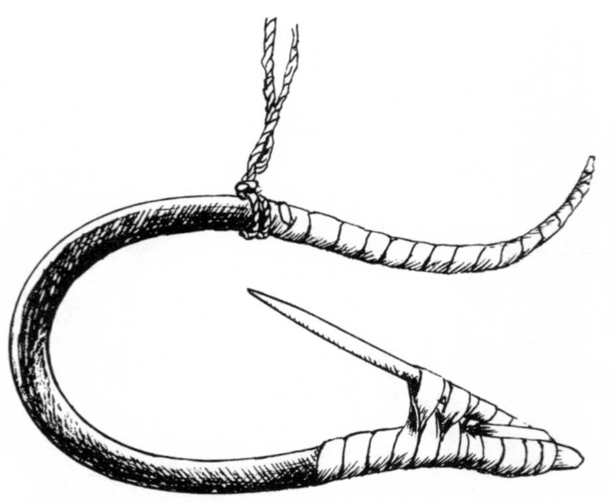

STEAM-BENT YEW WOOD HOOK, BONE BARB, CEDAR ROOT LASHING 15·8 cm. 16·MK

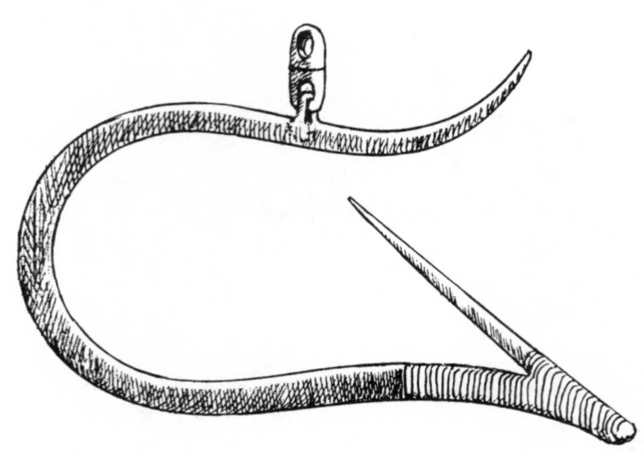

ALL METAL HOOK, WITH SWIVEL TOP, EMULATES TRADITIONAL BENTWOOD HOOK 13·5 cm 19·X

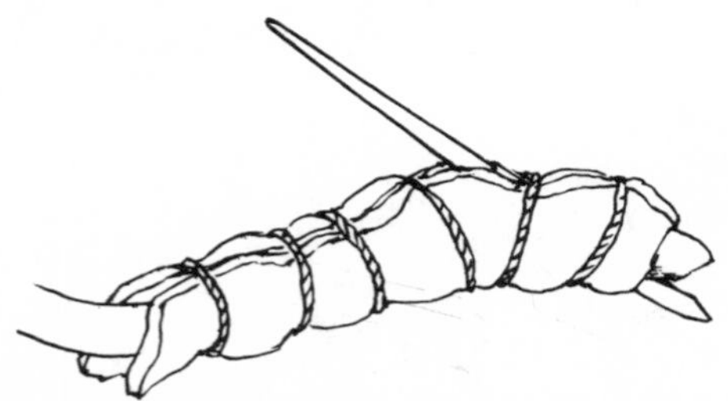

TWO STRIPS OF OCTOPUS OR OTHER BAIT TIED TO SIDES OF HOOK BELOW BARB. 56·CS

SMALL FISH PUT RIGHT OVER THE BONE BARB. 55·NK

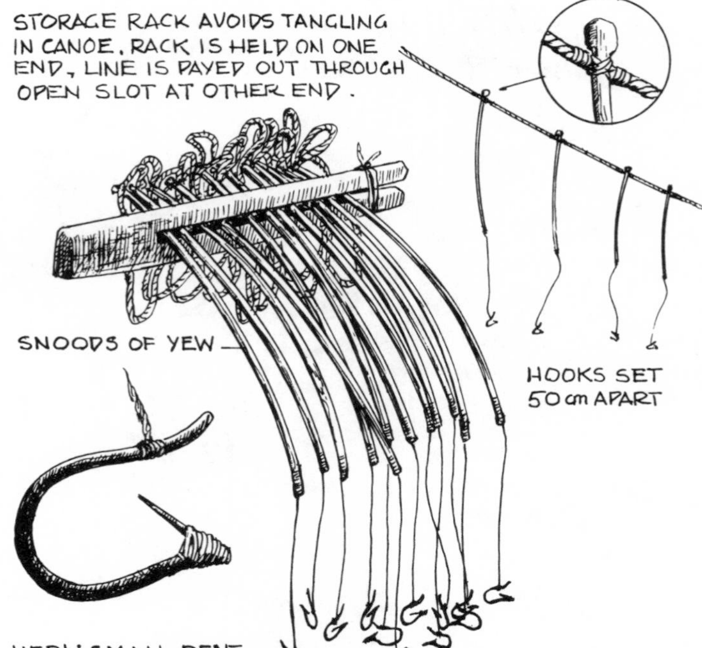

VERY SMALL BENT IRON HOOKS 4·8 cm 11·KW

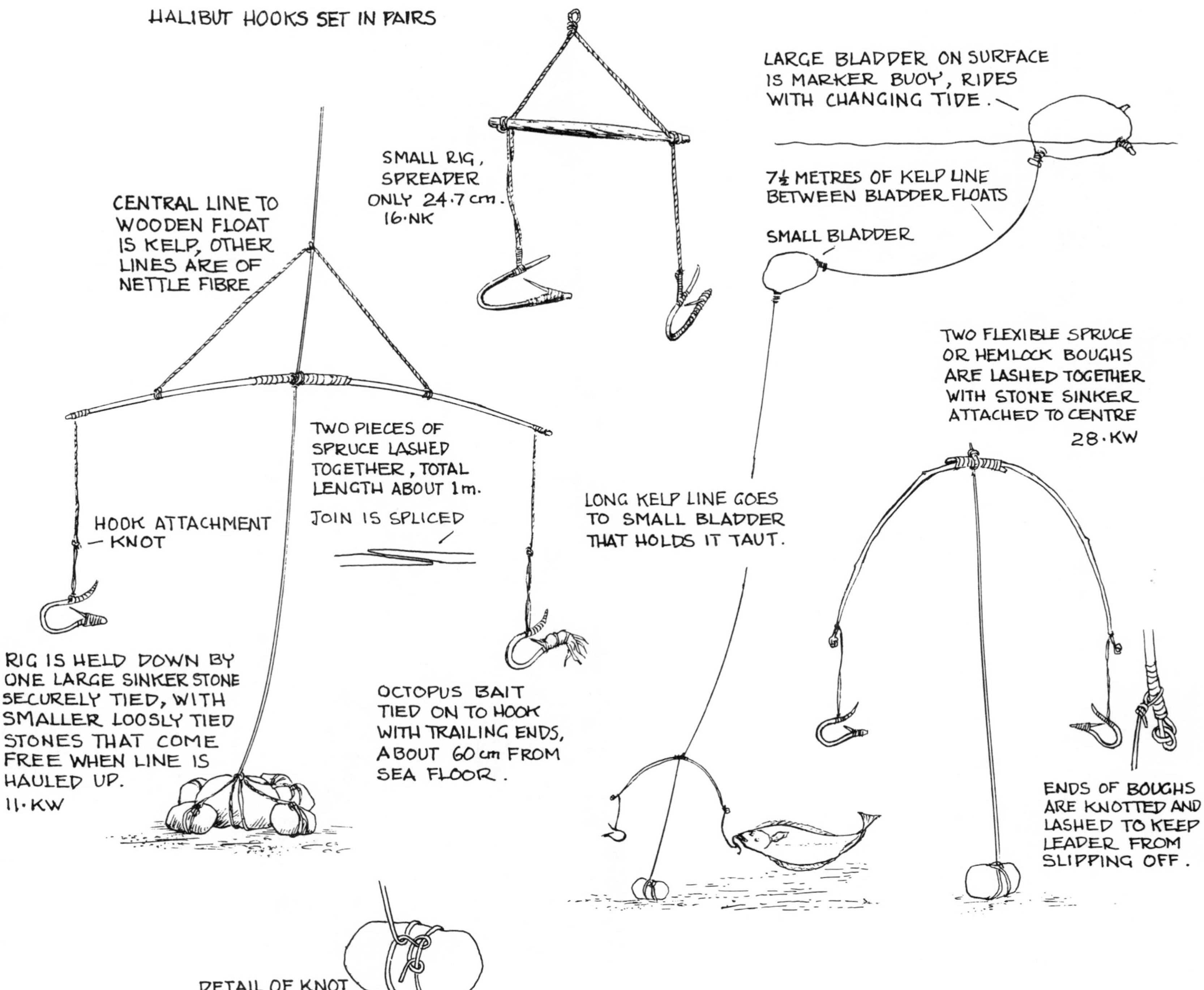

HALIBUT HOOKS SET IN PAIRS
SMALL RIG, SPREADER ONLY 24.7 cm. 16.NK
LARGE BLADDER ON SURFACE IS MARKER BUOY, RIDES WITH CHANGING TIDE.
7½ METRES OF KELP LINE BETWEEN BLADDER FLOATS
SMALL BLADDER
CENTRAL LINE TO WOODEN FLOAT IS KELP, OTHER LINES ARE OF NETTLE FIBRE
TWO PIECES OF SPRUCE LASHED TOGETHER, TOTAL LENGTH ABOUT 1m.
JOIN IS SPLICED
HOOK ATTACHMENT — KNOT
TWO FLEXIBLE SPRUCE OR HEMLOCK BOUGHS ARE LASHED TOGETHER WITH STONE SINKER ATTACHED TO CENTRE
28.KW
LONG KELP LINE GOES TO SMALL BLADDER THAT HOLDS IT TAUT.
RIG IS HELD DOWN BY ONE LARGE SINKER STONE SECURELY TIED, WITH SMALLER LOOSLY TIED STONES THAT COME FREE WHEN LINE IS HAULED UP.
11.KW
OCTOPUS BAIT TIED ON TO HOOK WITH TRAILING ENDS, ABOUT 60 cm FROM SEA FLOOR.
ENDS OF BOUGHS ARE KNOTTED AND LASHED TO KEEP LEADER FROM SLIPPING OFF.
DETAIL OF KNOT

BENTWOOD HOOKS

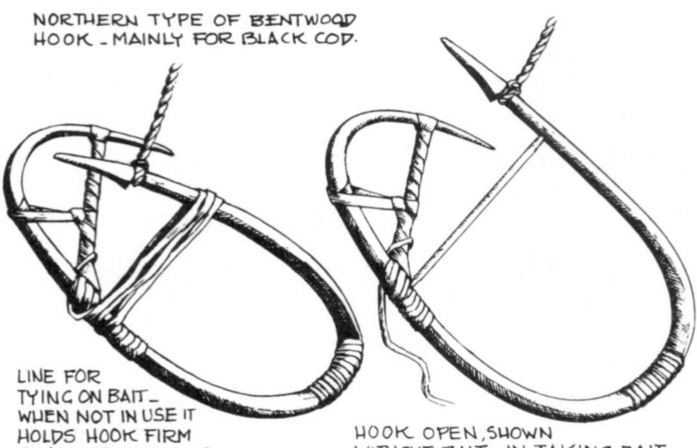

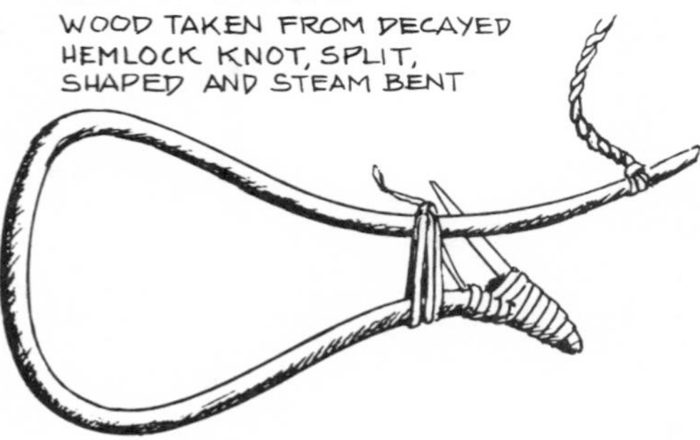

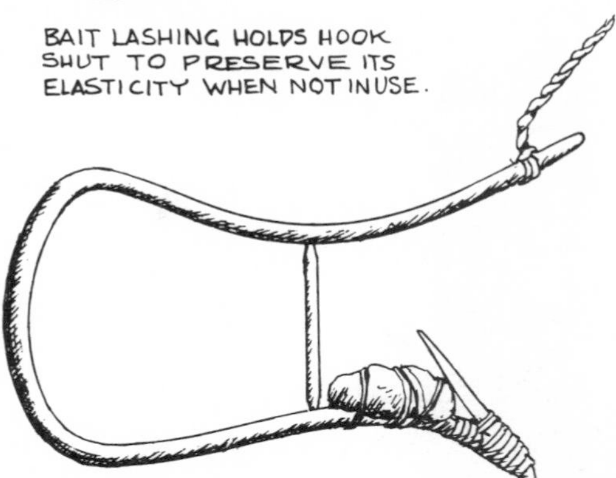

Totem poles at Masset, Queen Charlotte Islands. 25.HA

Salmon Trolling

Salmon could be caught in great numbers in traps and dams once they began their migration up river, but they were also successfully caught by trolling with hook and line in the bays and inlets, especially when they congregated prior to the run.

John R. Jewitt, a ship's armourer held captive by the famed Nootka Chief Maquinna for two years (1803-1805), describes the method of trolling in the narrative written from the diary he kept.

"One person seats himself in a small canoe, and, baiting his hook with a sprat, which they are always careful to procure as fresh as possible, fastens his line to the handle of the paddle; this, as he plies it in the water, keeps the fish in constant motion, so as to give it the appearance of life, which the salmon seeing, leaps at it and is instantly hooked, and by a sudden and dextrous motion of the paddle, drawn on board. I have known some of the natives take no less than eight or ten salmon of a morning, in this manner, and have seen from twenty to thirty canoes at a time in Friendly Cove thus employed."

The "sprat" referred to was most likely a shiner, which the Nootka caught for bait in small stone dams.

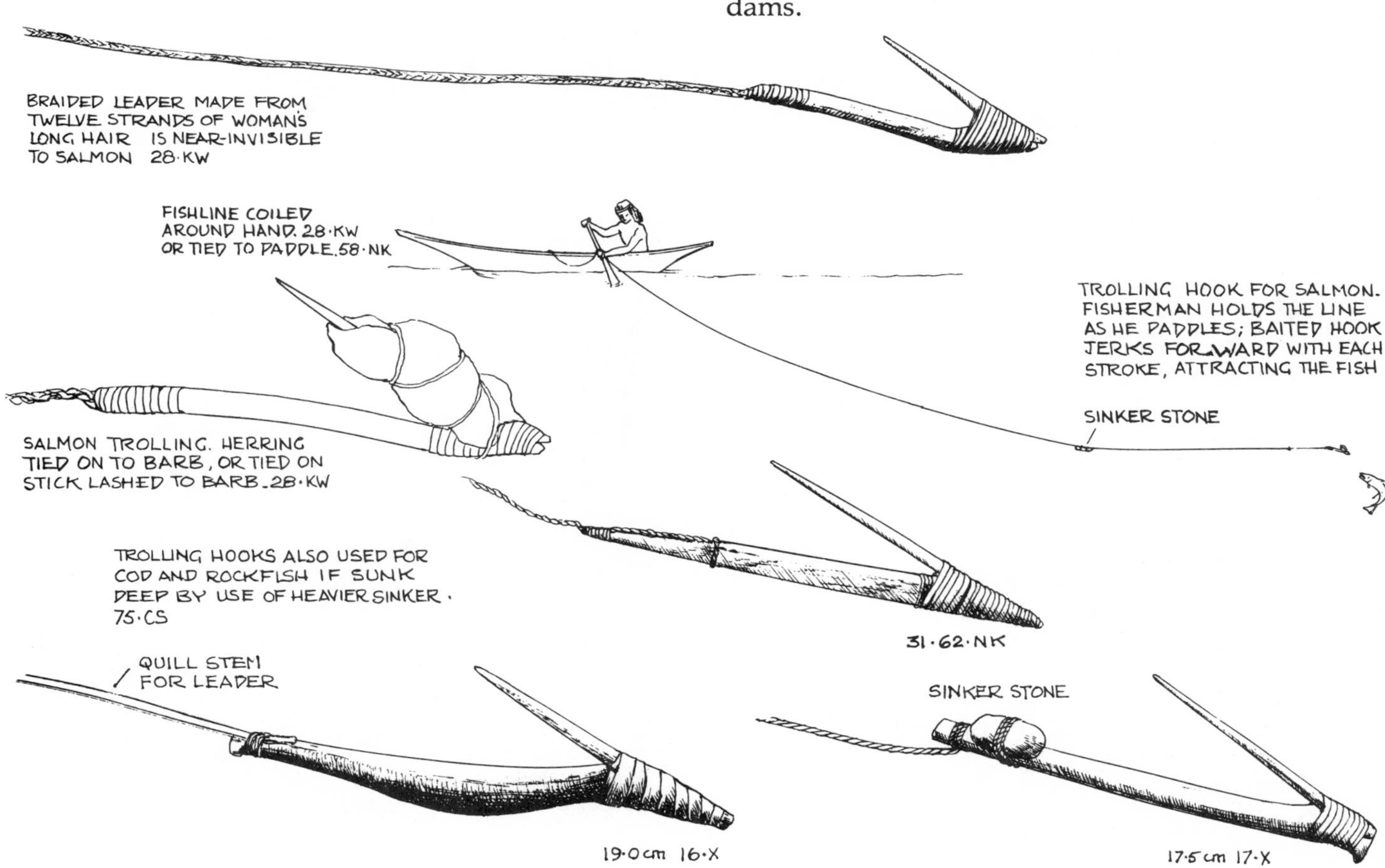

Carved and painted fish. Wood. 44.3cm (18½ inches) 60.10.X

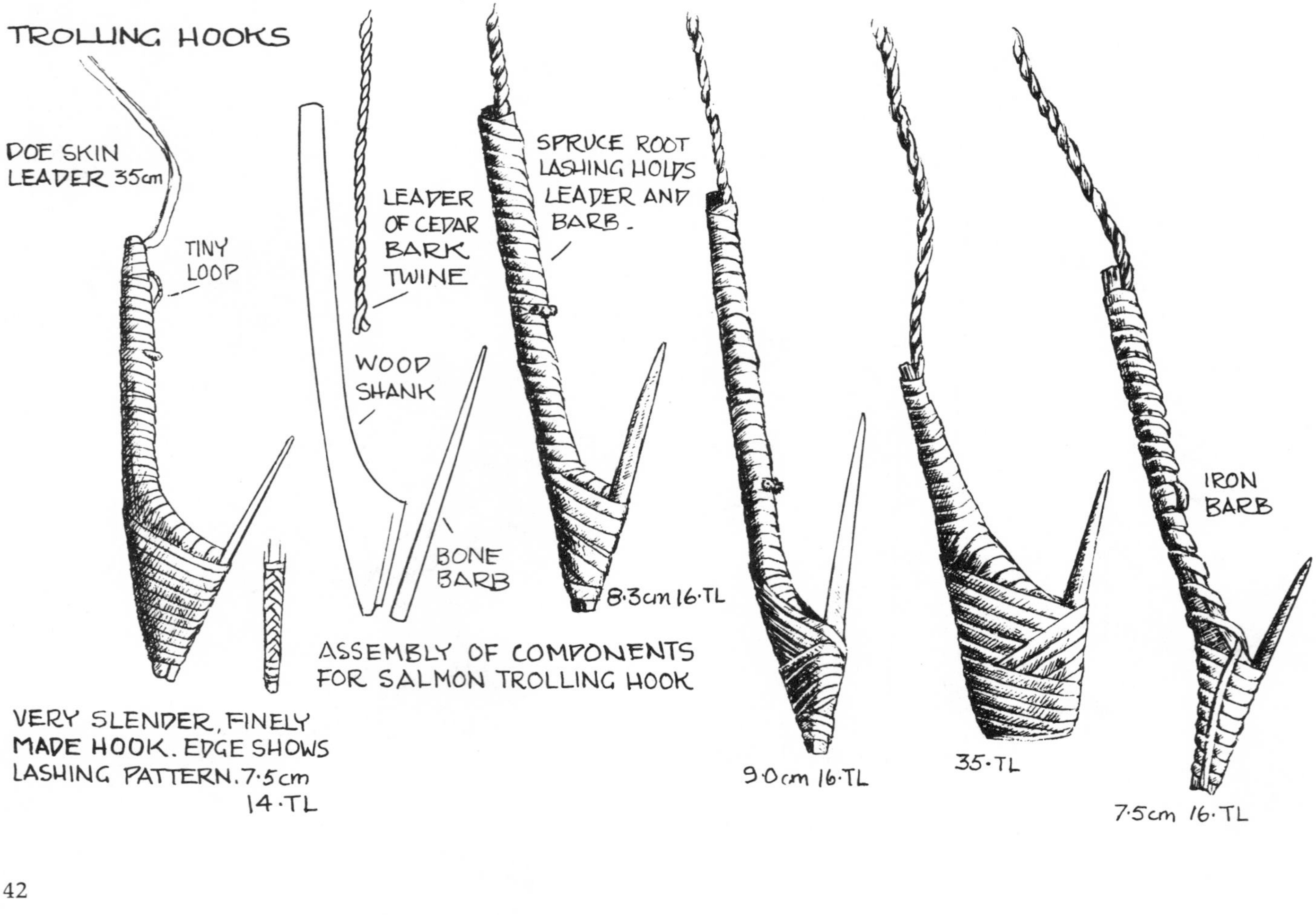

TROLLING HOOKS

DOE SKIN LEADER 35cm

TINY LOOP

LEADER OF CEDAR BARK TWINE

WOOD SHANK

BONE BARB

SPRUCE ROOT LASHING HOLDS LEADER AND BARB.

8·3cm 16·TL

ASSEMBLY OF COMPONENTS FOR SALMON TROLLING HOOK

VERY SLENDER, FINELY MADE HOOK. EDGE SHOWS LASHING PATTERN. 7·5cm 14·TL

9·0cm 16·TL

35·TL

IRON BARB

7·5cm 16·TL

MISCELLANEOUS HOOKS

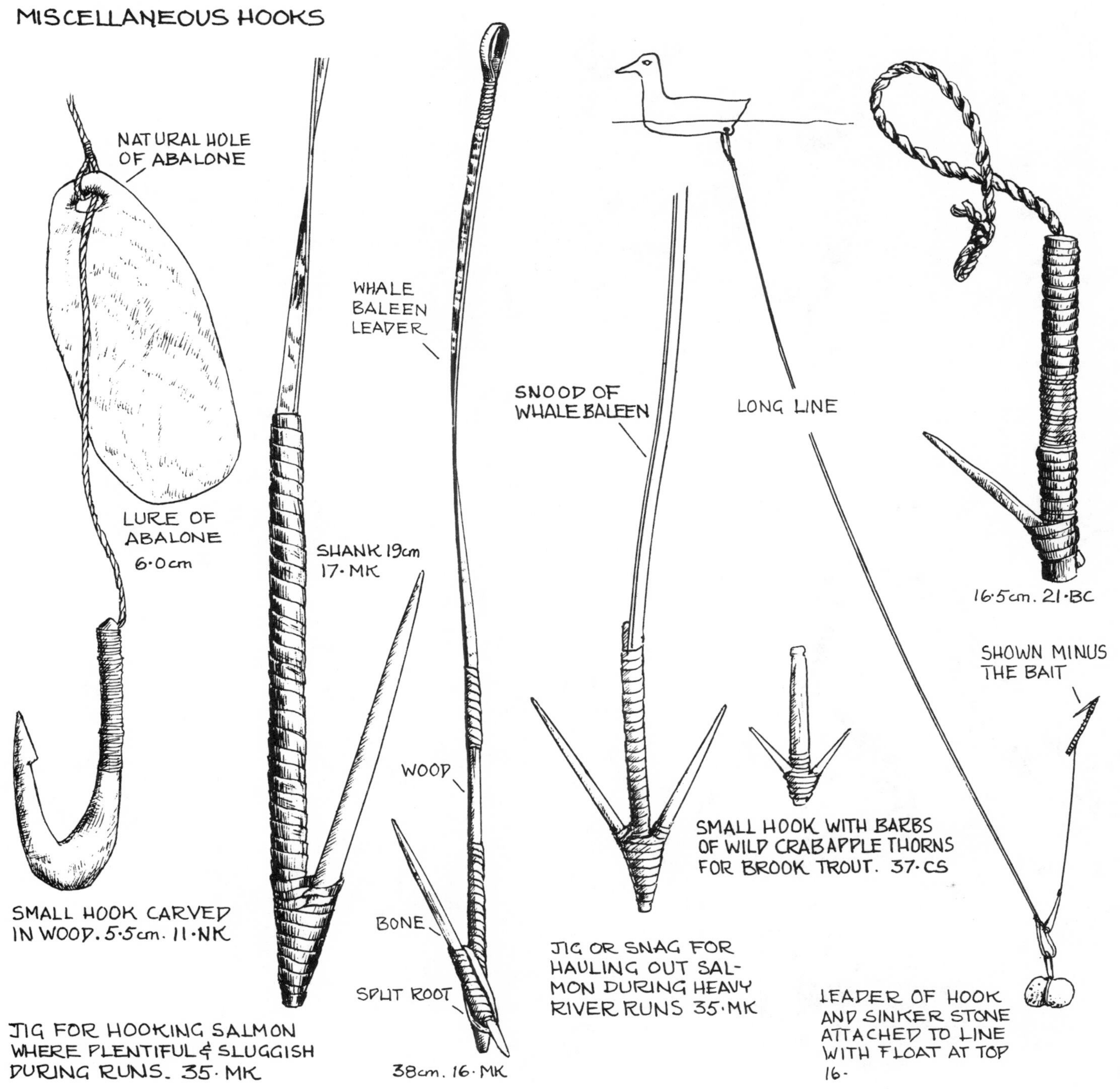

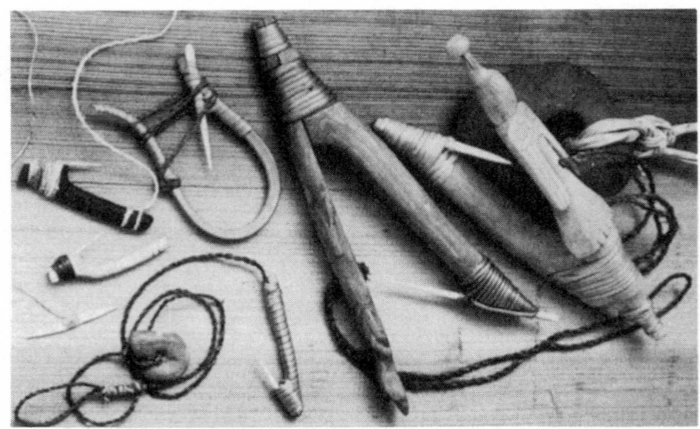

Variety of fish hooks made by the author. All cordage is two-strand inner cedar bark. 60.

FISH HOOK SHANKS MADE OF BONE.

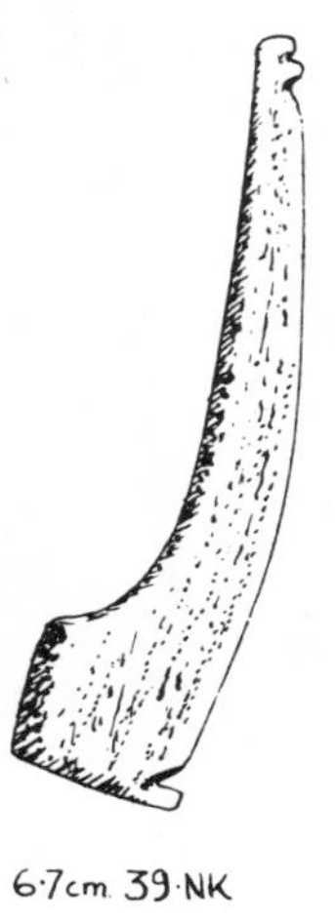

6·7cm 39·NK

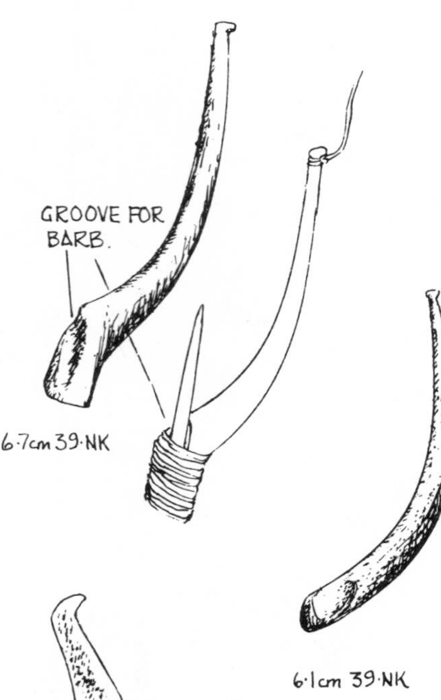

GROOVE FOR BARB.

6·7cm 39·NK

6·1cm 39·NK

FISH HOOK SHANKS MADE OF SLATE

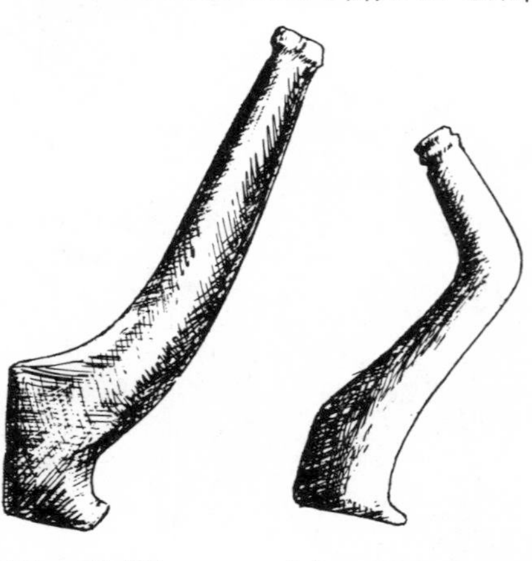

8·3cm 39·NK

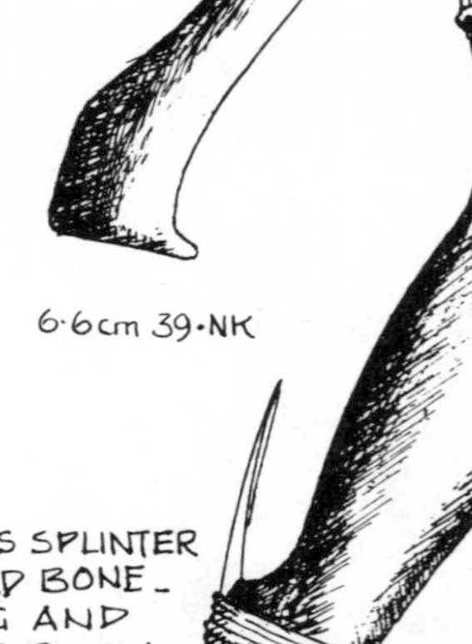

6·6cm 39·NK

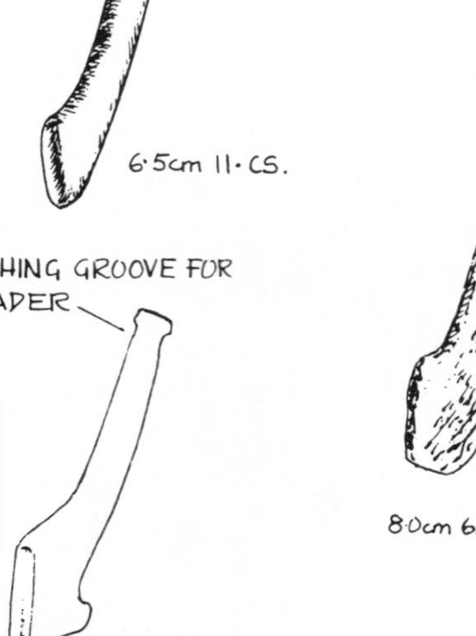

6·5cm 11·CS.

LASHING GROOVE FOR LEADER

BARB IS SPLINTER OF BIRD BONE. LASHING AND LEADER SINEW. SHANK IS SLATE. 9·3cm. 14·NK.

GROOVE TO HOLD BARB, AND SPUR TO HOLD LASHING

8·0cm 63·HA

5·0cm 63·HA

THROAT GORGES

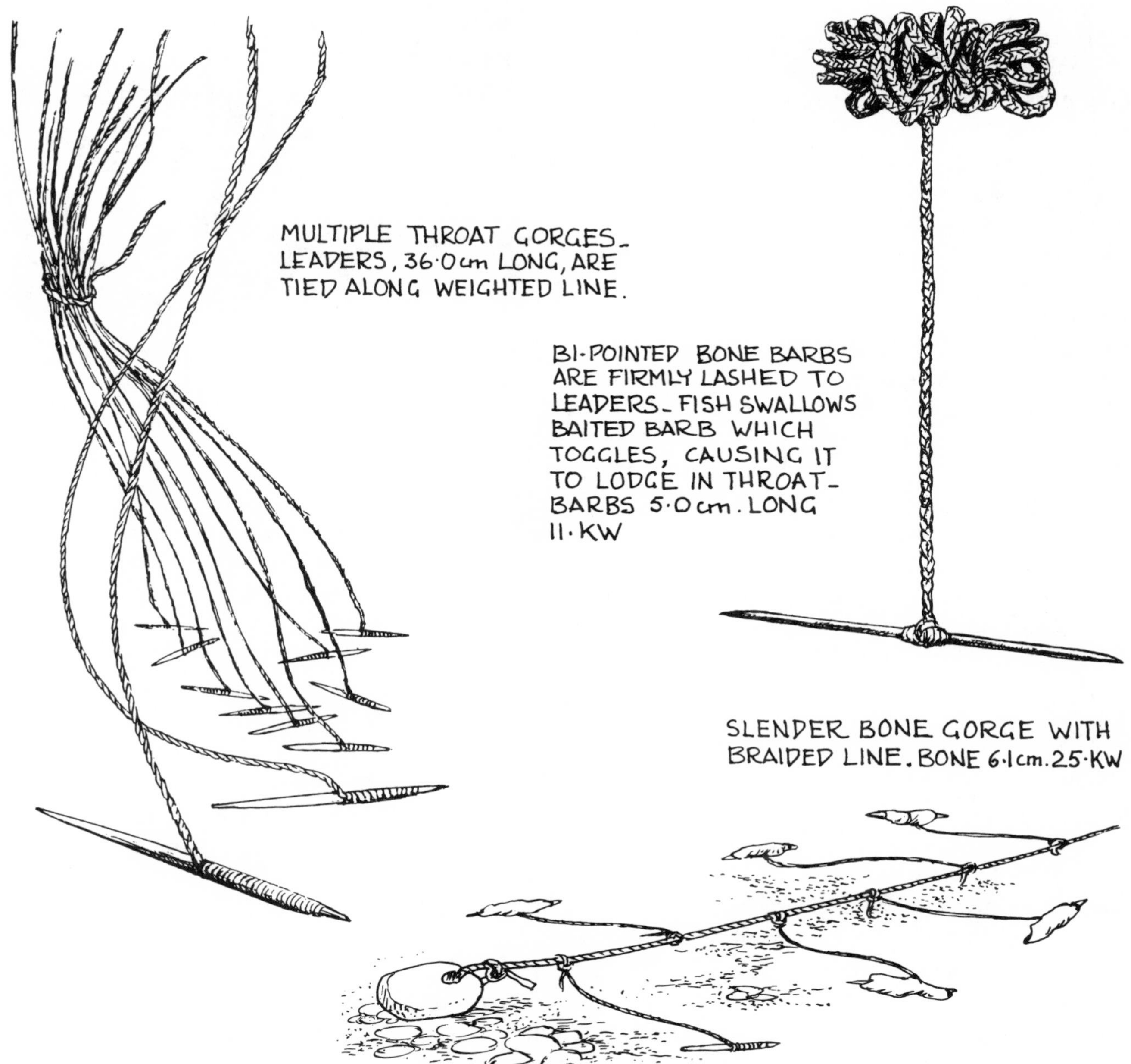

BAITED THROAT GORGES ATTACHED TO WEIGHTED LINE CATCH BOTTOM FEEDING FISH.

The Northern Halibut Hook

One of the largest fish to be caught along the coast, the halibut was particularly important to the people of the north coast, where the salmon was not caught in the quantities available to the more southern people.

Hatched in deep water, developing halibut float freely for the first six months of life. As they rise to the surface, these flat fish are carried by wind-driven currents onto the shallower section of the continental shelf. Here the fish rotates so that its broad surface is parallel to the sea bed. Now it is a bottom feeder, and to adapt to this change the fish's left eye migrates over the snout so that both eyes are on the upper surface. The mouth is then to one side, giving the head a strange, twisted look. The average weight of a halibut is between 30 and 36 pounds, but fish up to 200 pounds used to be taken by hook and line.

Although all coast tribes caught halibut, the Makah on the Olympic Peninsula in Washington and the Haida and Tlingit in the north were the most extensive harvesters of this fish, some venturing great distances to reach major halibut banks.

One of the most interesting and beautiful of all fish hooks is that used by the northerners for catching this great fish. This is the "clumsy hook" referred to by Niblack: two sections lashed together in a V shape. One arm of this "V" was often carved with a significant design. Since a halibut fisherman required a spirit helper, or power, to be successful in catching this very large and powerful fish, it seems likely that the designs had a significance relating to power. Two common figures were that of the octopus, or devil fish—a common bait for this hook—and that of a woman.

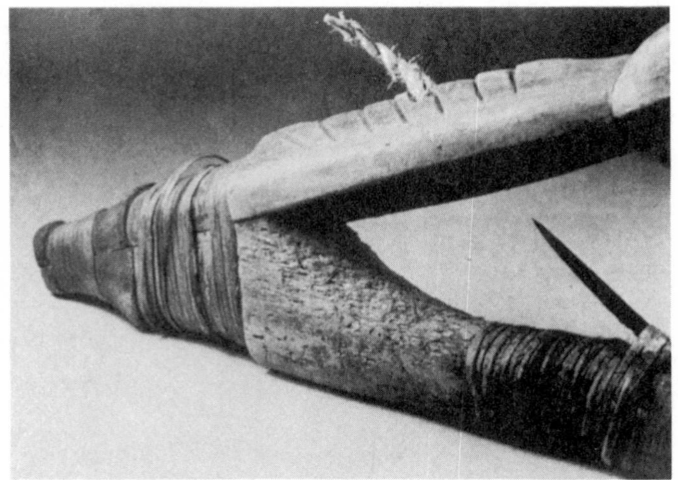

Halibut hook showing damage to lower arm caused by teeth of struggling fish. 60.HA

"Old Woman" was one of the many names used for the halibut; songs and legends were the sources for many others, including:

Scenting Woman
Wrinkled-in-the-Mouth
Born-To-Be-Giver-of-the-House
Flabby-Skin-in-the-Mouth
Squint-Eye
Old-Coming-Across-Going-Around-Island
Never-Appearing-Going-Around-the-Island
Big-One-Who-Comes-Taking-Pebbles-into-the-Mouth
Rising-Steeply
Great-One-Coming-Up-Against-the-Current

The undecorated arm of the V hook had a barb lashed to it, and it was this barb, impaled in the mouth of the fish, that held it firmly. Some of the barbed arms of hooks found in museums are rough and shredded from the frantic biting of the captive halibut; sometimes fish must have remained on the hook for some time before the fisherman returned to haul in the line. Since many of these hooks are comprised of two different woods which appear to be of different age, it seems very possible that a chewed-up section, when too badly damaged, would be discarded and a new piece fitted to the carved arm.

With the increasing introduction of metal to the coast cultures, iron replaced bone for the barbs of many fish hooks as they were made or repaired. Iron was a stronger ally against a large, fighting fish, but I believe that it also created a new problem. When baited with devil fish, which floats, the wooden hook maintained its correct position under the water, but when an iron barb was used, the equilibrium was destroyed and the hook sank. It became necessary to add a small float near the hook to counteract this effect. Among the many hooks I examined in the course of research for this book, these small floats were attached only to hooks having iron barbs. In one instance where the complete hook, not just the barb, was of iron, the float was correspondingly larger.

Sailing in the territorial waters of the northern Tlingit in 1787, Captain Dixon described the halibut fishing of the Indian people in his journal:

"They bait their hooks with a kind of fish . . . or squid . . . and having sunk it to the bottom they fix a bladder to the end of the line as a buoy . . . . One man is sufficient to look after five or six of these buoys; when he perceives a fish bite he is in no great hurry to haul up his line, but gives him time to be well hooked, and when he has hauled the fish up to the surface of the water he knocks him on the head with a short club. This is done to prevent the halibut (which sometimes are very large) from damaging or perhaps upsetting his canoe in their dying struggles."

To find out exactly how the halibut took its hook, I visited the Pacific Environment Institute in West Vancouver, where fish are kept outdoors in large round tanks for a variety of studies, including the effects of pollution.

In a tank housing half a dozen halibut, the water level was lowered to a few inches so that I could see the fish better and take photographs. Pieces of codfish were tossed into the tank and I saw that the halibut did not bite at the food the way a salmon or trout does, but drew it in with a strong sucking action, much like that of a vacuum cleaner. If the food taken in was acceptable, it was retained; otherwise it was expelled with equal force. The native V-shaped hook owes its success to a design that accommodates the flat shape of the fish and responds to the fish's method of eating. The bait, wrapped around the barb, was taken into the mouth, but because it could not be swallowed it was rejected. The forceful exit of the angled barb cause it to penetrate the cheek on the underside, and the fish was hooked. It could not go forward to release itself because of the V shape, and its attempts to withdraw only secured the barb more firmly.

I was curious to see this hook in action. Not having the nerve to ask a museum to lend me a halibut hook to go fishing, I made one, complete with deer bone barb, spruce root lashing, inner cedar bark leader and line, and a perforated stone sinker. For luck I carved a river otter on one arm of the hook, a creature well experienced in the art of fishing. With a "gone fishing" sign on my door I returned to the Pacific Environment Institute and their tank of halibut. Before tying on the bait with a string of cedar bark I rubbed my hands with seaweed and held them in the salt water, as was customary, to remove the human scent. Ever co-operative, the fisheries biologist Don McQuarry stood by with a small tank of sea water containing anesthetic so that the fish could be subdued and the hook removed.

Down went the stone sinker; up floated the baited hook attached to the sinker. I held onto the cedar bark line and watched, saying the Kwagiutl prayer to Scenting Woman to take the "sweet tasting food" and "not to keep me waiting long on the water." Twice a fish sucked at the barbed end of the hook only to reject it. A third attempt; the same. I then realized that the fish in the tank were too small to take the angled barb fully into their mouths, and I saw how the size of the halibut to be caught could be controlled by the size and angle of the barb, and the size of the hook.

I made another, smaller hook. This time I carved Raven flying with the sun in his beak, copied after the beautiful halibut hook in the Portland Art Museum that is one of my favorites. Then it was back to the Pacific Environment Institute. On went the bait and down went the sinker once more. From the bottom, Scenting Woman looked up and saw Raven taking the sun to the sky to bring daylight to all the world. The Old Woman smelled the squid wrapped on the hook, heard the words beseeching her to take the "sweet food," and obeyed. There was a violent thrashing as the hooked fish fought for its life. I saw the hook embedded in its mouth and hurriedly hauled in the cedar bark line. But as she reached the surface the old Squint Eye gave a mighty jerk, the leader broke, and she was free. Perhaps I should have been "in no great hurry to haul in the line." It might have been that I lacked a spirit helper—the power considered so necessary for halibut fishing. In any event, I understood the urgency of the fisherman's prayer to the hook, which he termed Younger Brother, when, hauling up the fish from a considerable depth, he said:

"Now hold this, my younger brother,
Don't let go this, my Younger Brother."

When the hook was eventually retrieved I found pitted scuff marks on the wood where the halibut had tried biting off the end of the hook. The fish was only a small one, but its strength and spirit left me with a finer respect for fishermen who made their tackle and took their dugout canoes out to the halibut banks to entice Scenting Woman to the bait—men who spent long cold hours on the water to ensure that their families had food for the winter.

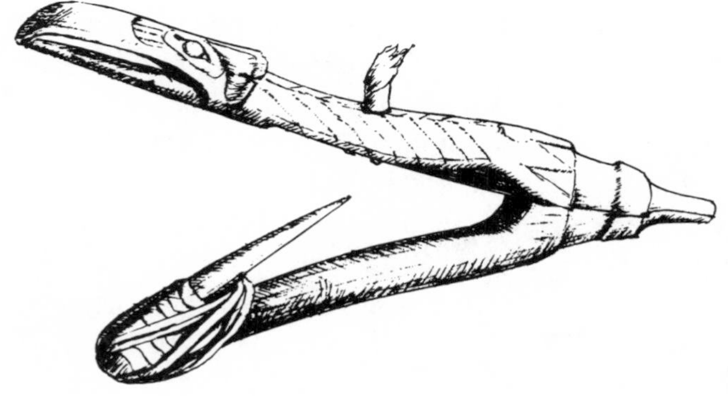

ONE-PIECE NORTHERN HALIBUT HOOKS

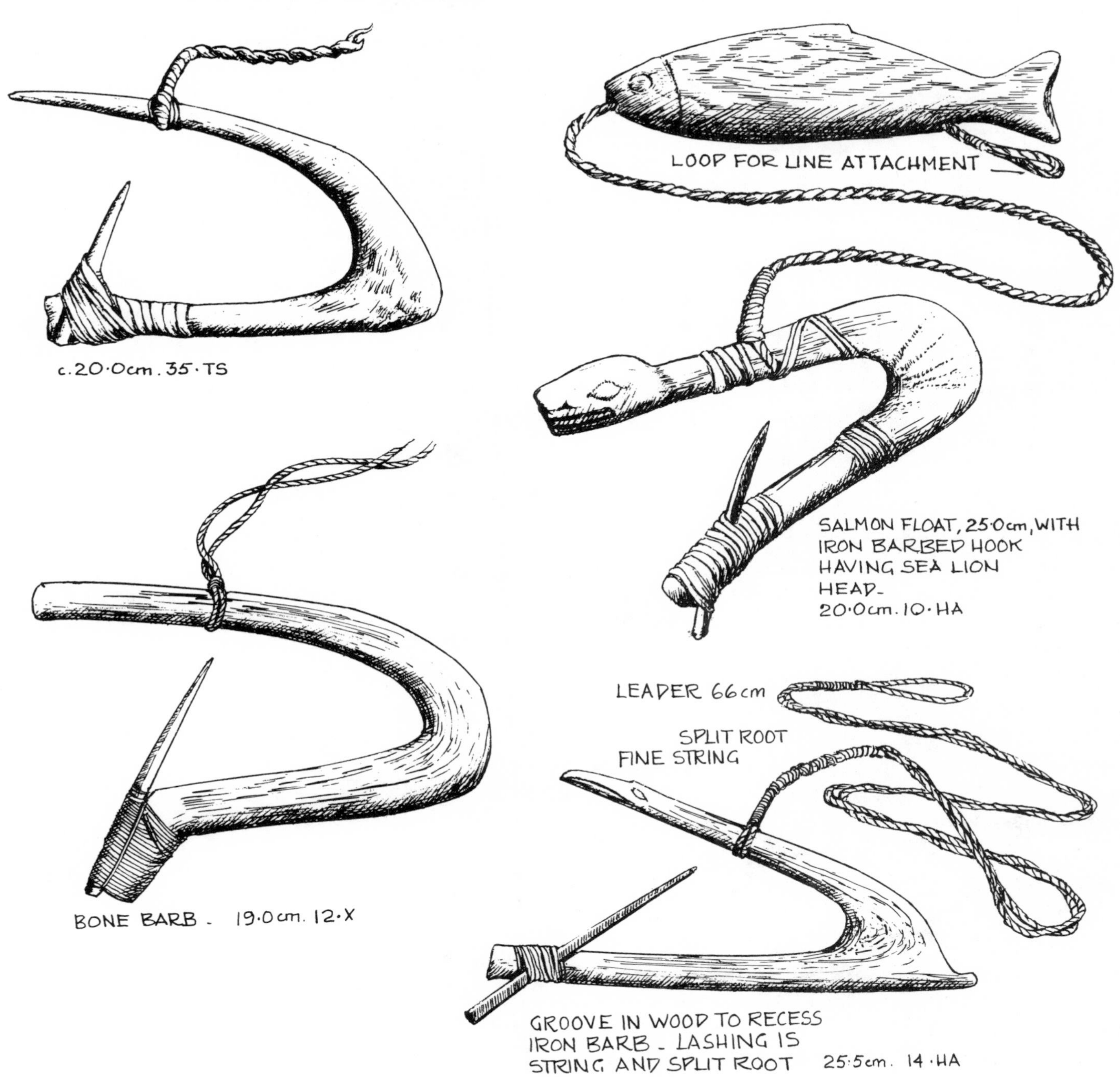

V HOOKS WITH ONE-PIECE SHANKS

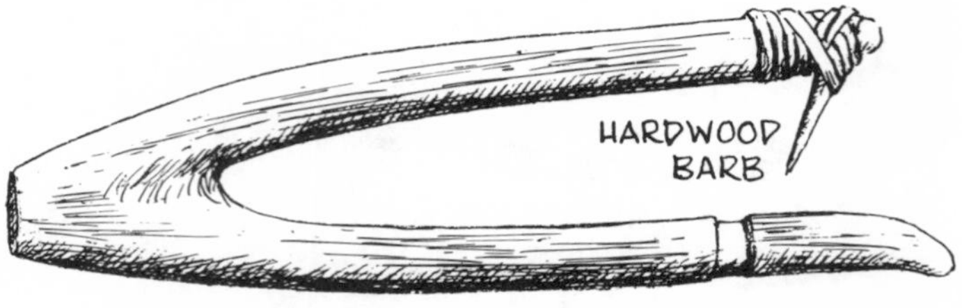

HARDWOOD BARB

BLACK COD HOOK. 23·6cm. 21·TL

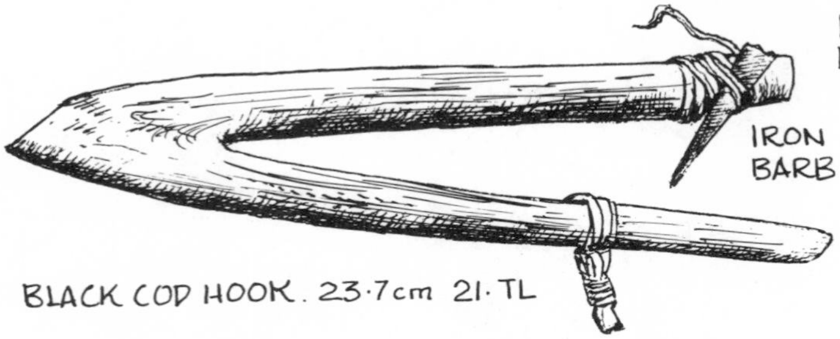

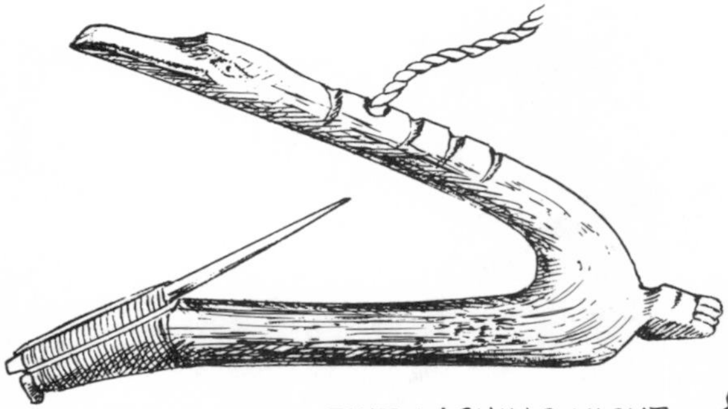

BONE BARB; VERY FINE LASHING MIGHT BE SAILMAKER'S THREAD - 25·0cm 14·HA

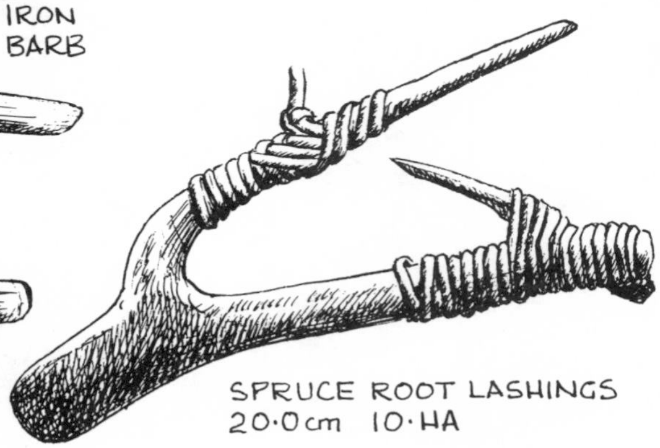

IRON BARB

BLACK COD HOOK. 23·7cm 21·TL

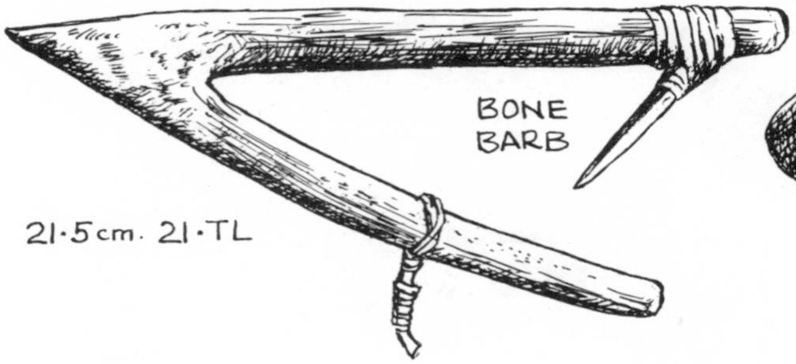

BONE BARB

SPRUCE ROOT LASHINGS 20·0cm 10·HA

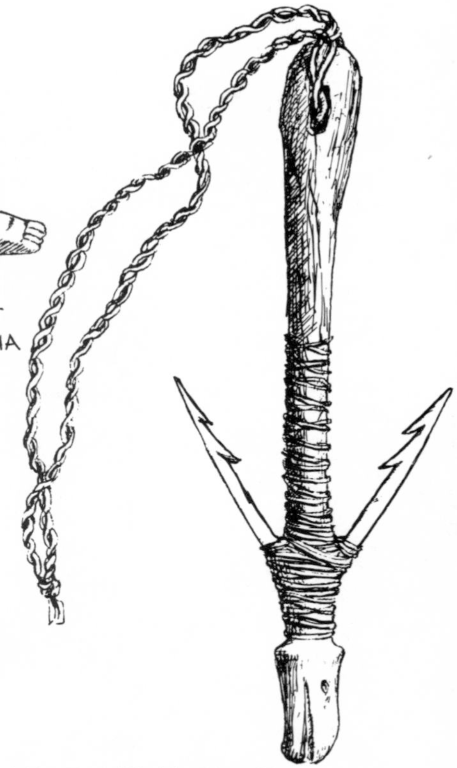

21·5cm. 21·TL

MODEL OF ANCIENT TYPE OF HALIBUT HOOK OFTEN REFERRED TO IN RAVEN STORIES - CARVING IS SEA DOG. 23·0cm. 25·HA

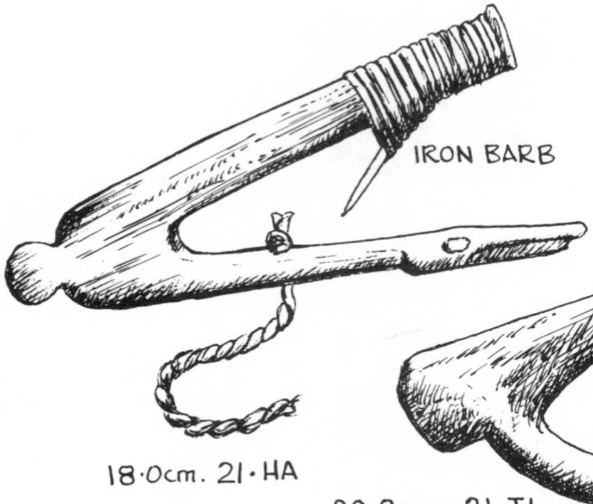

IRON BARB

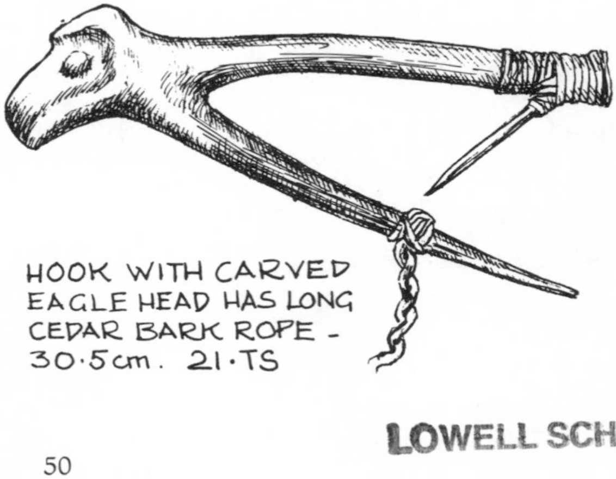

HOOK WITH CARVED EAGLE HEAD HAS LONG CEDAR BARK ROPE - 30·5cm. 21·TS

18·0cm. 21·HA

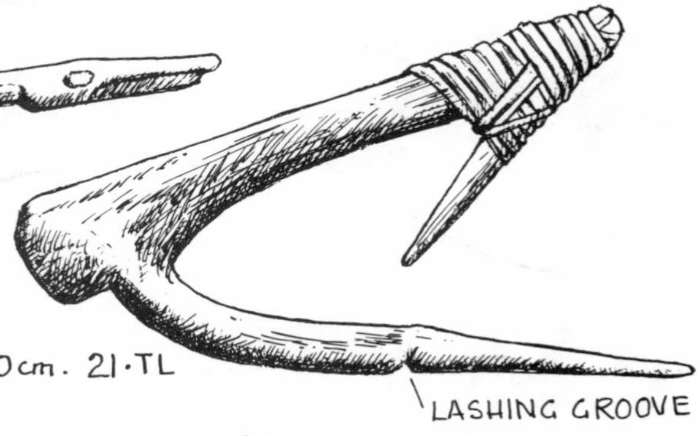

20·0cm. 21·TL

LASHING GROOVE

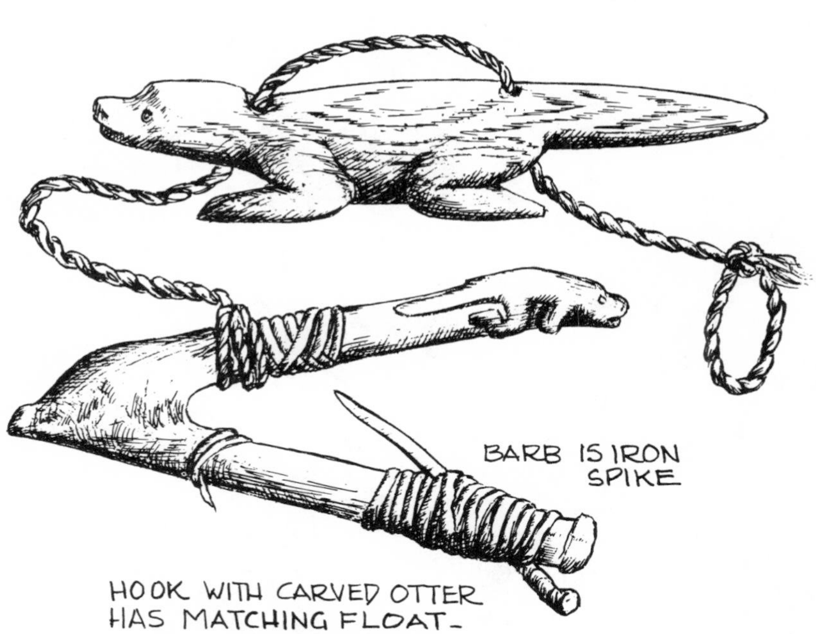

BARB IS IRON SPIKE

HOOK WITH CARVED OTTER HAS MATCHING FLOAT – OTTER REPRESENTS SUCCESS IN FISHING.
FLOAT 28cm. HOOK 25·7cm 10-HA

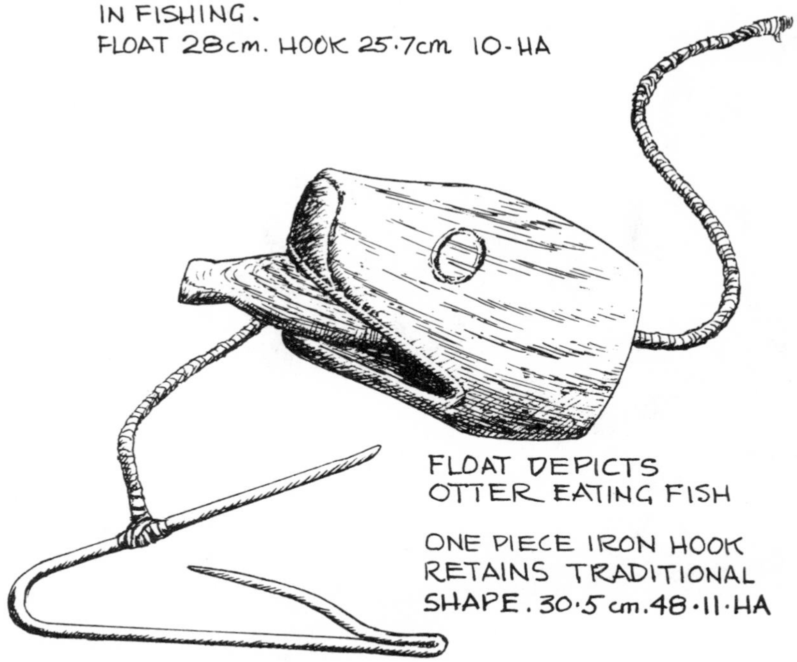

FLOAT DEPICTS OTTER EATING FISH

ONE PIECE IRON HOOK RETAINS TRADITIONAL SHAPE. 30·5 cm. 48·11·HA

Hilt of dagger representing dogfish. Yew wood, carved both sides. 60.19.X

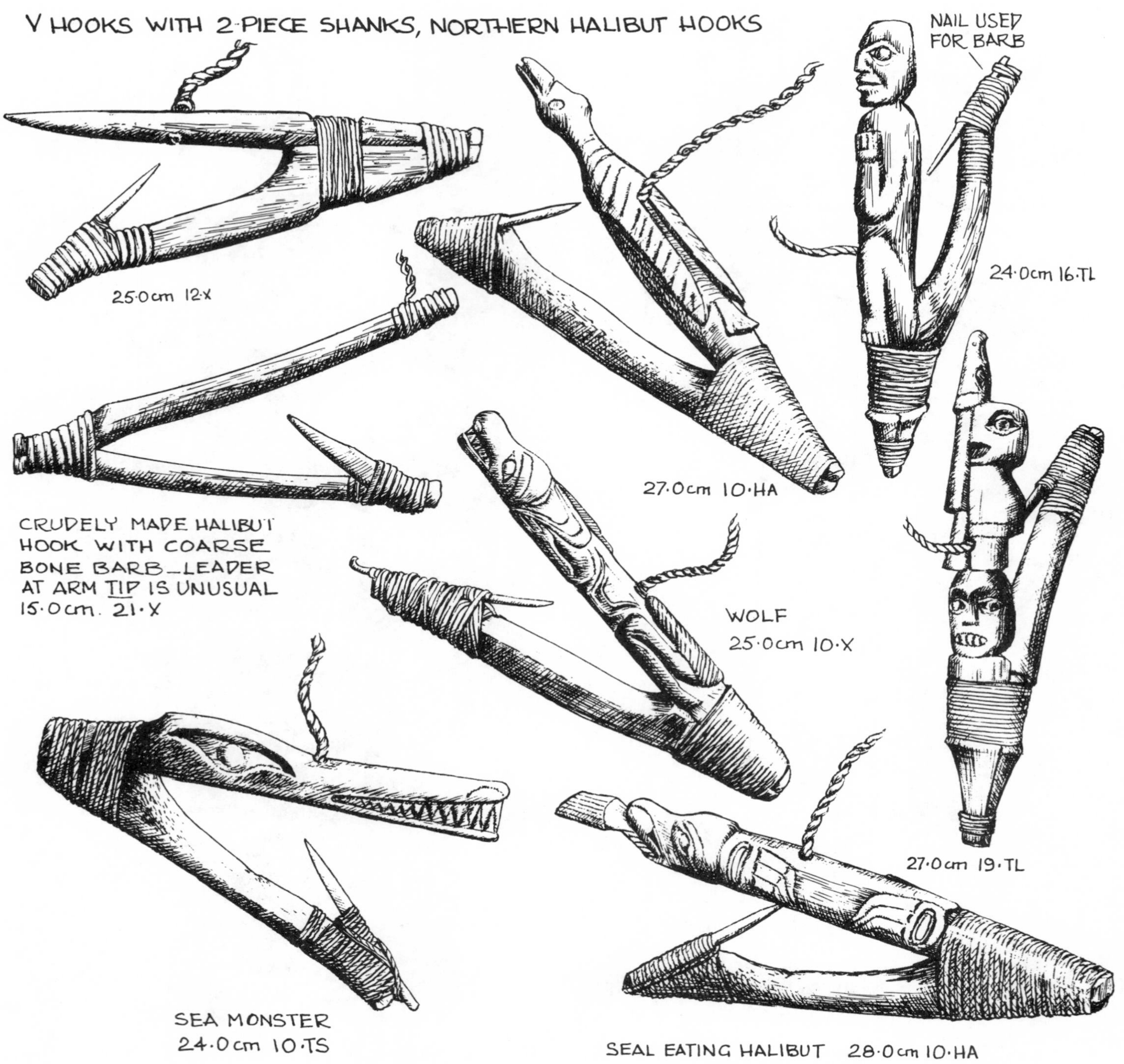
V HOOKS WITH 2-PIECE SHANKS, NORTHERN HALIBUT HOOKS
NAIL USED
FOR BARB
25·0cm 12·X
24·0cm 16·TL
27·0cm 10·HA
CRUDELY MADE HALIBUT
HOOK WITH COARSE
BONE BARB_LEADER
AT ARM TIP IS UNUSUAL
15·0cm. 21·X
WOLF
25·0cm 10·X
27·0cm 19·TL
SEA MONSTER
24·0cm 10·TS
SEAL EATING HALIBUT 28·0cm 10·HA

NORTHERN HALIBUT HOOKS WITH CARVED DESIGNS.

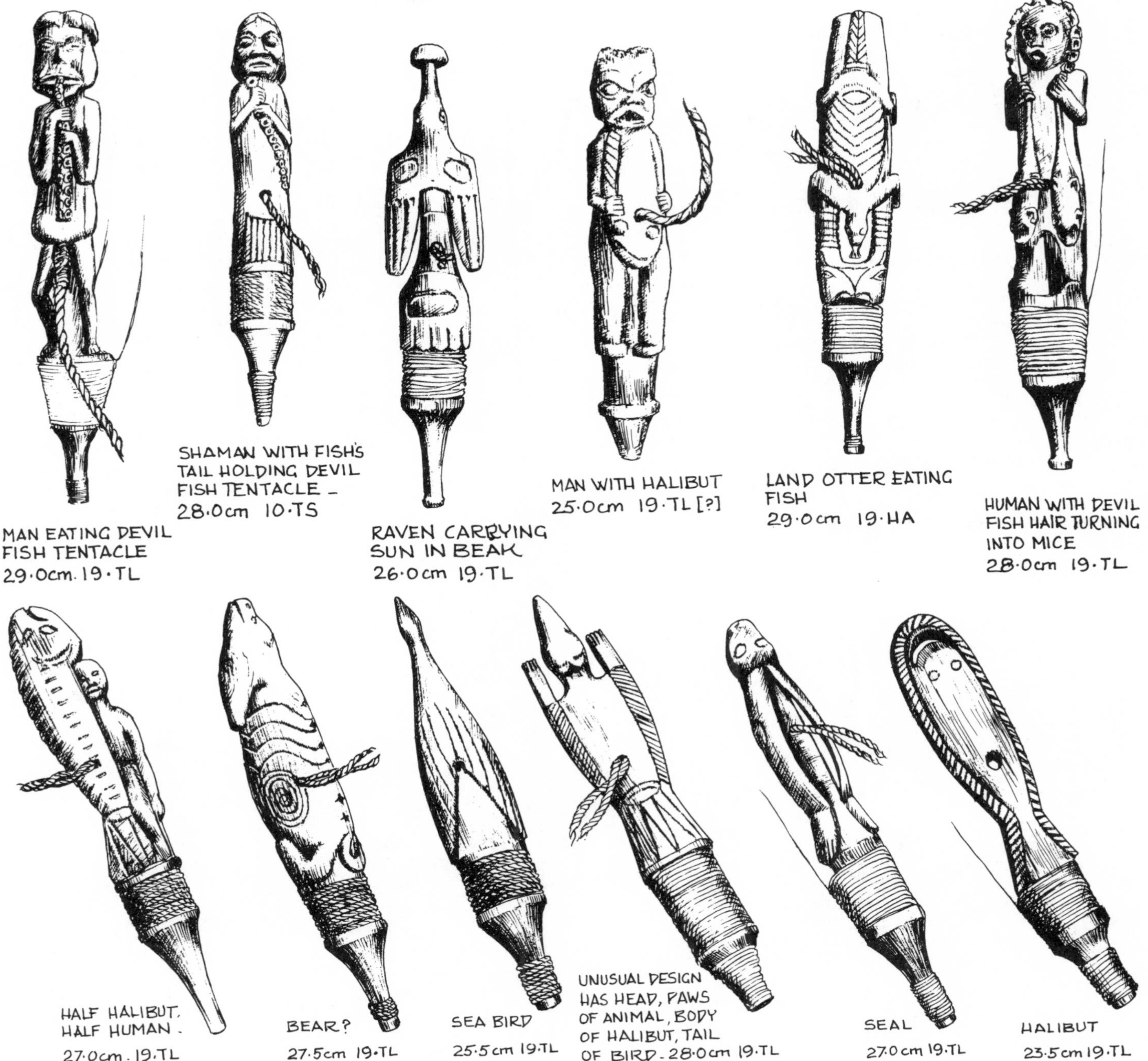

HOW A HALIBUT TAKES THE HOOK

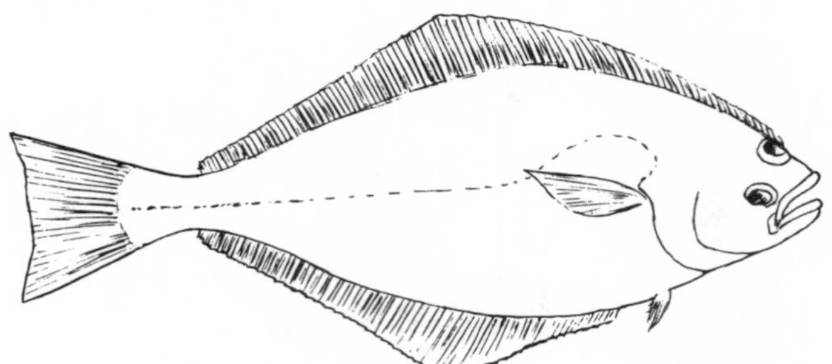

TOP VIEW OF HALIBUT SWIMMING.

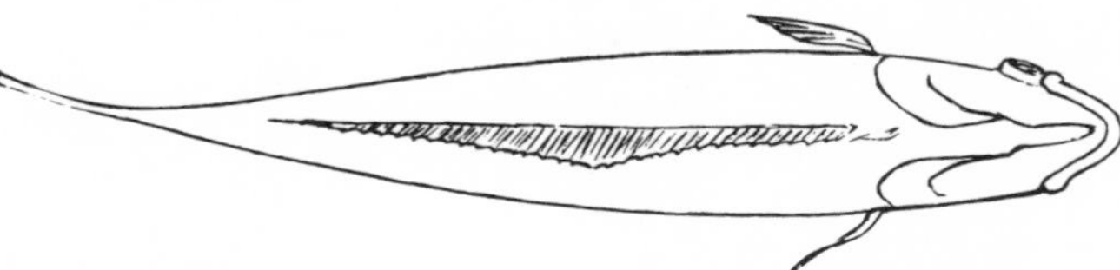

SIDE VIEW_ ADULT HALIBUT SWIMS HORIZONTALLY. JAWS HINGE SIDEWAYS.

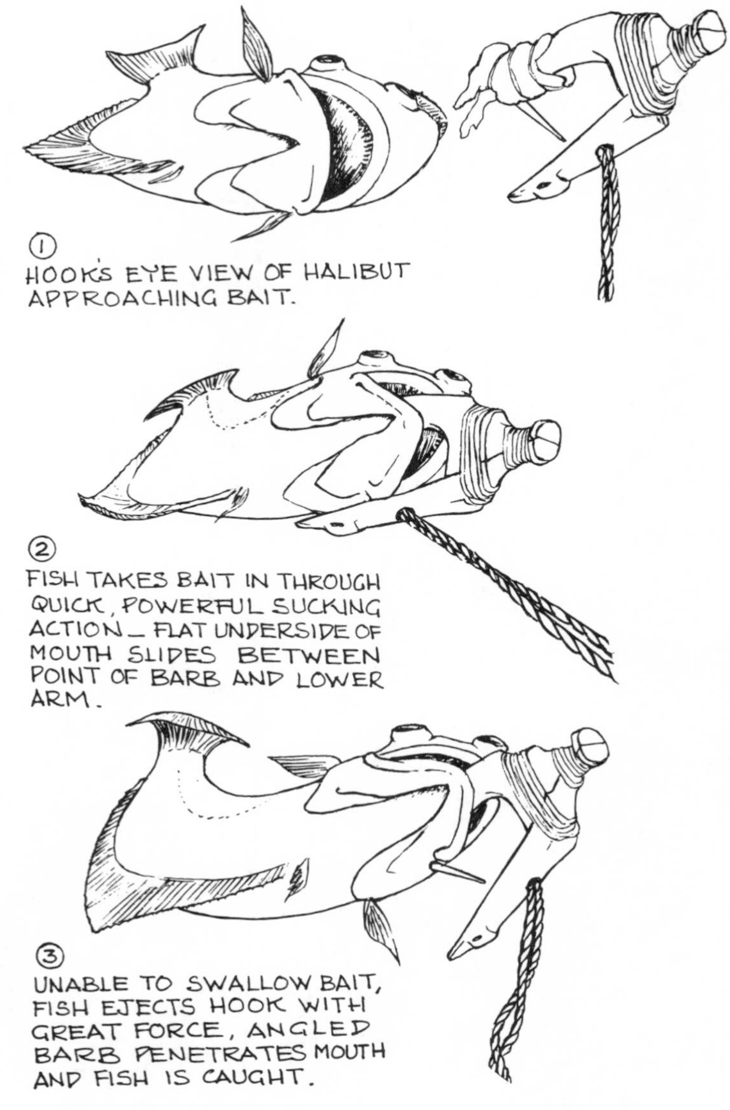

① HOOK'S EYE VIEW OF HALIBUT APPROACHING BAIT.

② FISH TAKES BAIT IN THROUGH QUICK, POWERFUL SUCKING ACTION_ FLAT UNDERSIDE OF MOUTH SLIDES BETWEEN POINT OF BARB AND LOWER ARM.

③ UNABLE TO SWALLOW BAIT, FISH EJECTS HOOK WITH GREAT FORCE, ANGLED BARB PENETRATES MOUTH AND FISH IS CAUGHT.

WHEN HALIBUT IS PLAYED OUT, LINE IS HAULED IN AND SHARPENED STICK THRUST THROUGH GILLS - STICK, ACROSS ONE KNEE AND UNDER THE OTHER, LIFTS FISH FROM WATER, AND IT IS CLUBBED. 75·CS

BONE BARBED HOOK

BAITED HOOK FLOATS STRAIGHT UP

LINE GOES TO FLOAT

LINE ATTACHED TO SINKER STONE – WHEN HALIBUT IS CAUGHT, FISHERMAN PULLS ON LINE TO FREE SINKER, HAULS UP FISH WITHOUT WEIGHT OF STONE.

IRON-BARBED HOOK

REPLACING BONE BARB WITH ONE OF IRON MAKES HOOK SINK – ADDING SMALL FLOAT COUNTERACTS THIS.

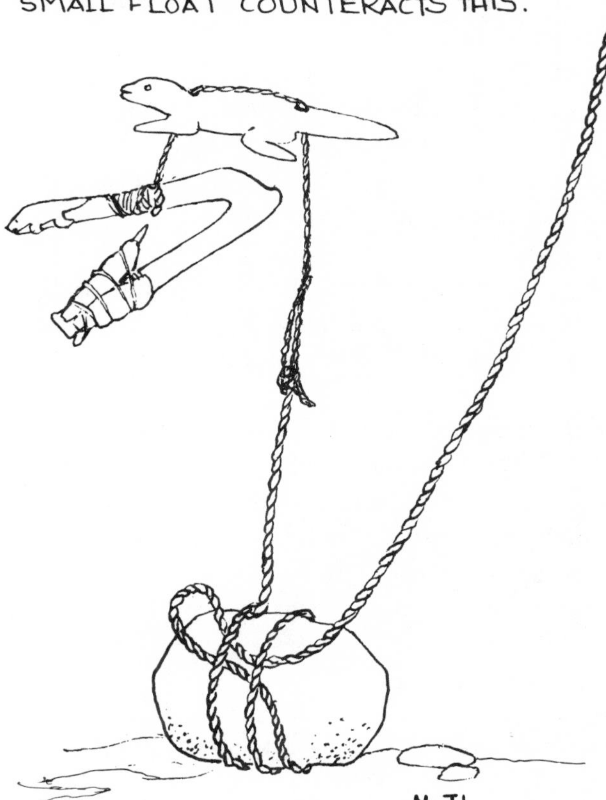

Lures

The Indians of the Northwest Coast used lures in ways that reflected close observation and intimate knowledge of marine life.

A sliver of willow — a white wood — carved in a fish shape with a slight curve gave a realistic imitation of a swimming fish as it was towed through the water. Uncarved pieces of willow in long strings trailing into the mouth of a net attracted the salmon by glimmering in the water. A piece of abalone glittering in the sunlight had the same effect as the polished metal flasher used by today's angler; it caught the attention of the fish.

Perhaps the most cleverly devised was the codfish lure. Pushed down into deep water on a long pole, it was designed to rise slowly and enticingly to the surface, where the fish that followed it up—with predictable cod-like curiosity—met the fisherman waiting with a spear or dip net in his hand.

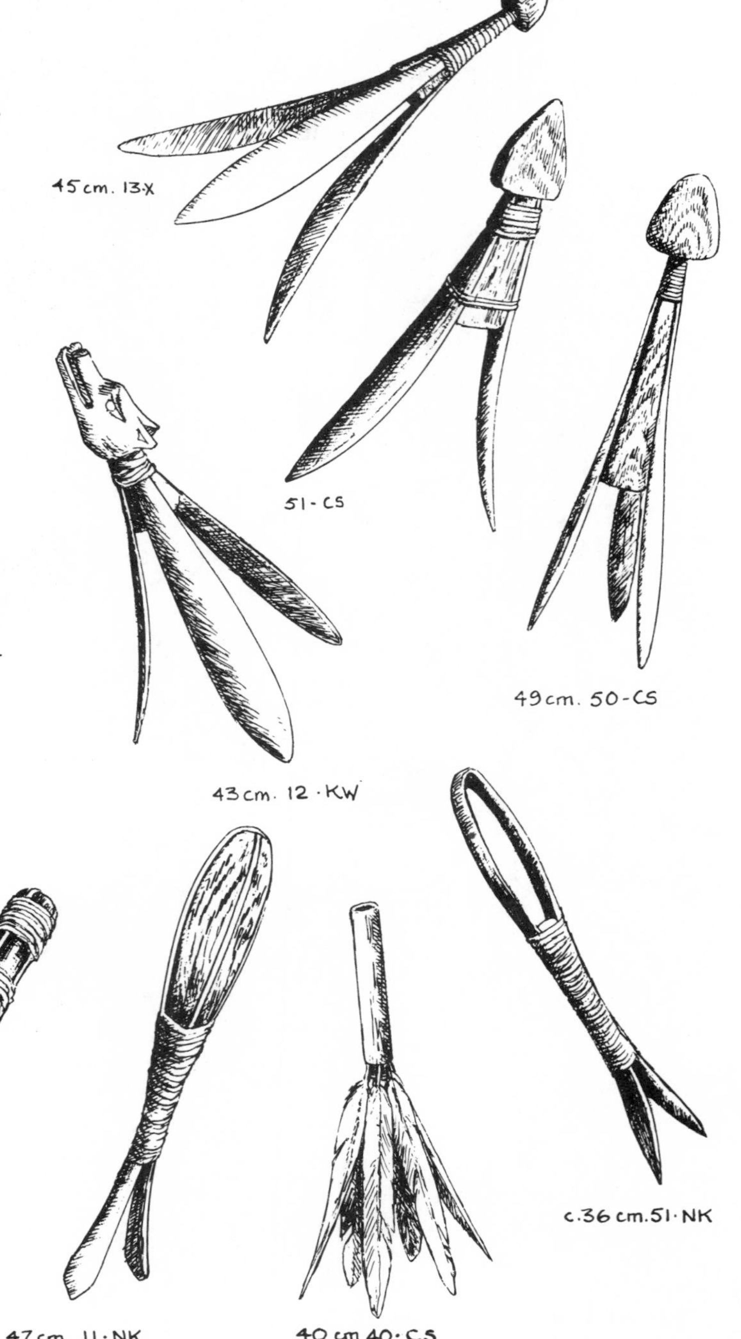

This 1899 photo shows 21 canoes at a landing on Koksila River, Vancouver Island. 25.CS

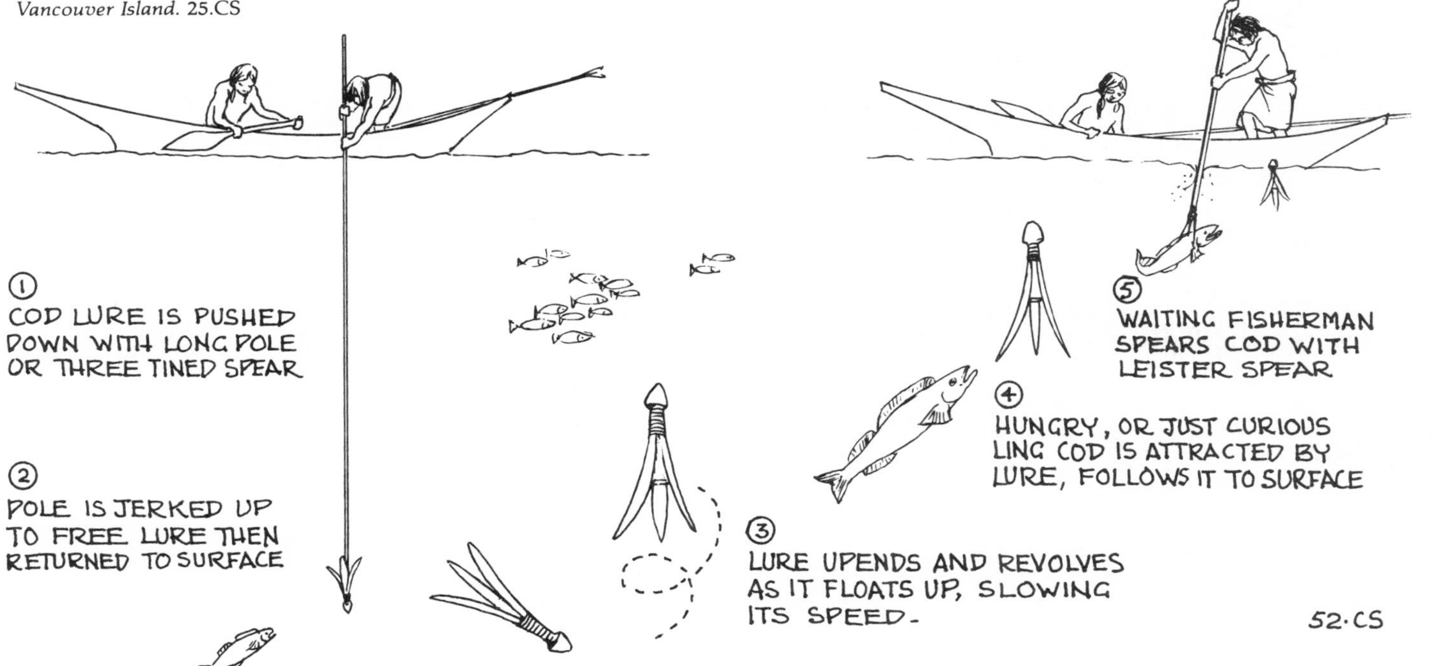

LURES

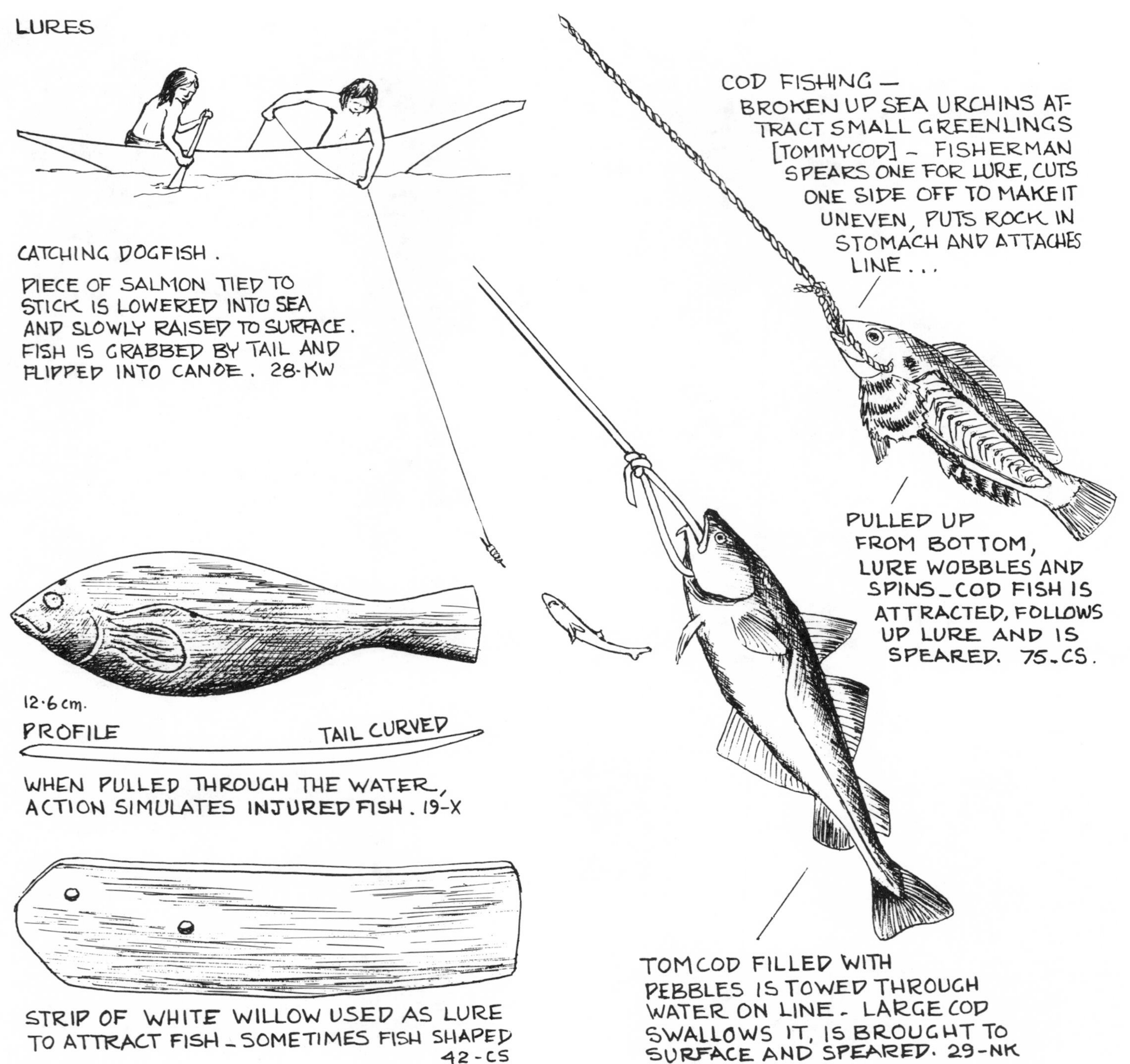
CATCHING DOGFISH.
PIECE OF SALMON TIED TO STICK IS LOWERED INTO SEA AND SLOWLY RAISED TO SURFACE. FISH IS GRABBED BY TAIL AND FLIPPED INTO CANOE. 28-KW
COD FISHING —
BROKEN UP SEA URCHINS ATTRACT SMALL GREENLINGS [TOMMYCOD] - FISHERMAN SPEARS ONE FOR LURE, CUTS ONE SIDE OFF TO MAKE IT UNEVEN, PUTS ROCK IN STOMACH AND ATTACHES LINE . . .
PULLED UP FROM BOTTOM, LURE WOBBLES AND SPINS_COD FISH IS ATTRACTED, FOLLOWS UP LURE AND IS SPEARED. 75-CS.
12·6 cm.
PROFILE
TAIL CURVED
WHEN PULLED THROUGH THE WATER, ACTION SIMULATES INJURED FISH. 19-X
TOMCOD FILLED WITH PEBBLES IS TOWED THROUGH WATER ON LINE. LARGE COD SWALLOWS IT, IS BROUGHT TO SURFACE AND SPEARED. 29-NK
STRIP OF WHITE WILLOW USED AS LURE TO ATTRACT FISH_SOMETIMES FISH SHAPED 42-CS

Floats

With characteristic aptitude for making a simple utilitarian object an item of beauty, the Indian fisherman frequently carved his wooden floats to represent a variety of creatures. Symbolism may have been part of the reason and perhaps it clarified ownership of the fishing gear, but the pleasure of seeing the gracefully carved sea bird, whale or swan riding the waves seems reason enough.

One of the most charming of these must surely have been the sea otter floating on its back, paws across its chest in the typical attitude of this animal.

Such floats mainly served to hold up and mark a halibut line, as did inflated seal skins or bladder floats. The small carved floats having a perforation from end to end were underwater floats used to maintain the correct position of some of the V-shaped hooks of the north.

Simpler, undecorated floats of wood supported the upper edge of fish nets; small ones along the length of the net, large ones at the ends.

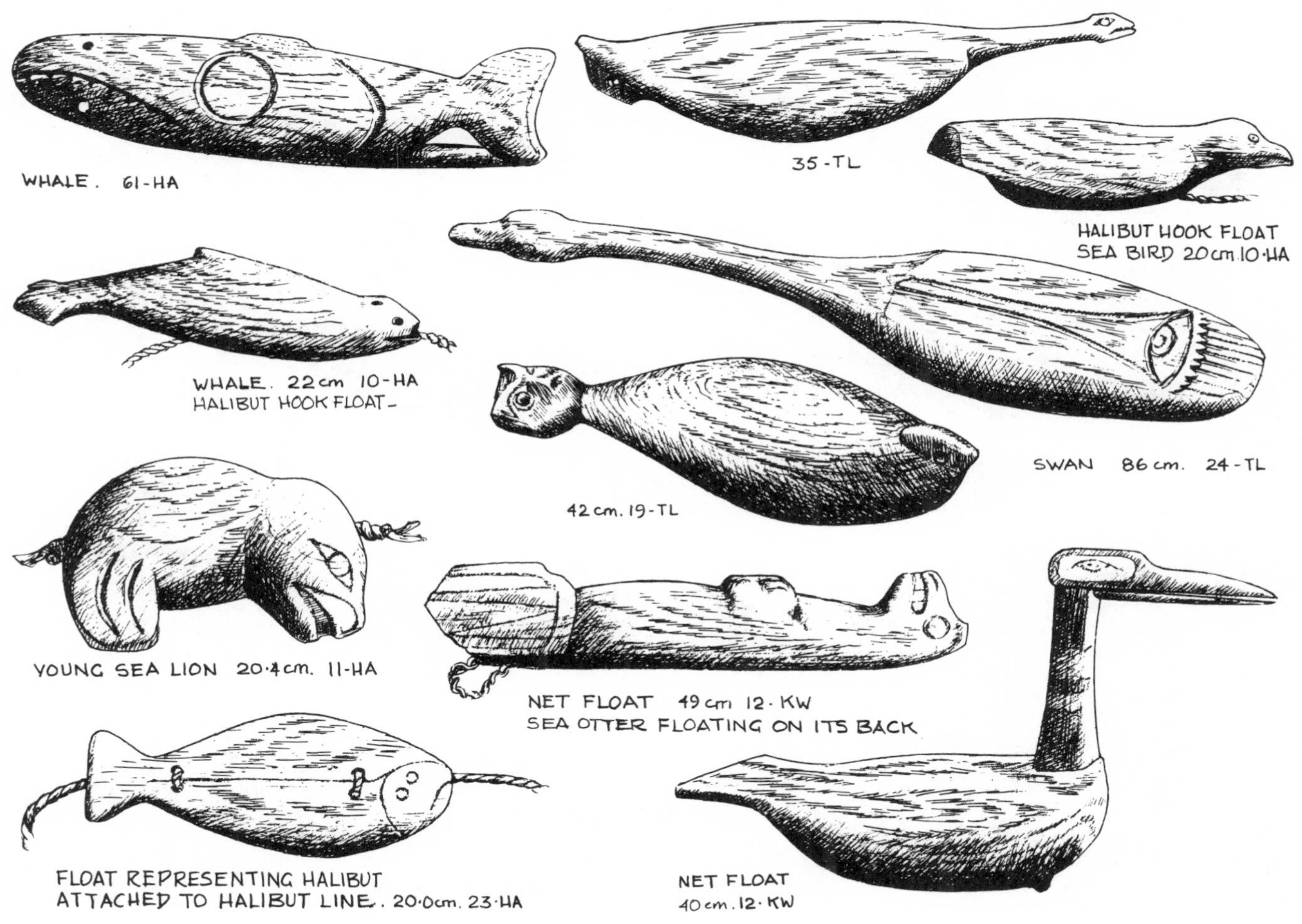

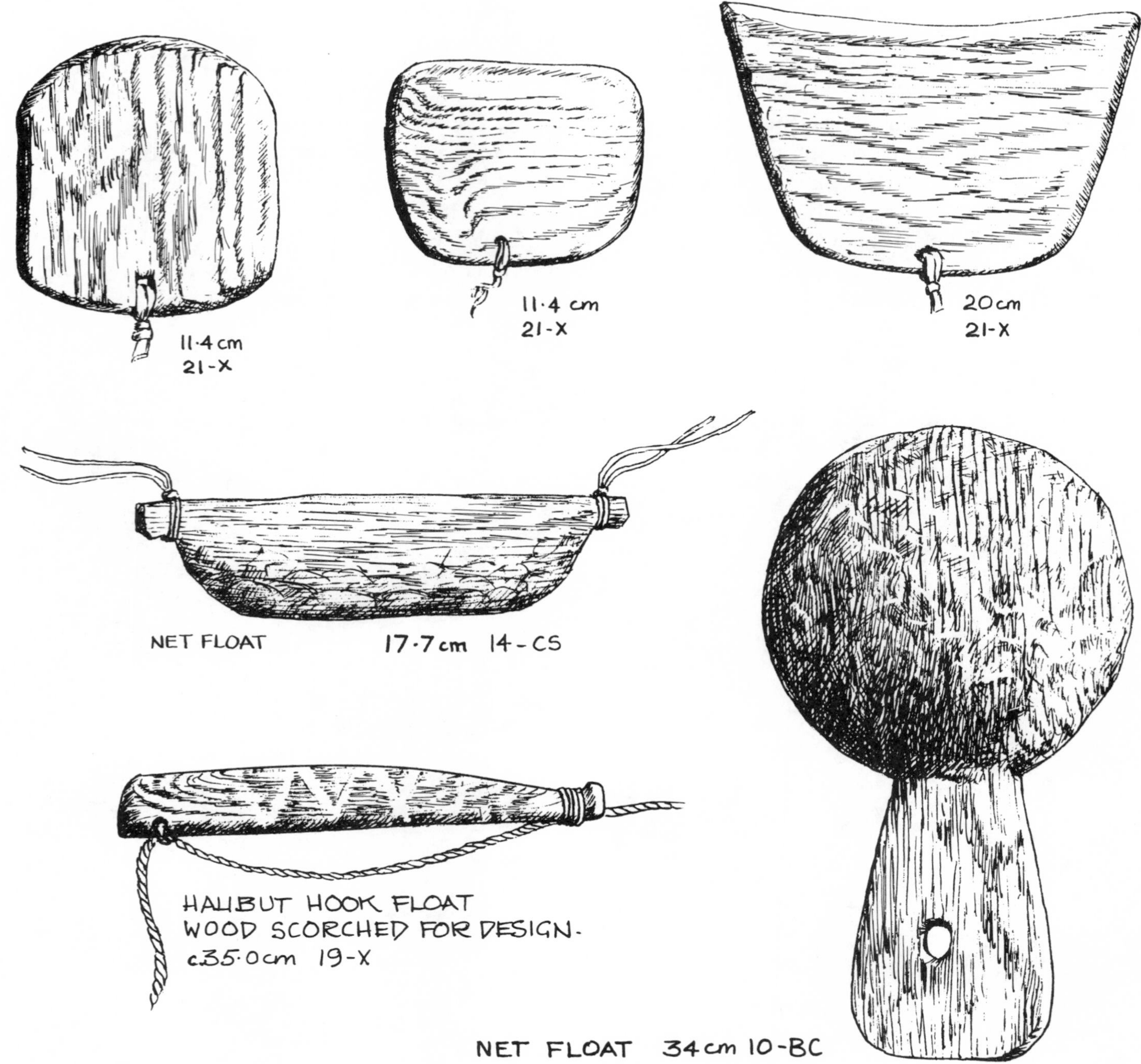
FLOATS TO SUPPORT TOP EDGE OF FISHNET
11·4 cm
21-X
11·4 cm
21-X
20 cm
21-X
NET FLOAT
17·7 cm 14-CS
HALIBUT HOOK FLOAT
WOOD SCORCHED FOR DESIGN.
c.35·0 cm 19-X
NET FLOAT 34 cm 10-BC

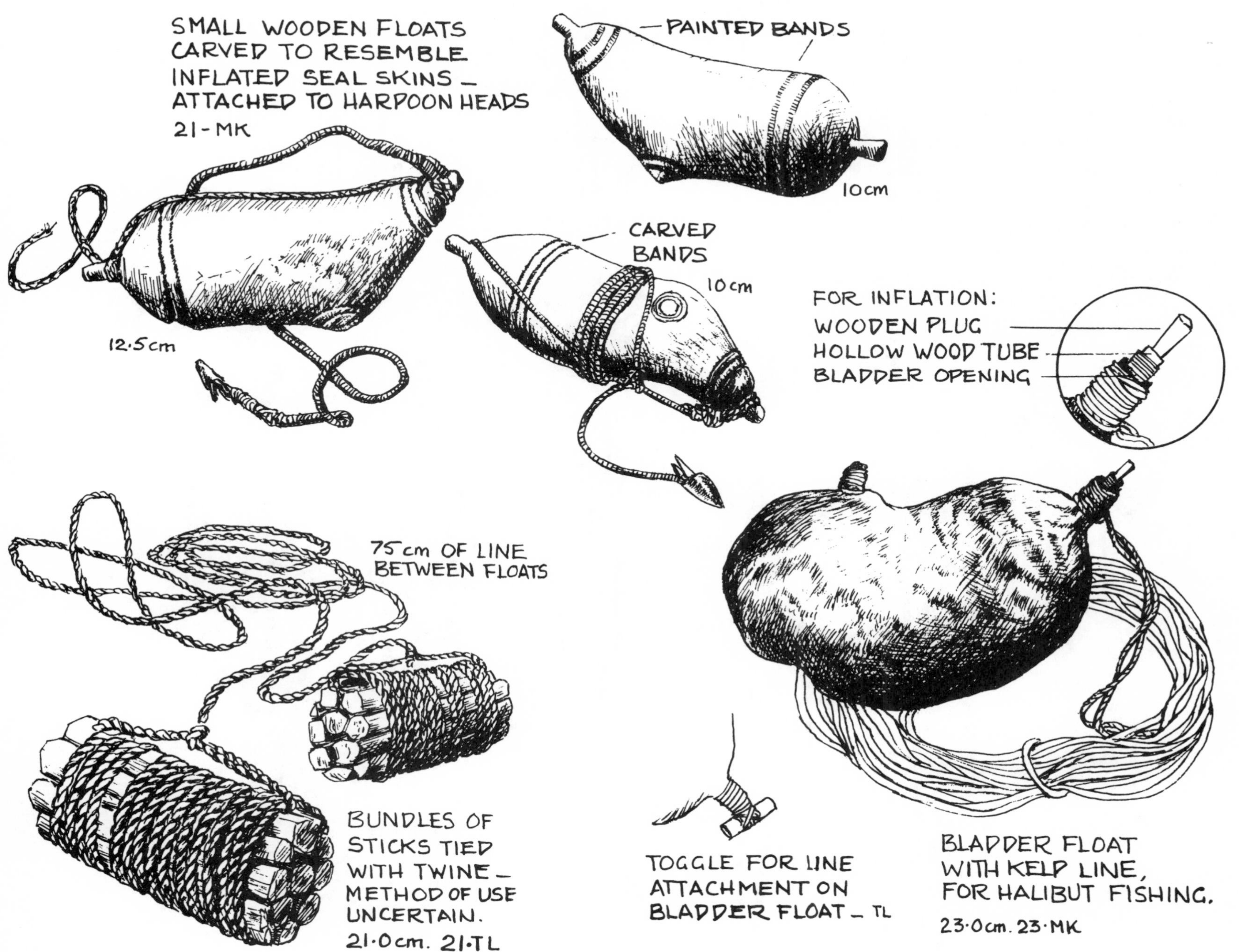
SMALL WOODEN FLOATS
CARVED TO RESEMBLE
INFLATED SEAL SKINS _
ATTACHED TO HARPOON HEADS
21-MK
PAINTED BANDS
10cm
CARVED
BANDS
10cm
12.5cm
FOR INFLATION:
WOODEN PLUG
HOLLOW WOOD TUBE
BLADDER OPENING
75cm OF LINE
BETWEEN FLOATS
BUNDLES OF
STICKS TIED
WITH TWINE _
METHOD OF USE
UNCERTAIN.
21·0cm. 21·TL
TOGGLE FOR LINE
ATTACHMENT ON
BLADDER FLOAT _ TL
BLADDER FLOAT
WITH KELP LINE,
FOR HALIBUT FISHING.
23·0cm. 23·MK

Clubs

Part of a fisherman's gear that he carried in the canoe, or used at the fish weir or trap, was the heavy wooden club for quickly killing the fish. These ranged from simple, bulbous-ended truncheons to highly decorated and even three-dimensionally carved works of art. Elaborate shaping and carving would not have been easy in the hardwood that was necessary for the making of these clubs.

In their book *Indian Art of the Northwest Coast*, William Reid and Bill Holm discuss the fine qualities of a large, slender and beautifully made club with superb carving. Artists and carvers both, they feel that the care expressed in the design and craftsmanship of the club might well have showed respect for the creature whose death it would bring about through its brutal but necessary use.

Compared with the Tlingit and Haida clubs, those of the south tended to be less elaborate and without decoration, but almost all were well carved and finished.

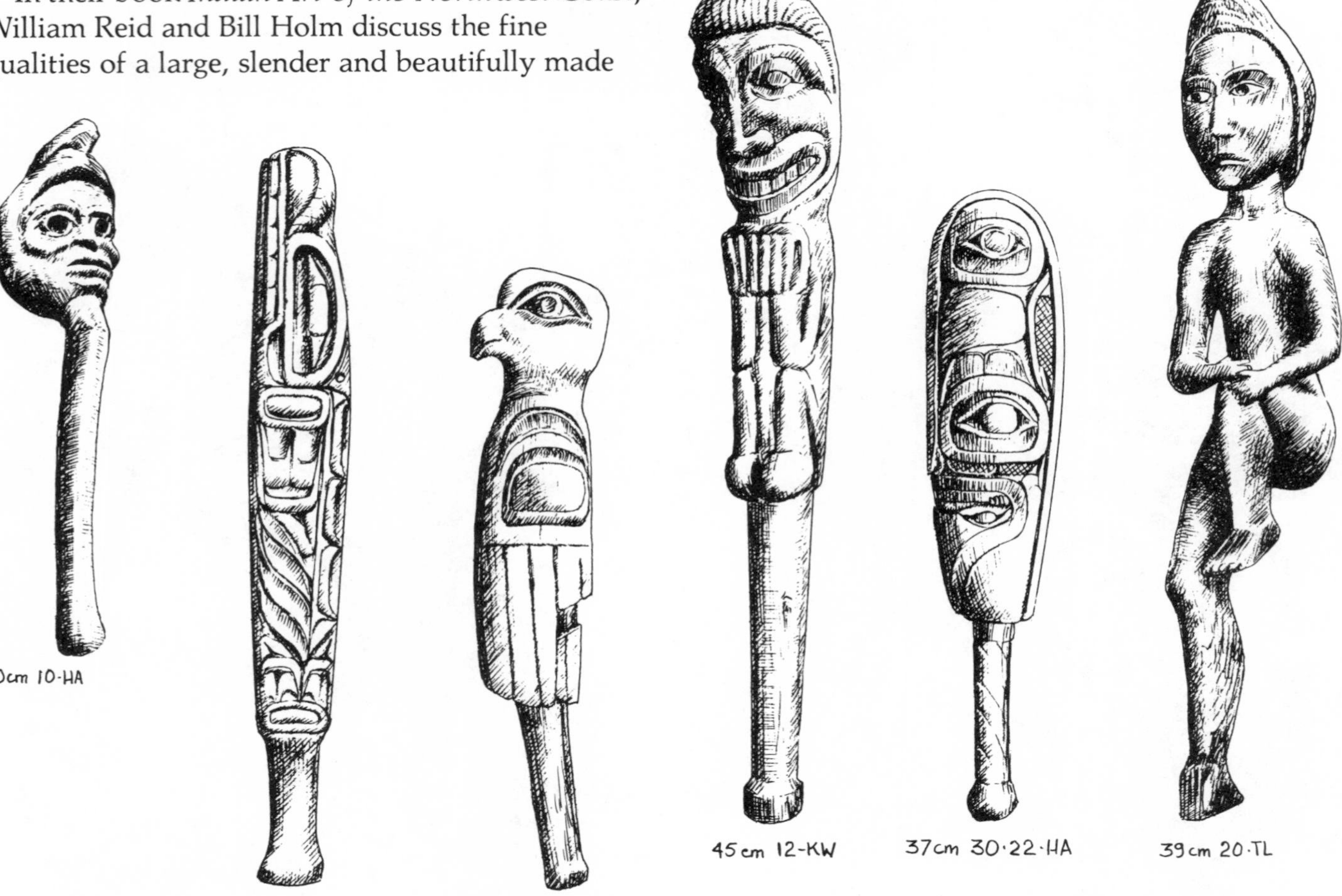

Wooden tobacco mortar with dogfish design. 35cm (14 inches) 16.TL

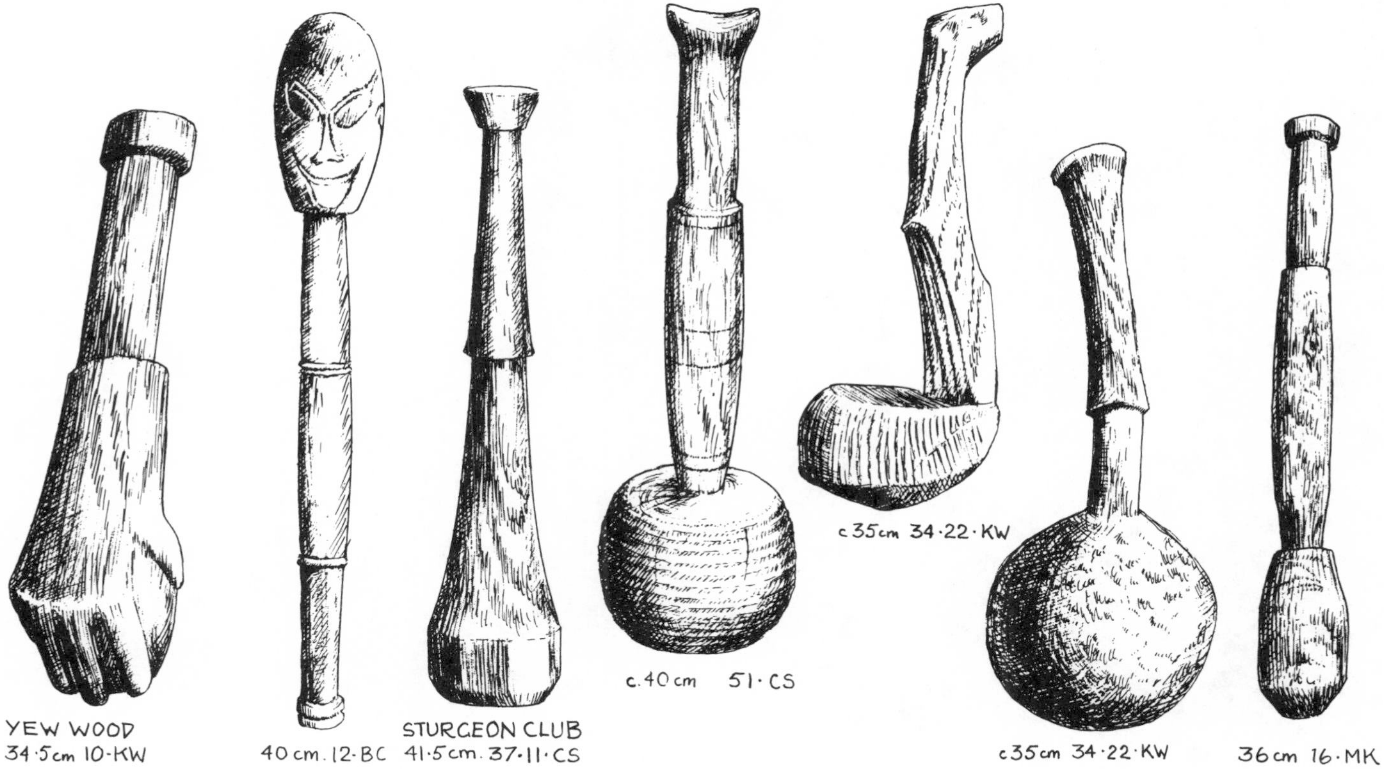

YEW WOOD
34·5cm 10·KW

40 cm. 12·BC

STURGEON CLUB
41·5cm. 37·11·CS

c.40 cm 51·CS

c35cm 34·22·KW

c35cm 34·22·KW

36cm 16·MK

13.X

Spears and Harpoons

Thrusting his harpoon with just enough power to impale the fish, but not too much to break the gear if he should miss, a man learned to judge the depth of water and the speed of the swimming fish, allowing for light refraction at the same time. Referring to the skill and success of this type of salmon fishing, John Jewitt comments:

"Such is the immense quantity of these fish, and they are taken with such facility, that I have known upwards of twenty five hundred brought into Maquinna's house at once; and at one of their great feasts, have seen one hundred or more cooked in one of their largest tubs.

"I used frequently to go out with Maquinna upon these fishing parties, and was always sure to receive a handsome present of salmon, which I had the privilege of calling mine; I also went with him several times in a canoe, to strike the salmon, which I have attempted to do myself, but could never succeed, it requiring a degree of adroitness that I did not possess."

The implement Maquinna used to "strike the salmon" was probably a harpoon. The difference between the spear and harpoon lay in the manner of its use and the nature of the head of the weapon. The spear point was firmly fixed to the end of the shaft, which was thrust at the prey and remained in the fisherman's hands. The harpoon head became detached from the prong or foreshaft when it struck the fish. It was tethered to the shaft by the lanyard. Some harpoons combined two and even three heads on separate prongs. A throwing harpoon had a finger grip at the butt end from which the shaft was propelled towards the fish, and it was afterwards hauled back in by the attached retrieving line.

While a large, struggling fish impaled on a fixed spear point could break the shaft or point, or free itself by thrashing about, the detachable harpoon head allowed the fish to move in the water without putting direct strain on the gear, while its struggles imbedded the barbs well into the flesh.

The harpooning of salmon was generally limited to rivers and streams with clear water, but it was also practicable in bays and inlets, especially where the fish congregated prior to ascending the rivers. If a stream was not navigable by canoe, the fisherman walked up it or along its banks finding suitable places to fish.

So specialized was the art of fishing by harpoon that different types of harpoons were devised for different river conditions. Among the Nootka, for instance, there was a harpoon made for use in a small stream, a river with deep pools in it, a shallow river with rapids, and a wide expanse of river water.

The spear seems to have had its best use with the smaller species of salmon which were close at hand and readily available: for example, at a trap or dam where they were concentrated and could quickly be flipped onto the bank or into the canoe.

An efficient spear for salmon and cod was the leister spear with its reverse-angle barbs that held a fish very firmly. Used with a downward, vertical thrust, the leister was effective in taking salmon lurking beneath a log jam in a river, and was sometimes employed in conjunction with the cod lure. Another specialized spear was for flounder. This had two wooden prongs with tips sharpened to a point, probably to pierce right through the flat fish as it lay half hidden in the sand.

The spear for dragging the tenacious octopus from its den had a reverse barb a short distance from the long point. Chief Charles Jones described for me the catching of the "devil fish." The long point was pushed into the hunched-up mass of octopus; the barb prevented it from slipping out. By maintaining strong and steady pull on the spear, the fisherman eventually forced the creature to let go its hold. Devil fish was extensively used for bait.

Harpoon and spear shafts were frequently of cedar so as to be lightweight. Strong, durable cherry bark was used for lashing on prongs of a tougher, often springy wood: yew, ironwood, or service berry wood.

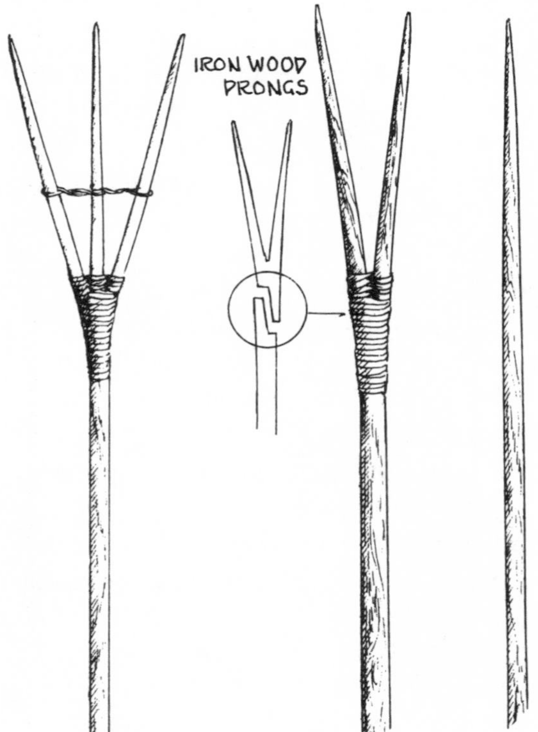

FLOUNDER SPEAR, PRONGS OF IRONWOOD. 75·CS

FLOUNDER SPEARS

SPEARING FLOUNDER

GROUPS OF YOUNG FISHERMEN WADE ON MUD FLATS OR SAND BARS FEELING OUT PARTIALLY BURIED FLOUNDER WITH THEIR FEET. THEY MAKE A SPORT OF TRYING TO STAND ON FLAT FISH TO SPEAR IT. 30·CS _ 28·KW

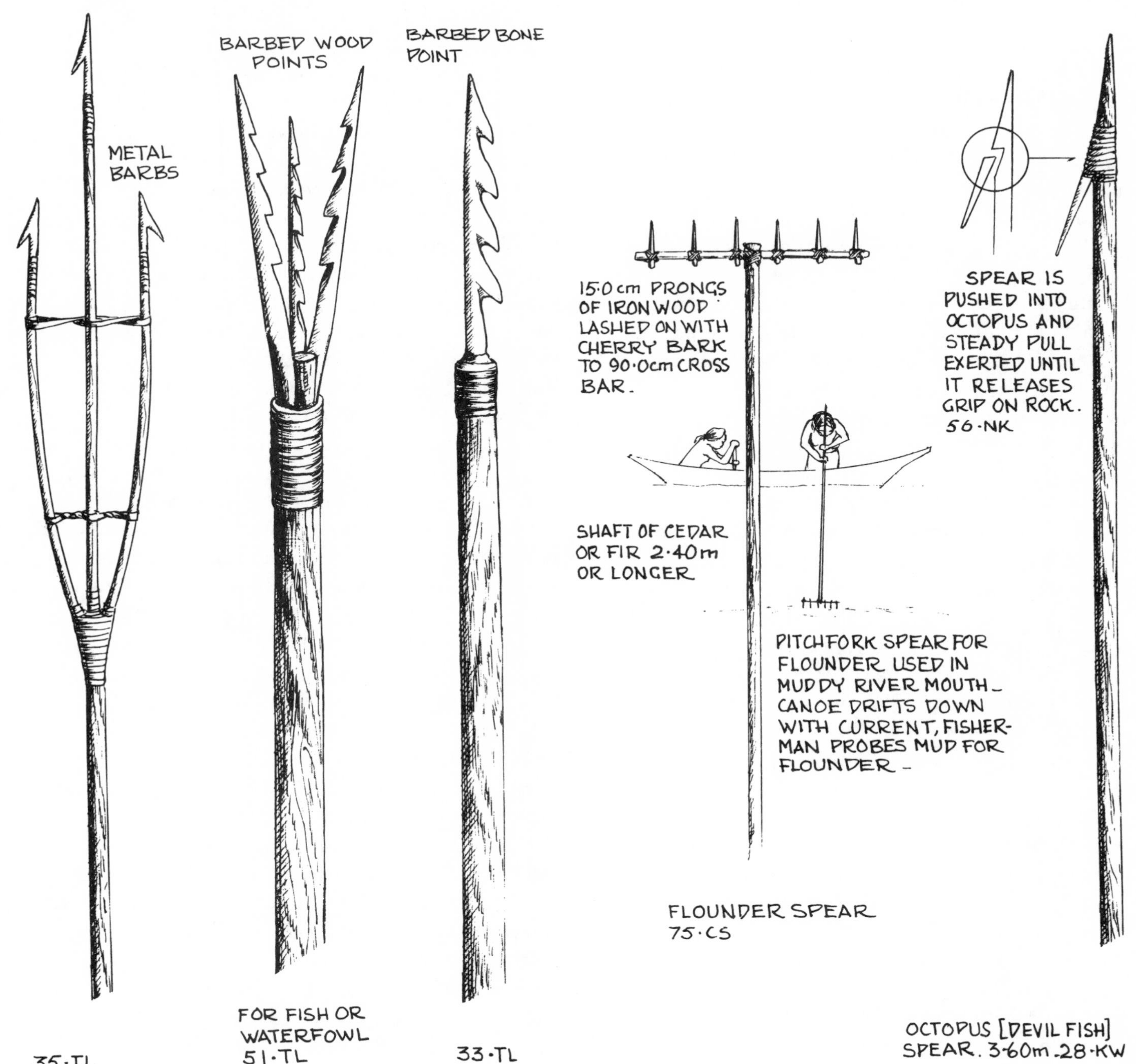
METAL BARBS
BARBED WOOD POINTS
BARBED BONE POINT
15·0 cm PRONGS OF IRONWOOD LASHED ON WITH CHERRY BARK TO 90·0cm CROSS BAR.
SHAFT OF CEDAR OR FIR 2·40m OR LONGER
PITCHFORK SPEAR FOR FLOUNDER USED IN MUDDY RIVER MOUTH. CANOE DRIFTS DOWN WITH CURRENT, FISHERMAN PROBES MUD FOR FLOUNDER.
SPEAR IS PUSHED INTO OCTOPUS AND STEADY PULL EXERTED UNTIL IT RELEASES GRIP ON ROCK.
56·NK
FLOUNDER SPEAR
75·CS
35·TL
FOR FISH OR WATERFOWL
51·TL
33·TL
OCTOPUS [DEVIL FISH] SPEAR. 3·60m. 28·KW

Sturgeon Fishing

Probably the largest of the fish caught by the coast Indians was the sturgeon, a long-lived freshwater fish that can grow to about six metres (20 feet), and range in weight up to 812 kilos (1,800 pounds). While the sturgeon inhabits the major rivers of the Northwest Coast, the Coast Salish people were the great pursuers of this fish.

The sturgeon, sluggish in winter, lay in deeper water during this time and was not difficult to locate by probing with a two-pronged harpoon with an extended shaft. In the early summer the sturgeon came in to shallower water to spawn, and from April through summer could be taken in the sloughs by fence weir, set net, trawl net and harpoon. Harpoons, the same ones used for seal and porpoise with a trident butt, were used in the daytime on low tides. At night, on any tide, a fish swimming about 2.4 metres (8 feet) deep could be seen well ahead by its phosphorescence, and became an easy target.

A large sturgeon, struck with a harpoon, would take off into deeper water, speedily towing the canoe behind it. The late Chief August Jack Khahtsahlano (born 1887 in Vancouver) once described how a heavy stone on a cedar bark rope would be dropped from the stern of the canoe to help slow down and steady the erratic craft being powered by a captive sturgeon. When eventually the fish tired and sank to the bottom, the line went vertically down—a signal to the fishermen to bring it to the surface. With sufficient lines embedded in the flesh, the fish was hauled up and clubbed on the side of the head.

In a well practised manoeuvre the canoe was then tipped, the sturgeon rolled in over the gunwale, and the water bailed out. Sometimes an outrigger was made to steady the canoe for hauling in a large fish. A pole, with a block of wood at one end, was put across the canoe and lashed to the thwart. Another method of getting the catch home was to simply reverse the fish-towing-the-canoe procedure and have the canoe tow the fish.

The 1827 journal of Fort Langley, on the Fraser River, has a July 21 entry reading:

"We procured a small supply of fresh sturgeon from the Indians today. These fish are as large as those of the Columbia, and are killed in this River with Spears fifty feet in length, having a fork at the end, Barbed occasionally with iron, but oftener with a piece of shell. When the fish is struck, the barbs having a cord, attached to their middle, and held at the end of the Spear, are drawn from their socket and remain in the fish across the wound, til it is drawn up and killed."

On August 2 the fort traded "two hundredweight of sturgeon" and at a later date "Bought a sturgeon from the Cowichans—weight 400 lbs. the guts out."

Another eye witness to sturgeon fishing was Sir Arthur Birch, Colonial Secretary at Government House in New Westminster. In a letter to his brother John, dated 7 May 1864, he writes: "I have got a very nice little Wooden Office & my room is charming now though I fear very cold in the winter. It is close onto the Fraser & the balcony & veranda over hang the water. All the Indians now fishing and it is great fun to watch them spearing Sturgeon which here run to the enormous size of 500 & 600 lbs. The Indians drift down with the stream perhaps 30 canoes abreast with their long poles with spear attached kept within about a foot of the bottom of the River. When they feel a fish lying they raise the spear and thrust it at the fish seldom missing. The barb of the spear immediately disconnects from the pole but remains attached to a rope & you see sometimes 2 or 3 canoes being carried off at the same time down river at any pace by these huge fish."

"Sturgeon Spearing on the Fraser River." From A Naturalist in British Columbia, Vol. 1, *by John Lord. 1866.*

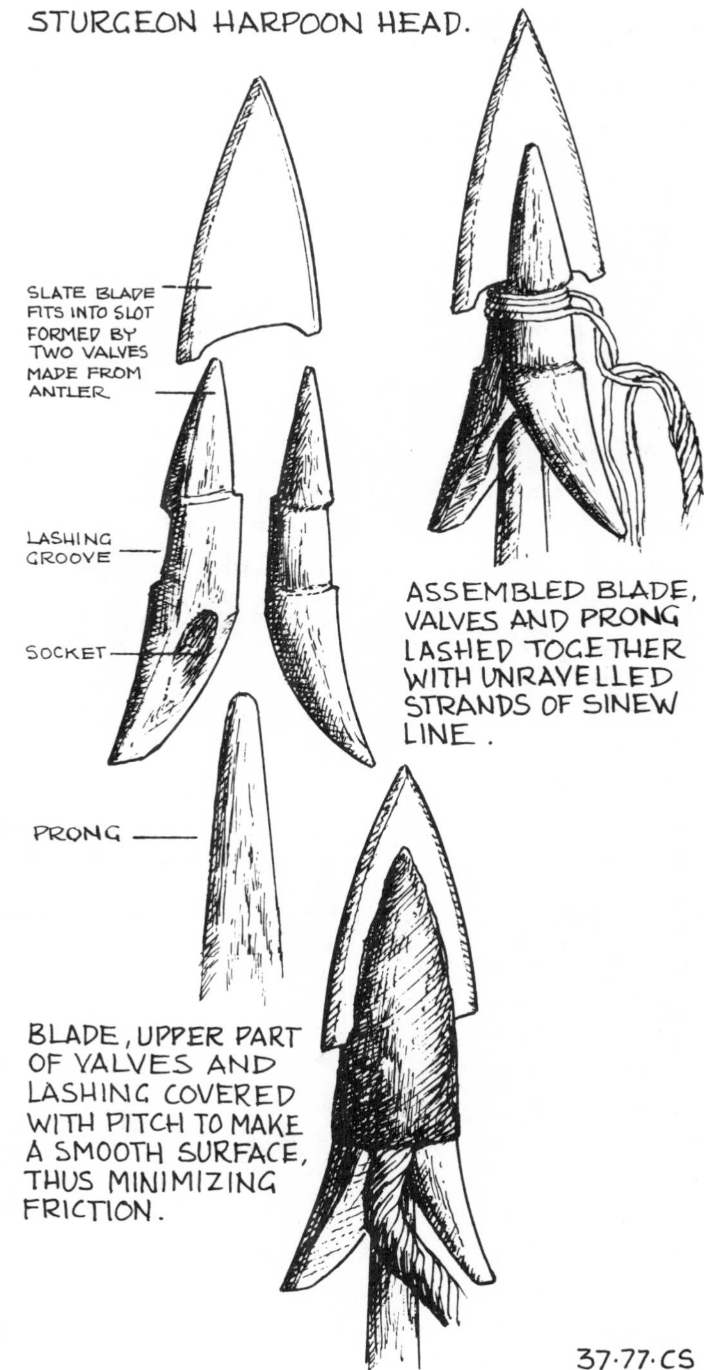

STURGEON HARPOON

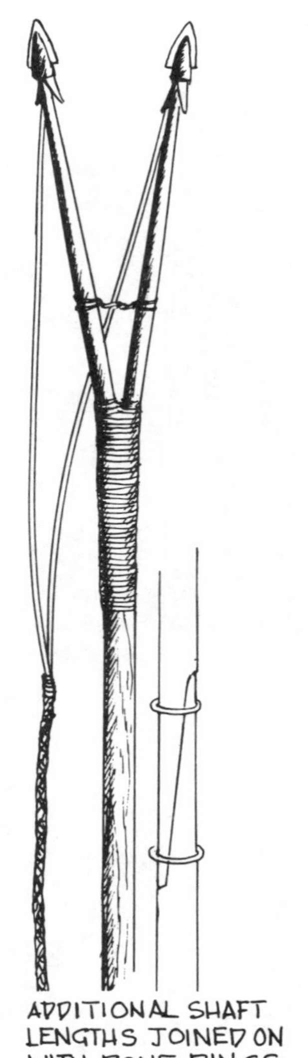

ADDITIONAL SHAFT LENGTHS JOINED ON WITH BONE RINGS.

HARPOONING STURGEON

STANDING IN STERN, FISHERMAN GENTLY RAISES AND LOWERS HARPOON, PROBING RIVER BOTTOM TO FEEL FOR STURGEON IN WATER UP TO 20m. DEEP.

IN VERY DEEP WATER EXTRA SHAFT LENGTHS ARE JOINED ON.

CANOE DRIFTS DOWN RIVER, PADDLER KEEPS BOW POINTED UP STREAM, HOLDING LINE TAUT TO HELP KEEP SHAFT VERTICAL.

RIVER FLOW ⇨

ENOUGH LINES ARE USED TO ENSURE LARGE FISH CAN BE HAULED UP.

STURGEON RESTS ON RIVER BOTTOM, HEAD DOWN, FACING UPSTREAM.

EAGLE FEATHERS ON PRONG TIPS ACT AS SENSORS FOR FEELING THE BOTTOM AND CONTACT WITH FISH. ON CONTACT, HARPOONER THRUSTS DOWN TO HARPOON STURGEON AND SHAFT IS WITHDRAWN.

37. CS

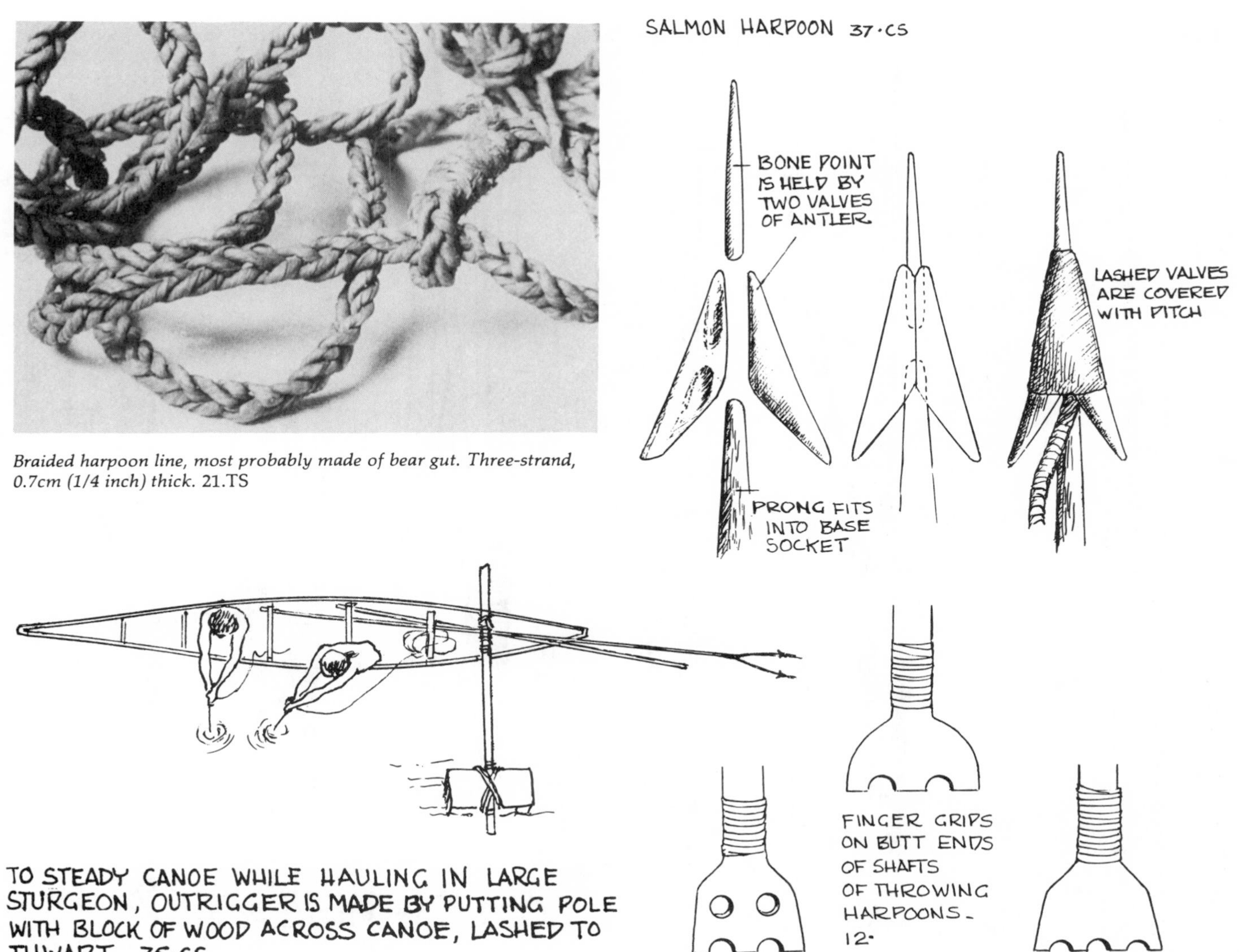

Braided harpoon line, most probably made of bear gut. Three-strand, 0.7cm (1/4 inch) thick. 21.TS

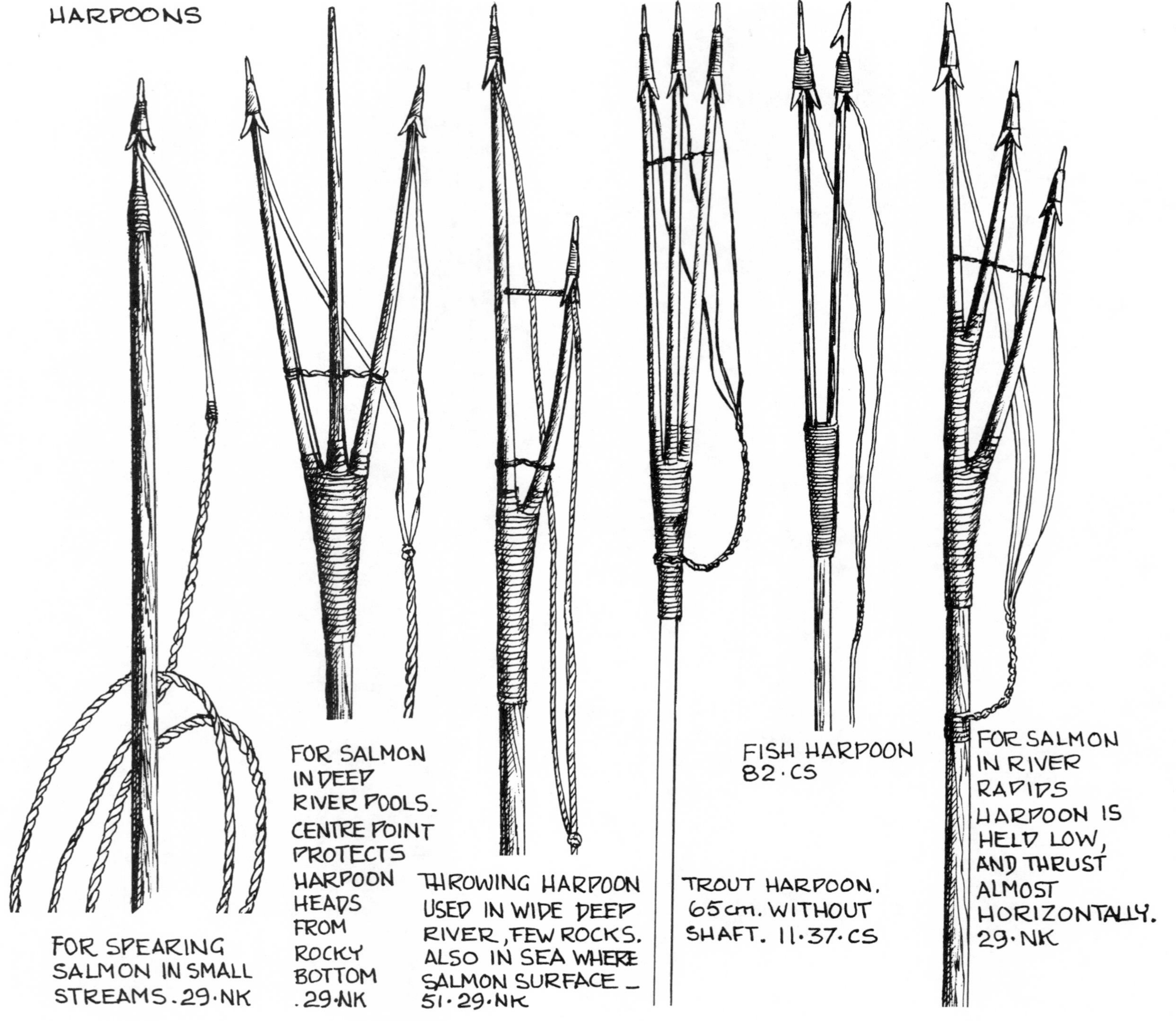
HARPOONS
FOR SPEARING SALMON IN SMALL STREAMS . 29·NK
FOR SALMON IN DEEP RIVER POOLS. CENTRE POINT PROTECTS HARPOON HEADS FROM ROCKY BOTTOM . 29·NK
THROWING HARPOON USED IN WIDE DEEP RIVER, FEW ROCKS. ALSO IN SEA WHERE SALMON SURFACE _ 51·29·NK
TROUT HARPOON. 65cm. WITHOUT SHAFT. 11·37·CS
FISH HARPOON 82·CS
FOR SALMON IN RIVER RAPIDS HARPOON IS HELD LOW, AND THRUST ALMOST HORIZONTALLY. 29·NK

HARPOONING SALMON IN SEA

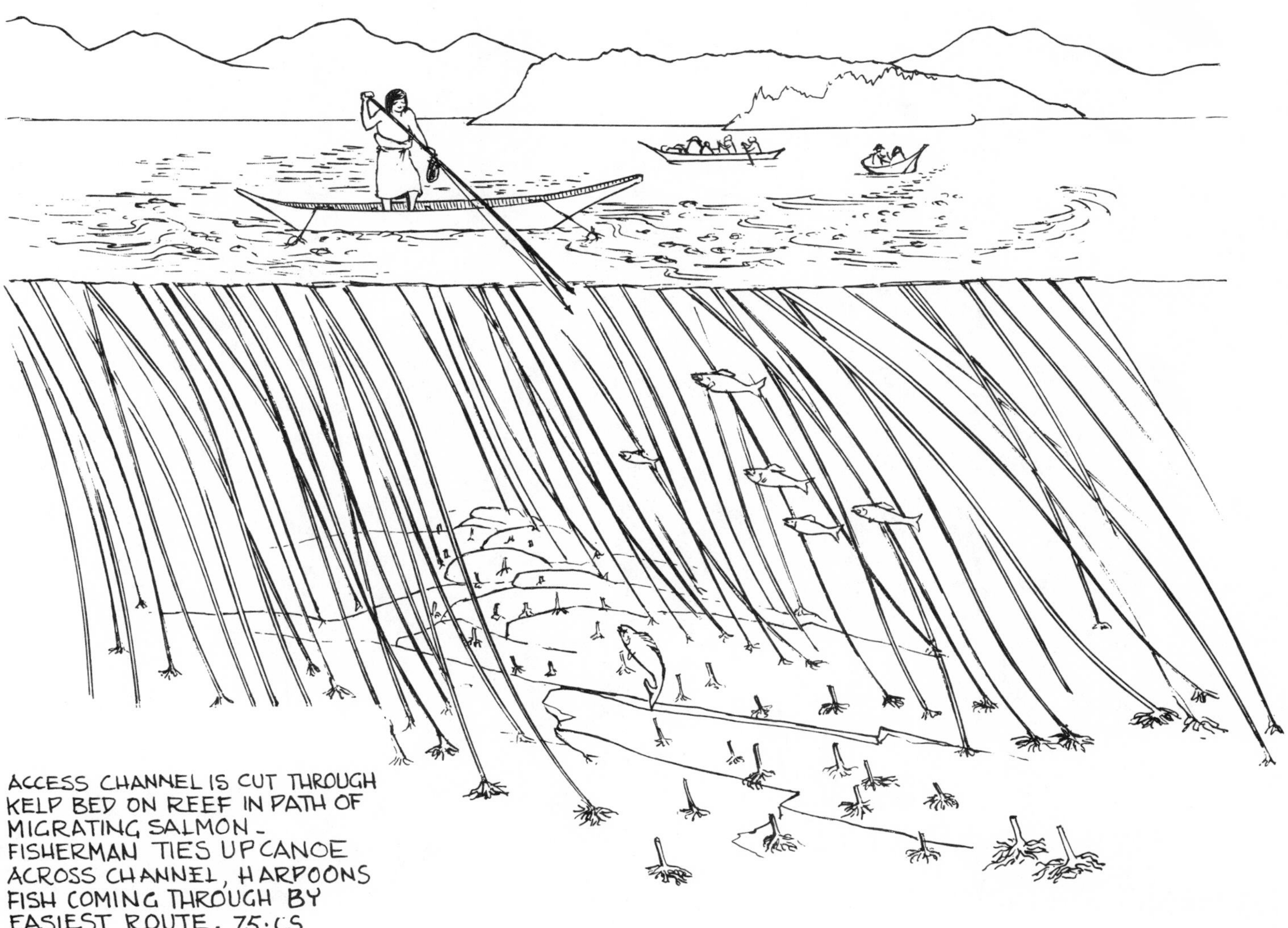

ACCESS CHANNEL IS CUT THROUGH KELP BED ON REEF IN PATH OF MIGRATING SALMON - FISHERMAN TIES UP CANOE ACROSS CHANNEL, HARPOONS FISH COMING THROUGH BY EASIEST ROUTE. 75·CS

LEISTER SPEARS.

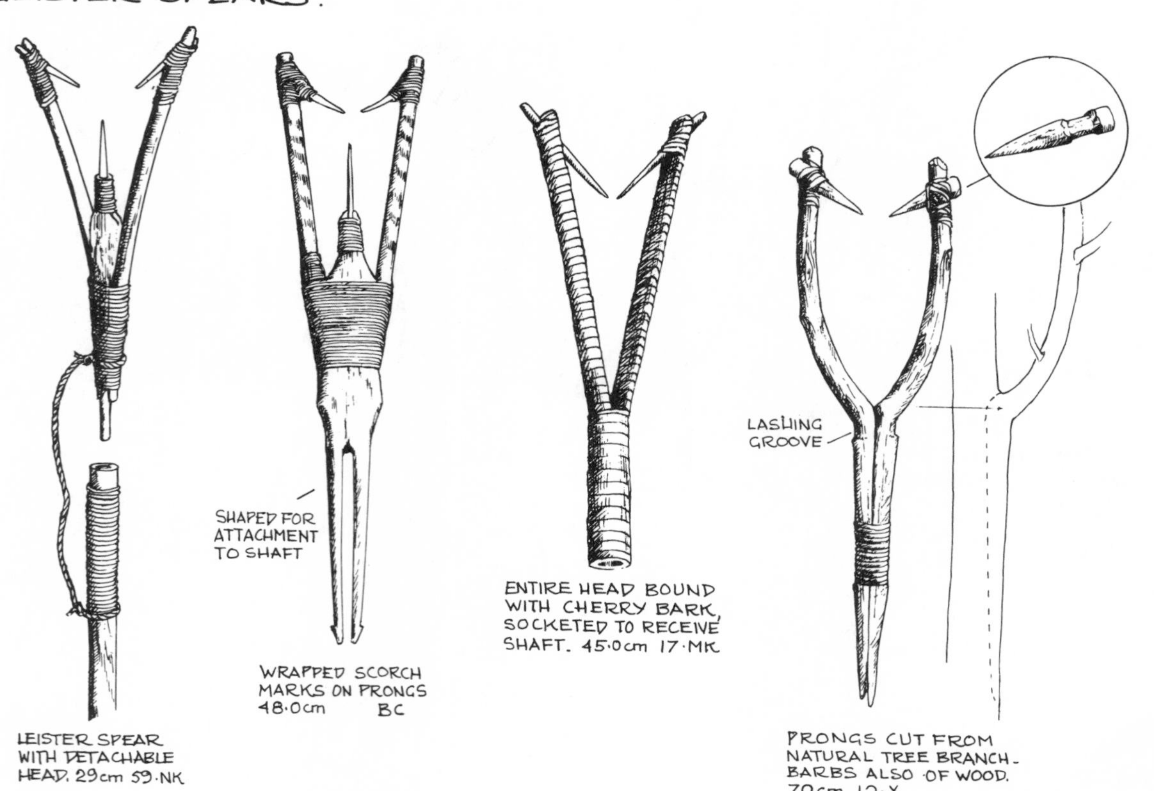

Gaff Hooks

Another method of taking fish, mostly salmon, was by gaff hook. Working from a platform built at an eddy or by rapids, or standing in his canoe, the fisherman quickly jerked the hook upward to impale the fish.

At night or in murky water, the feel of the fish brushing against the hook was the signal for him to strike. A gaff with a detachable hook prevented a struggling salmon from breaking the shaft or tearing itself free.

When the run of salmon was heavy, the fisherman stood on the river bank or in his canoe, and used the gaff with a quick raking motion along the bottom. He also used it at fish traps and weirs to haul out the catch.

Gaff hooks of iron, introduced through trading, eventually replaced those of wood, bone and antler. The metal hooks came fitted with a short handle designed for the white man's way of using it, but the Indian replaced it with a long shaft to suit his own needs. It is legal for Indian people to gaff salmon and many of them still pursue this practice today.

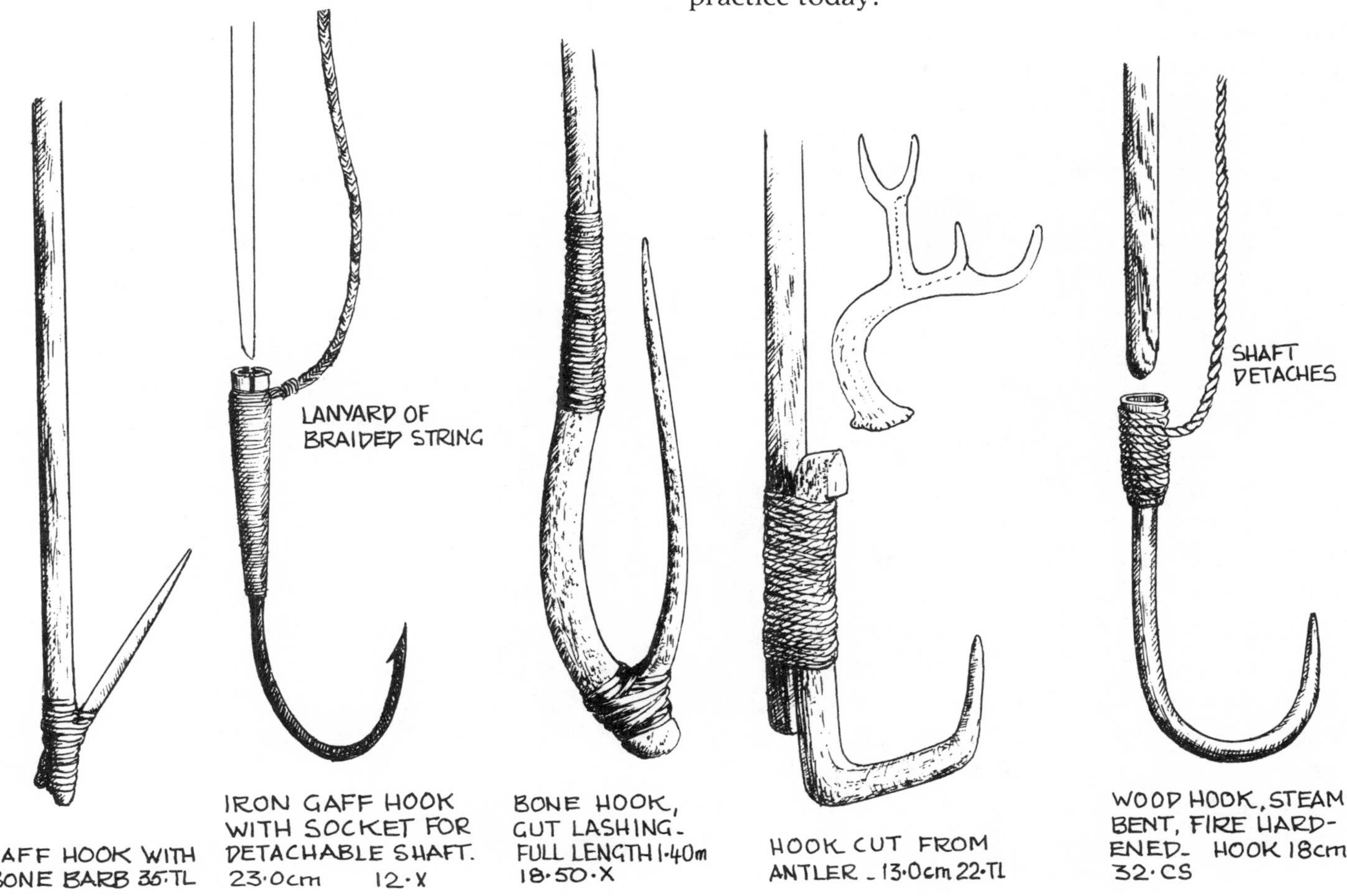

GAFF HOOK WITH BONE BARB 35·TL

IRON GAFF HOOK WITH SOCKET FOR DETACHABLE SHAFT. 23·0cm 12·X

BONE HOOK, CUT LASHING. FULL LENGTH 1·40m 18·50·X

HOOK CUT FROM ANTLER _ 13·0cm 22·TL

WOOD HOOK, STEAM-BENT, FIRE HARD-ENED. HOOK 18cm. 32·CS

The Herring Rake

Today fishermen complain that herring runs are depleted by overfishing. Once Indians went out in canoes to meet herring that schooled in uncountable numbers. So thick were the fish that they were easily harvested by running a rake through the water to impale them. It was a method of fishing used extensively along the coast, and a single village might have ten or fifteen people on herring rakes gathering up the fish.

For bone barbs, splinters from the leg bone of deer were made by hammering the bone lightly until it began to crack. The crack was followed up until it split, and the splinters then shaped and sharpened on both ends by using a sandstone abrader. With the shaft set sideways between pairs of stakes in the ground, holes were drilled along the edge and the barbs driven in with a yew hammer, or set in with spruce gum.

For wooden barbs, sharpened points of ironwood were driven through the cedar shaft with a hammer so that they protruded on the opposite side in much the same way that nails would.

One account of making a Kwagiutl rake describes the barbs as being "three finger widths long and two finger widths apart," but a rake I looked at in the B.C. Provincial Museum had barbs more closely spaced, about 1.5 centimetres (5⁄8 inch) apart. This more closely fits a Nootka rake described by Jewitt:

"A stick of about 7 feet long, by 2 inches broad, and a half an inch thick . . . formed from some hard wood, one side of which is set with sharp teeth made from whalebone, at about half an inch apart."

To strengthen and waterproof it, the rake was smoked over a fire for four days, with tallow rubbed in each morning to make the soot from the fire adhere as waterproofing.

Early March brought the herring run and with it the eagles, the gulls, the seals and all the creatures eager for a share of the easily caught fish that would run in such abundance for about twenty days. The best time for herring raking was between sunrise and sunset, when the fish moved up off the bottom. When the fisherman and his wife reached the herring grounds in their canoe, she sat in the bow facing the stern and he sat in the stern facing the same way.

Observing the herring rake in action Jewitt declared:

"It is astonishing to see how many are caught by those dextrous at this kind of fishing, as they seldom fail, when shoals are numerous, of taking as many as ten or twelve at a stroke, and in a very short time will fill a canoe with them."

In addition to herring, the rake was used with equal success in catching smelt. Sir Arthur Birch, who watched sturgeon fishing from his Government House office window, did more than merely observe the use of the rake. In a letter to England he wrote:

"I took a canoe from below my window and paddling with a rake had in about an hour 600 smelts in the bottom of the canoe. The rake is so — [he made a sketch] about 8 ft. long, you sit right forward and use the rake as a paddle bringing it behind you into the boat each stroke sometimes I would bring up 9 or 10 at a stroke very large smelts and delicious eating."

HERRING RAKING

Nootka man with herring rake. Early Spanish picture courtesy Dr. Erna Gunther.

HARDWOOD OR BONE TEETH SET INTO DRILLED HOLES, OR HAMMERED IN FROM THE BACK.

LENGTHS VARY FROM 2·5cm - 4·0cm. SPACING FROM 1·5 cm - 2·8 cm.

A VARIATION HAS ANGLED TEETH. 12·X

WHEN NAILS BECAME AVAILABLE, THESE REPLACED TEETH OF WOOD AND BONE. RAKES ARE ALSO USED FOR TAKING SMELT AND EULACHON.

FROM RIGHT SIDE OF CANOE, FISHERMAN IN STERN SWEEPS HERRING RAKE THROUGH WATER IN PADDLE-LIKE MOTION, DRAWING IT UP AND UNDER FISH.

WIFE, IN BOW, PADDLES CANOE IN OPPOSITE DIRECTION TO INCREASE FORCE OF RAKE THROUGH WATER. IN ONE CONTINUOUS MOTION, MAN LIFTS RAKE OUT AND RAPS IT SHARPLY ON GUNWALE, CAUSING FISH TO DROP INTO CANOE. 29·NK

16.TL

Nets and Netting

Indians today still use fishing nets in many ways, but the spun nettle, cedar (and occasionally hemp) fibres of the coast have been replaced by nylon net, while the carved wooden netting needle is now of moulded plastic.

As with fish hooks, spears and harpoons, coastal Indians devised a great many different styles of nets for the taking of fish. A material much used was the well known stinging nettle *(Urtica lyallii)* that grew tall in the rich soil of forest clearing or river bank. In an amazing evolution of plant knowledge, the Indians discovered that one part of a plant as formidable as the nettle could be cut, split, dried, peeled, beaten, shredded and spun into a fine two-strand twine of exceptional strength. Interestingly, the preparation and manufacture of nettle fibre into thread was known in early European times and it was considered to be stronger than flax. In fact the word "net" is derived from "nettle."

On the Northwest Coast, nettles were gathered in late summer or early fall when they were mature, the fat, hollow stems towering over a person's head. With the leaves stripped off, the stalks were split before being dried. One account of the fibre preparation says that the splitting was done with the thumbnail. I tried it in my experiments in making nettle twine, and although it worked well I found after a while the need to resort to a tool. A bone herring knife, shaped from a deer ulna, made a fine substitute, running smoothly and easily up the stem to split it.

It was the nettle's cortical "bark" and not the woody inner part that produced fibres. After this was peeled off it was beaten and then cleaned of its outer covering by drawing the lengths of fibre over a section of bone (bear rib) held between thumb and little finger, the other fingers pressing the fibres against the bone.

Long, fine fibres, clean and separated, were the result of much labouring, and these were spun into a two-strand twine by using a spindle, or rolling the fibres on the naked thigh with the palm of the hand. Finding that I was not at all proficient at using the spindle I had made, I tried out the other method, and with blue jeans around ankles eventually came up with a few metres (about four yards) of reasonably good nettle twine. It was then I understood and appreciated the time involved and the skill required to gather, prepare and spin sufficient of the fibre to make a net.

The bark of willow saplings *(Salix hookeriana)* was spun into two-ply twine for reef nets by some of the southern Coast Salish, while up the Fraser Valley the prepared fibre of a plant now known as Indian Hemp *(Apocynum cannibinum)* was utilized for netting. The ubiquitous inner cedar bark was also often used for netting.

Net making by hand is another ancient skill still practised in many parts of the world. The size of the mesh must differ according to the species of fish to be caught, and to ensure uniformity of any one size a mesh gauge was usually employed. I was fascinated to watch a young native boy in Hawaii sitting on the deck of his fish boat making a net with agile fingers. The tip of the conical net was fastened to the stay above him, and he worked around the edge as it hung down, adding to the number of meshes every few rows. He measured and knotted several meshes around the gauge before taking them off, thus minimizing labour. The same technique was used by the coast Indians.

Many of the nets on the coast were attached to a hoop or frame of some sort. These served to dip out or scoop up the fish massed in migratory schools or congregated in a trap or dam. Hoops were often of bent vine maple *(Acer circinatum)* with the net lashed around the rim. I have found that a slender fresh length of vine maple will bend into the hoop shape without steaming.

Pausing on a river raft trip down waterways of the interior of British Columbia one year, I with my companions pulled into the bank on a remote part of the Fraser River. On the other side of a ridge an Indian family had set up their annual fish camp and I visited with them a while. Fish hung on racks above a smoking fire tended by an older woman; tents, bedding, pots and pans, food and an array of belongings indicated a fairly lengthy stay. Every year around this time — it was August — they came to this spot on the river for a few weeks.

For generations their families had been coming, the husband standing on the end of a rocky point jutting into the river, sweeping his dip net downstream with the current, the wife butchering and smoking the fish that would see them through the winter. Children played nearby. I watched the man on the point of rock repeatedly dipping in and taking out the net in a slow steady rhythm, over and over again, hoping for a catch. When a salmon on its upstream journey became caught in the net being swept downstream, it was quickly lifted out and put into a low stone wall enclosure built up of loose rocks. I noticed that the fisherman's dip net was not nylon but chicken wire! This material was obviously heavy, but he explained its advantage: the salmon would not get entangled and so could be emptied out more easily and quickly.

The fish were few and far between, partly because it was too early in the afternoon (the fishing is better when the sun is off the water; then the salmon rise nearer the surface) but also because there were fewer fish going up the river now. Not as in the old days, he told me, when there were lots of fish and no government regulations. There were plenty of fish in those days and you got one, sometimes two, with every dip of the net. You caught more fish than you needed and you shared it with others in the village, with old people who could no longer go to the fish camps.

Many of the older people are so accustomed to the dried, smoked fish that they can eat little else in the way of protein, and having to do without it creates a real hardship for them.

We ran into similar complaints about the diminishing salmon runs much farther down the river, near Yale, where for countless generations the people have come to their hereditary fishing grounds on the Fraser River. Evidence from an archaeological site on the other side of the river (Site number DjRi-3) dates its occupation back to

9,000 years ago, and in all probability the people then were down at the river for the very same reason: the catching of salmon.

Fishermen here set out gill nets in the quiet backwaters, where the salmon pause to rest in their upriver migrations. In the summer, nets with their wooden floats bobbing on the water can still be seen not far from the highway. In some places a long pole, one end anchored on the rocky bank, holds the net out into the muddy, silt-laden river.

It was early morning. We had set our sleeping bags on a ledge high above the river the night before. Waking to the spectacular sight of shafts of sunlight stabbing diagonally into the canyon through mist clouds on mountain tops, I peered over the rocky ledge to the river below. Two men were striding over the rocks towards a quiet bay with a net stretched across it, and I watched in anticipation. They hauled in the long net by its rope and there, hanging in the net caught behind the gills, was a solitary salmon.

Later I walked along a path to another net and

Fraser River salmon net is suspended from pole anchored to river bank. This adaptation of net that originally used anchor stone to hold it out into current was devised around 1930, is still in use today. CS talked with a woman who said that new government regulations had cut down on the number of days a week they were allowed to have their nets out, and now it was hardly worth coming to the fish camps, spending so much time, to catch so few fish. Each year fewer people were spending less time at the camps.

I recalled visiting this same area 14 years before when the river banks were alive with families busily catching, butchering and drying salmon, stacking it between branches of alder to keep it from wasps. Drying racks high on rocky pinnacles were loaded with the bright red sockeye, and warm winds blowing down the canyon worked the miracle of preservation the way it had always done.

But there were a lot fewer fish now, and the blame was tossed in various directions: too many salmon being taken on the high seas, too much commercial fishing at the mouth of the river, pollution of the river by industrial waste.

The following spring, by arrangement with the Masset Band Council, I was at a fish camp at the mouth of the Yakoun River, at the end of Masset Inlet on the Queen Charlotte Islands. The water was shallow, especially when the tide was out, and gill nets were stretched right across one arm of the river. Neat one-room cabins, drying racks and smoke houses dotted the bank on both sides. The falling tide left small boats sitting on mud banks the way canoes might have once been. An eagle circled the gray sky and raven cries brought to mind the myths and legends of the Haida people who had been coming to fish the Yakoun for longer than anyone could remember. A few of them were still lured back each season by their love for the rich, succulent salmon.

Long racks in cedar plank smoke houses were hung with the silver-sided strips of sockeye; alderwood fire smoke made the brilliant hued fish flanks a deeper red as it added to the already delicious flavour.

Inside a comfortable cabin a family of noble lineage made their evening meal of fresh roasted salmon. Outside, stapled to the cedar plank wall, a government permit from the Department of Fisheries and Forestry, issued under the Authority of the Fisheries Act, signed by the Director of Fisheries, gave them limited permission to catch the fish.

DEPARTMENT OF FISHERIES AND FORESTRY
INDIAN PERMIT — 1975 9446
HAIDA INDIAN BAND COUNCIL
HAIDA, B.C.
IN THE WATERS OF THE YAKOUN, AIN OR AWUN RIVERS, FR[illegible]
RESERVE LAND, BETWEEN MAY 1 AND JUNE 15, 197[illegible]
ALL FOOD FISH ARE TO BE MARKED AS SUCH AND CATCH NUMBERS [illegible]
GILLNETS 50 FATHOMS OR LESS IN LENGTH ONE THIRD [illegible]
THE RIVER TO BE OPEN AT ALL TIMES
FROM MIDNIGHT WEDNESDAY TO MIDNIGHT SUNDAY
THIS PERMIT IS ISSUED UNDER THE AUTHORITY OF THE FISHERIES ACT AND IS NOT TRANSFERABLE
W. R. HOURSTON
REGIONAL DIRECTOR OF FISHERIES
Masset April 25/75
ORIGINAL

Split and dried nettle stalks, with coil of rough nettle fibre, coil of prepared fibre and hank of spun twine. Experimental work by the author. 60.

GROOVED ON REVERSE, USED IN PREPARATION OF NETTLE FIBRES – OUTER BARK IS PEELED FROM DRIED STALKS AND BEATEN TO SOFTEN AND CLEAN READY FOR SPINNING. 12·44·KW.

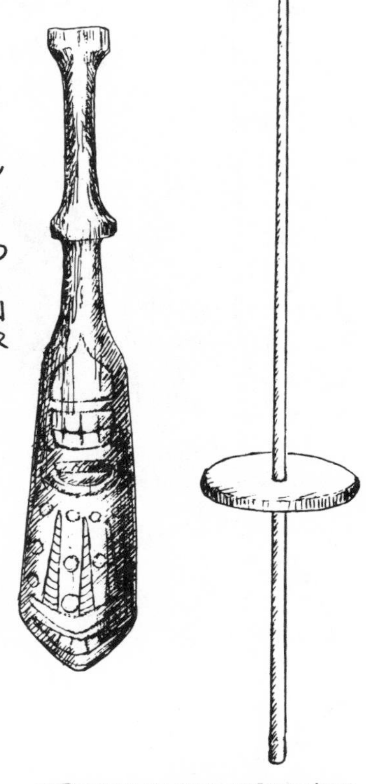

SPINDLE FOR SPINNING NETTLE FIBRES HAS SMALL BONE WHORL TO ACT AS FLYWHEEL. LENGTH ABOUT 30 cm. 77·BC

TWO METHODS OF SPINNING NETTLE FIBRE FOR NETTING – LENGTHS OF PREPARED FIBRES COILED INTO BASKET ARE PULLED OUT AND SPUN:

1) BY ROLLING ON THIGH WITH PALM OF HAND –

2) BY USING A SPINDLE ROTATED ON THE THIGH OR LEG BY ROLLING –

Plastic netting needle and nylon net of modern Haida fisherman differ only in material, not form. 60.HA

NET GAUGES

GAUGE FOR NETTING FOR SPRING SALMON -MAPLE WOOD. 11·4x9cm. 16·CS

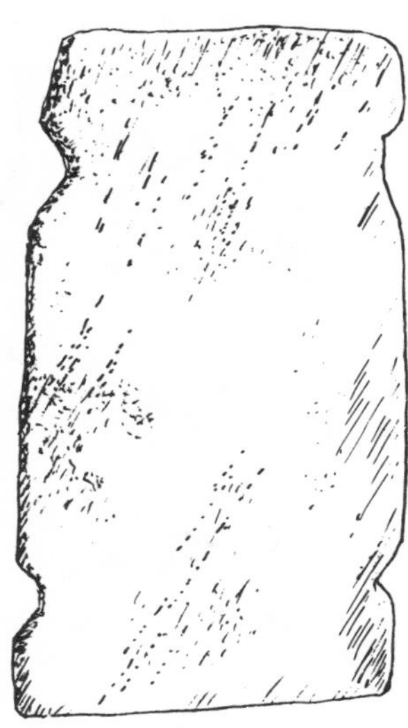

BONE. 6x4cm 13·CS

NETTING NEEDLES

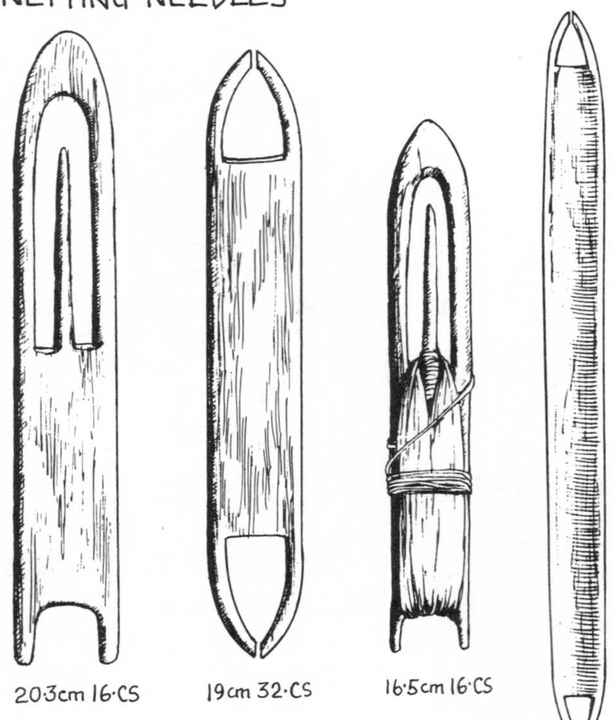

20·3cm 16·CS

19cm 32·CS

16·5cm 16·CS

24cm 11·X

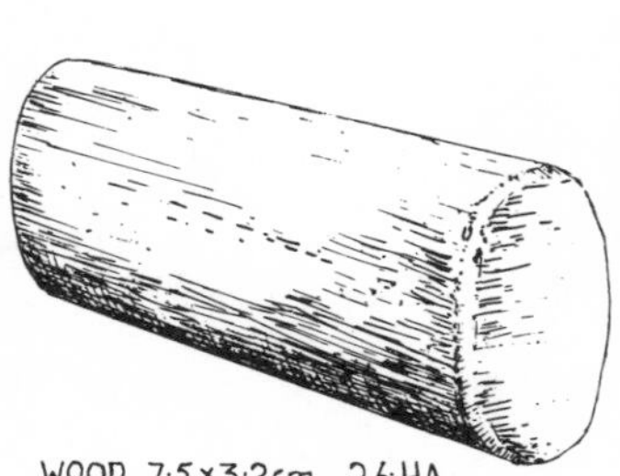

WOOD. 7·5x3·2cm. 26·HA

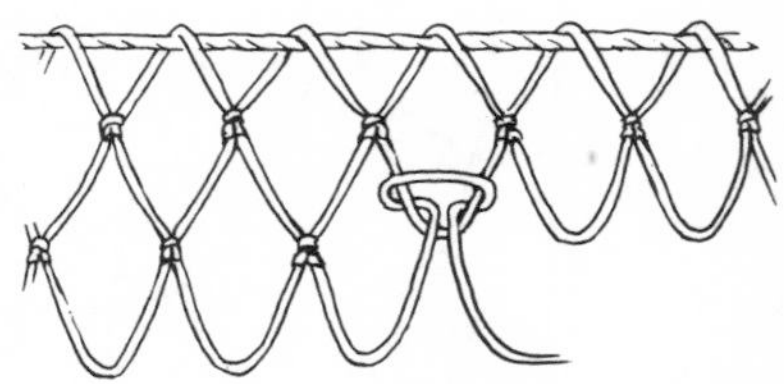

NETTING KNOT

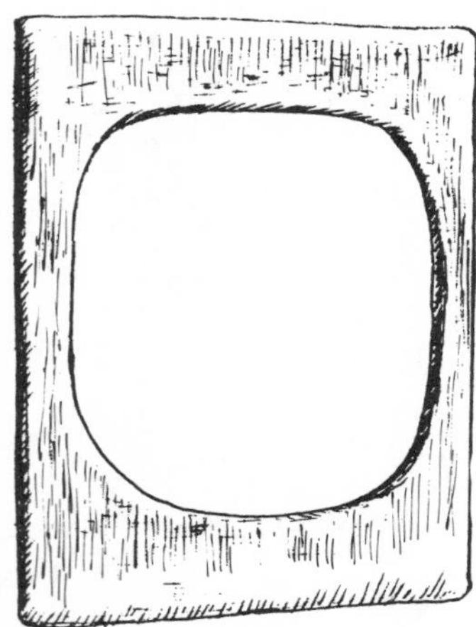

MAPLE WOOD. 10·4cm x 7·5cm. 16·CS

NETTING FLOUNDER

75·CS
SEINE NET FOR CATCHING FLOUNDER IS SET IN SHALLOW BAY AT LOW TIDE. GROUP OF MEN AND BOYS WADE IN, SPLASHING WATER _ FISH, RESTING ON BOTTOM, ARE CHASED INTO NET.

Surf fishing for smelt. 17 . MK (?)

GILL NETS

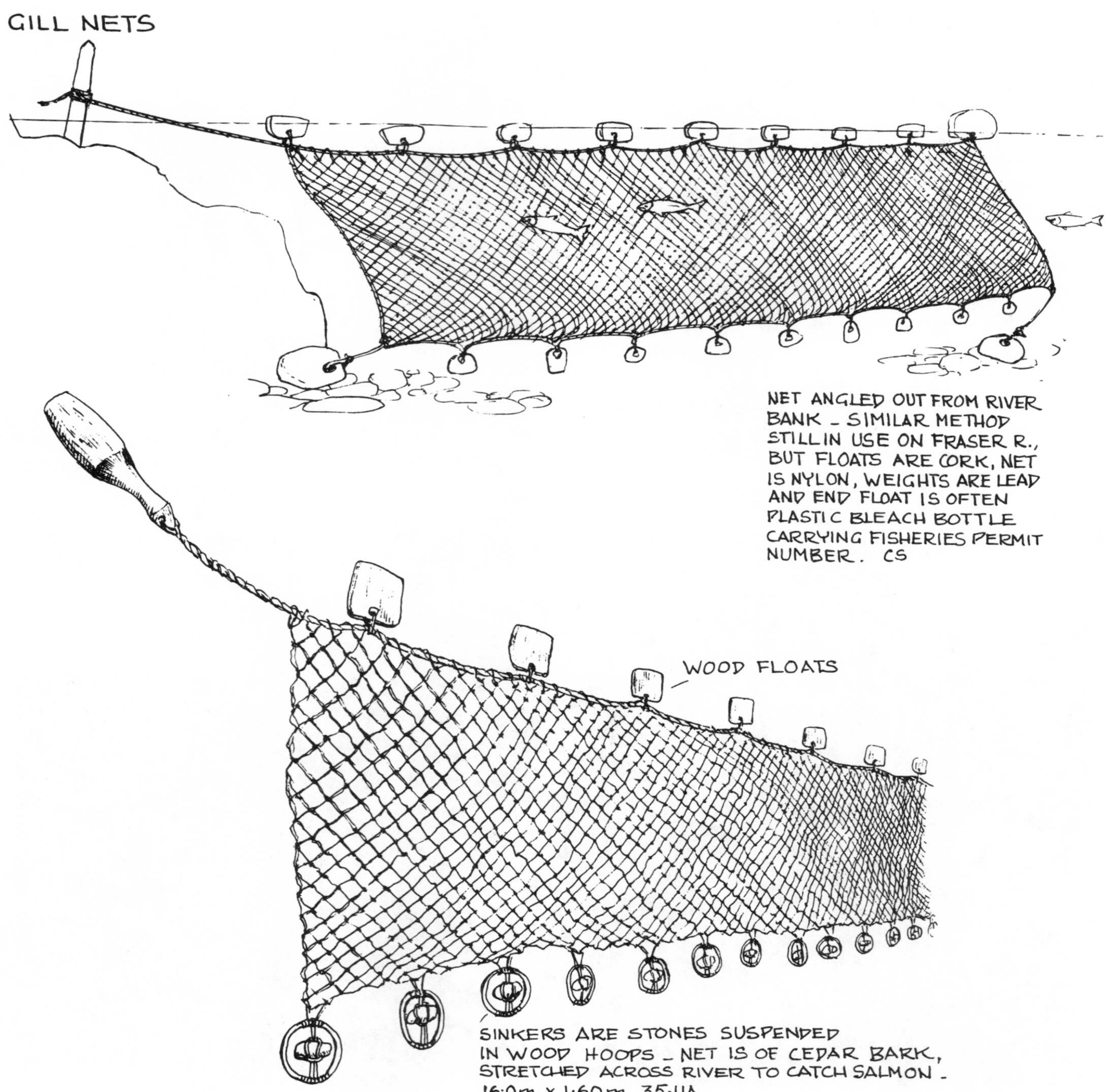
NET ANGLED OUT FROM RIVER BANK _ SIMILAR METHOD STILL IN USE ON FRASER R., BUT FLOATS ARE CORK, NET IS NYLON, WEIGHTS ARE LEAD AND END FLOAT IS OFTEN PLASTIC BLEACH BOTTLE CARRYING FISHERIES PERMIT NUMBER. CS
WOOD FLOATS
SINKERS ARE STONES SUSPENDED IN WOOD HOOPS _ NET IS OF CEDAR BARK, STRETCHED ACROSS RIVER TO CATCH SALMON _ 16·0m. x 1·60m 35·HA

BEACH SEINE NET

(A) SETTING OUT BEACH SEINE NET AT HIGH TIDE –

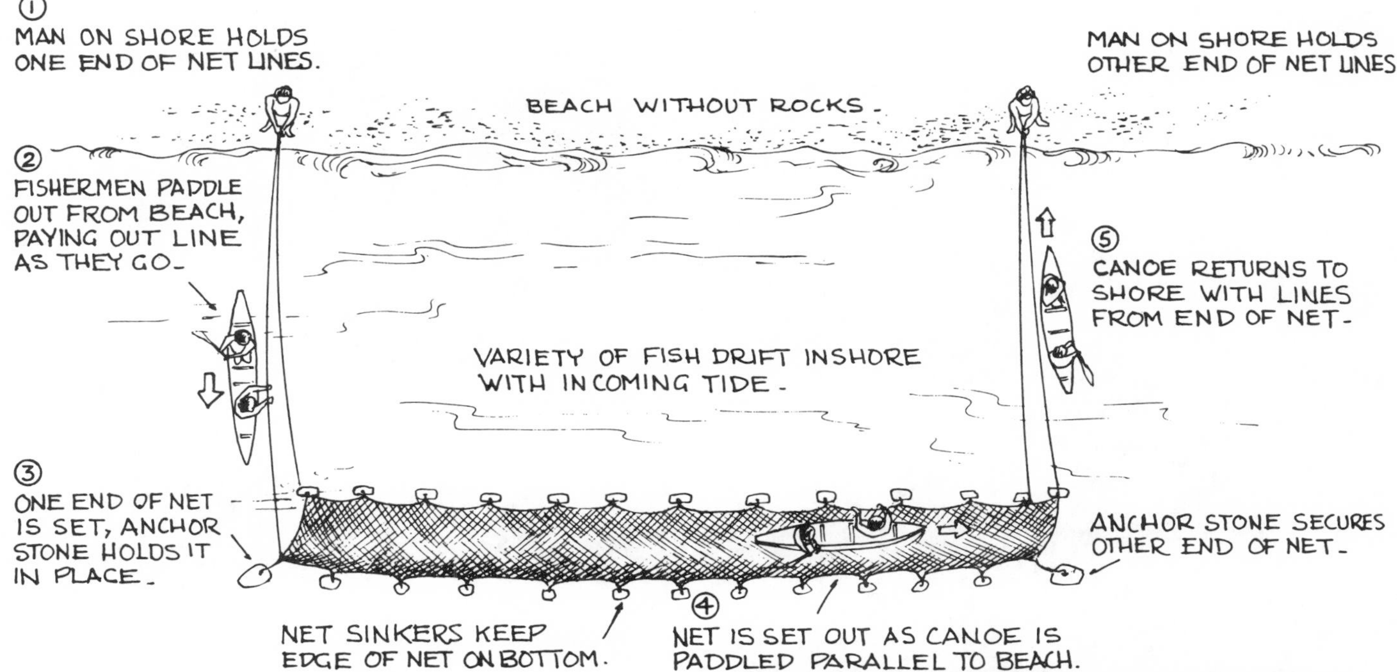

(B) HAULING IN BEACH SEINE NET.

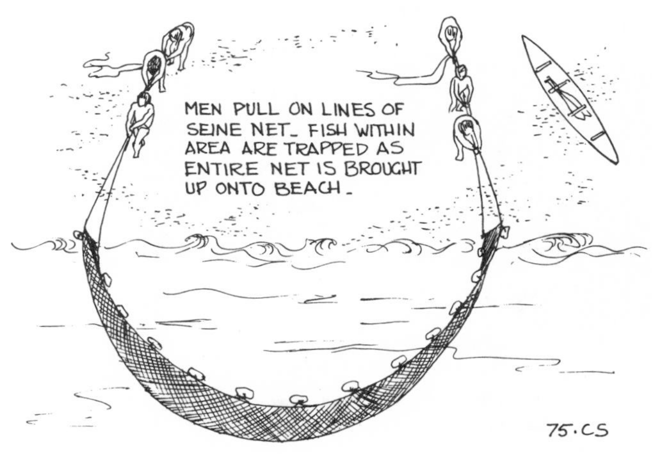

Face of shark carved on intervertebrate bone. 18cm (7 inches). 60.21.TL

Cover engraving for New York *magazine dated September, 1890, shows men dip netting salmon on the Fraser River near Yale, with fish drying on rack nearby.* 62.CS

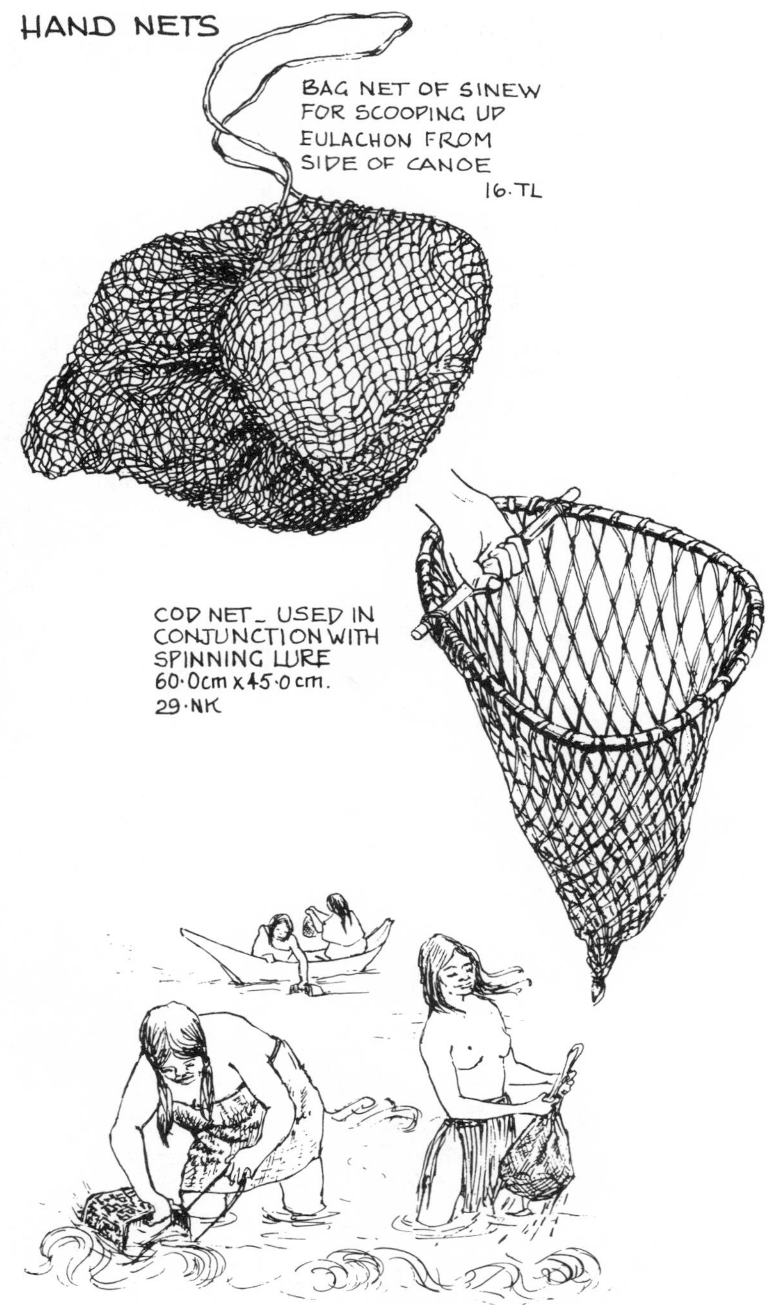

Netting eulachon, Chilkat River. 22.TL

Eulachon fishing on the Chilkat River. 22.TL

NETS FOR SMALL FISH

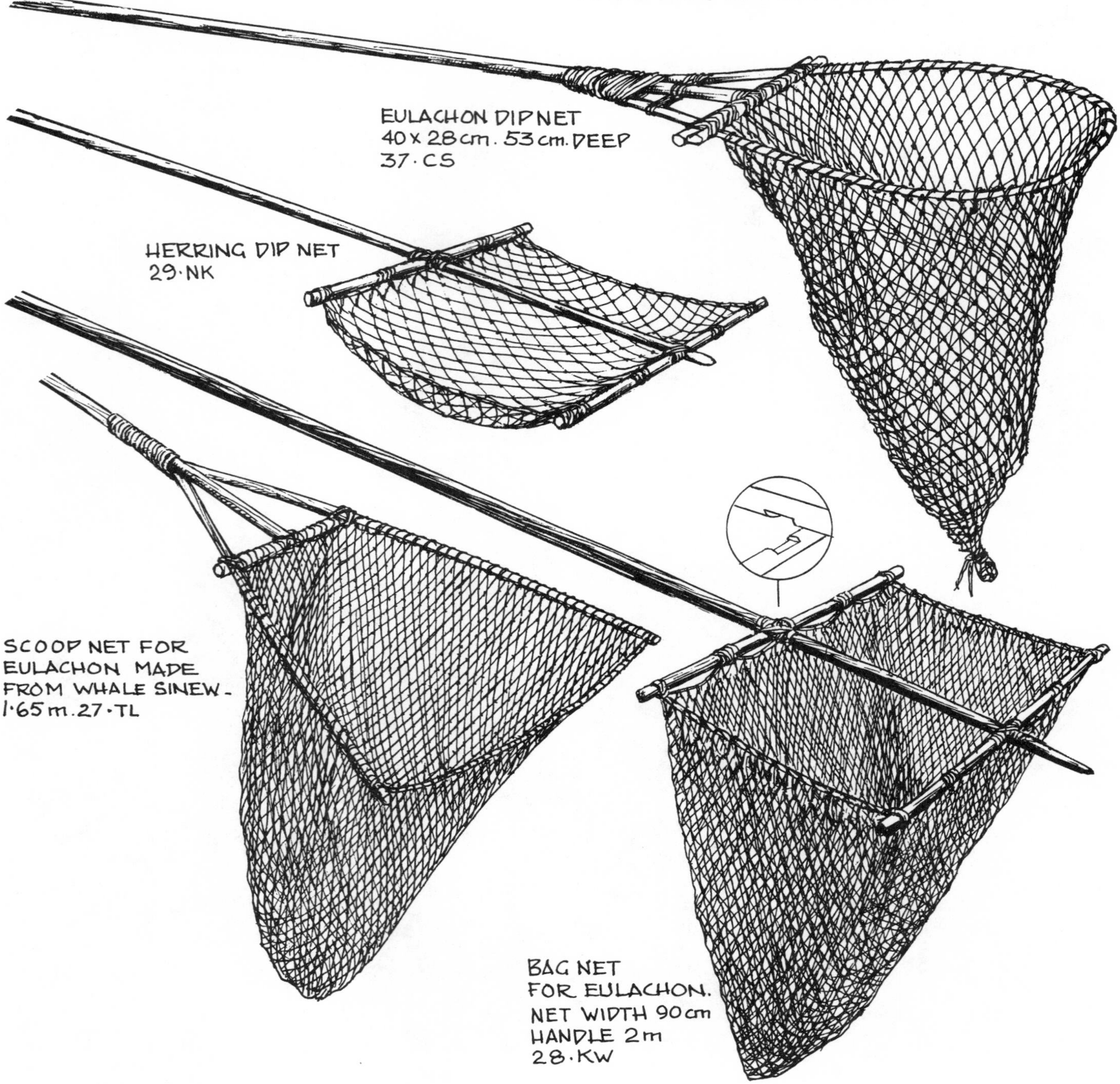

EULACHON DIPNET
40 x 28 cm. 53 cm. DEEP
37 · CS

HERRING DIP NET
29 · NK

SCOOP NET FOR
EULACHON MADE
FROM WHALE SINEW -
1·65 m. 27 · TL

BAG NET
FOR EULACHON.
NET WIDTH 90 cm
HANDLE 2 m
28 · KW

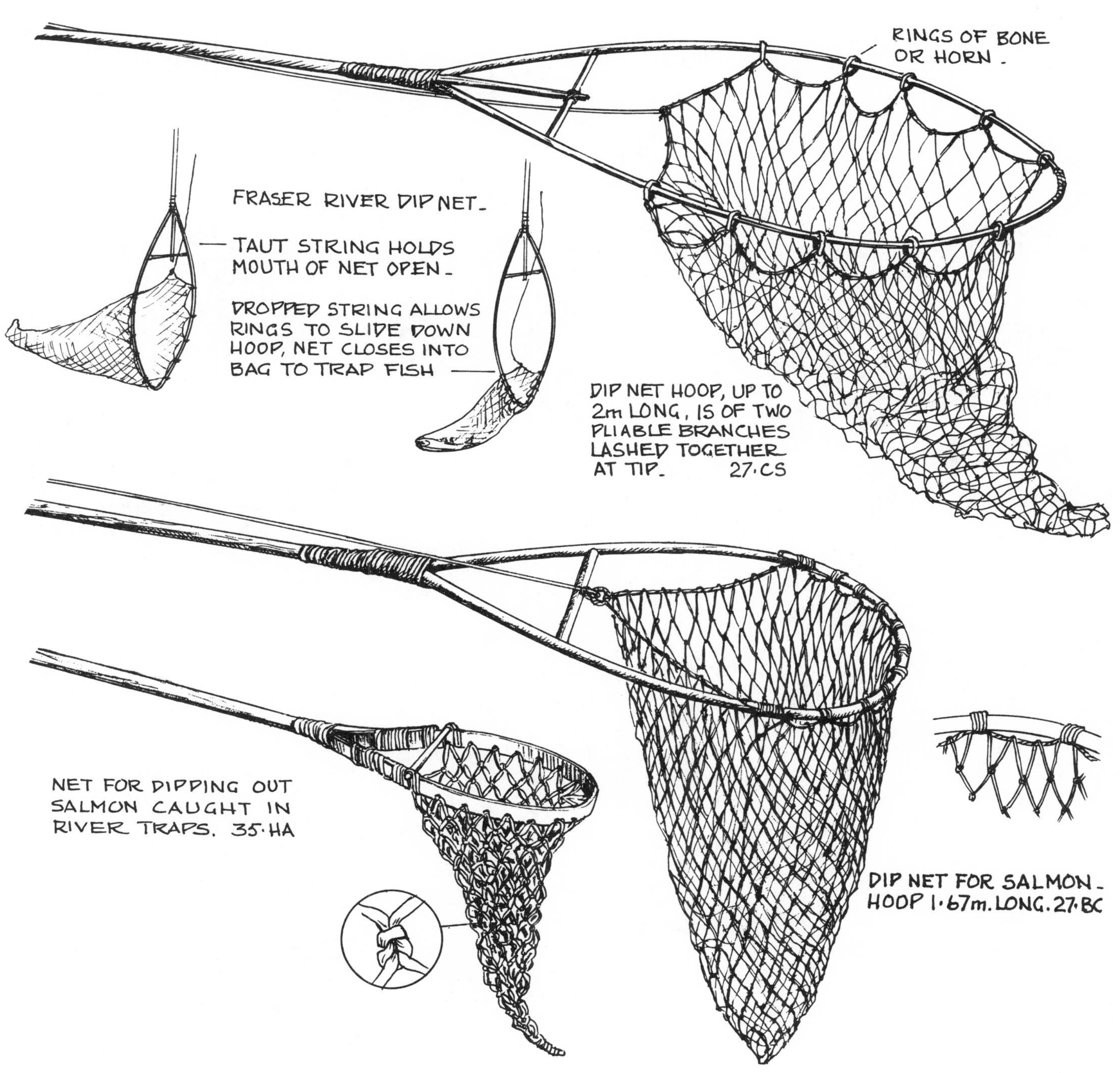
RINGS OF BONE
OR HORN.
FRASER RIVER DIP NET.
TAUT STRING HOLDS
MOUTH OF NET OPEN.
DROPPED STRING ALLOWS
RINGS TO SLIDE DOWN
HOOP, NET CLOSES INTO
BAG TO TRAP FISH
DIP NET HOOP, UP TO
2m LONG, IS OF TWO
PLIABLE BRANCHES
LASHED TOGETHER
AT TIP. 27·CS
NET FOR DIPPING OUT
SALMON CAUGHT IN
RIVER TRAPS. 35·HA
DIP NET FOR SALMON.
HOOP 1·67m. LONG. 27·BC

DRAG NET OR BAG NET

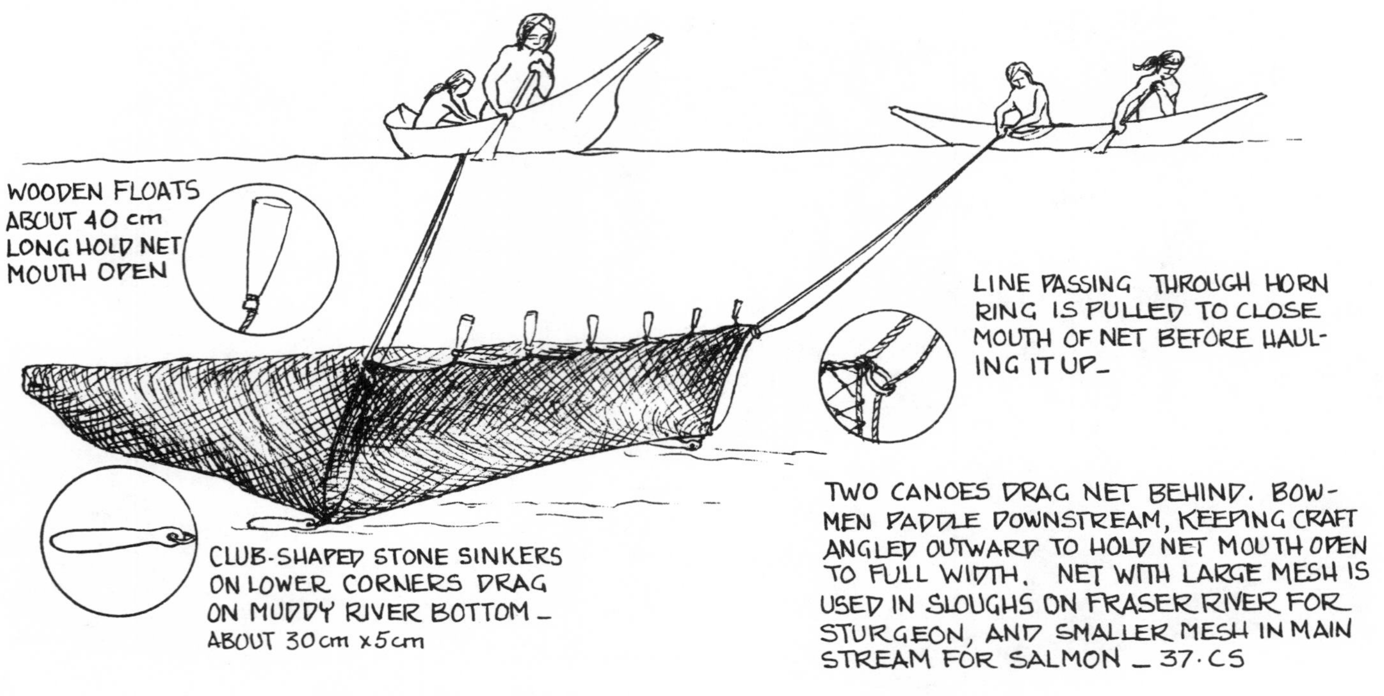

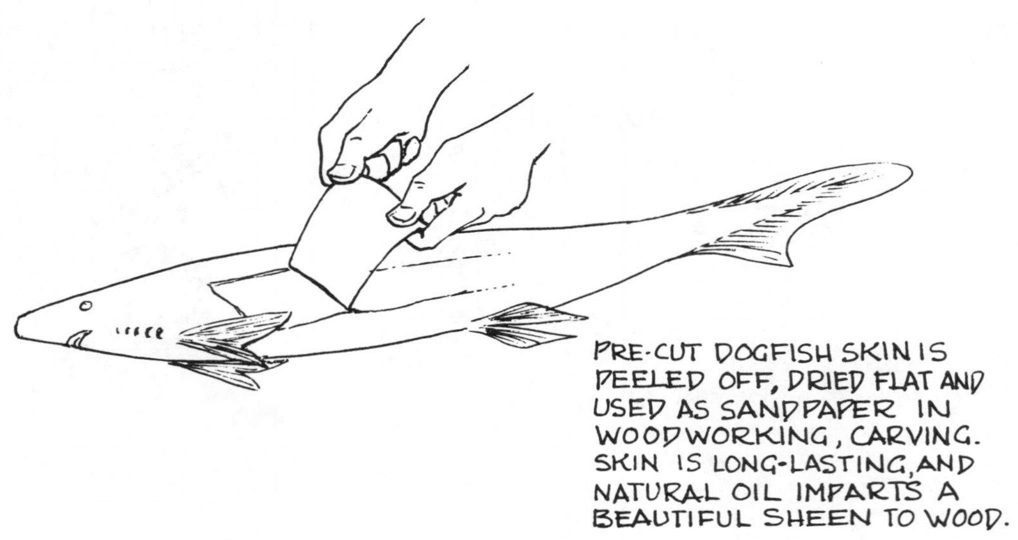

REEF NET

① SINGLE REEF NET_USUALLY SET JUST OFF SHORE OVER KELP COVERED REEF, IN PATH OF MIGRATING SALMON. CHANNEL IS CUT THROUGH KELP TO FUNNEL FISH TOWARD NET.

② WATCHMEN IN CANOE STERNS KEEP LOOKOUT FOR SALMON ENTERING NET. AT THE RIGHT MOMENT, WATCHMAN IN OFF-SHORE CANOE [THE CAPTAIN] SIGNALS CREW TO RAISE NET

③ WHEN NET SIDES ARE UP OVER GUNWALES, MAN LETS OUT SLACK ON ANCHOR LINE, ALLOWING CANOES TO SWING TOGETHER.

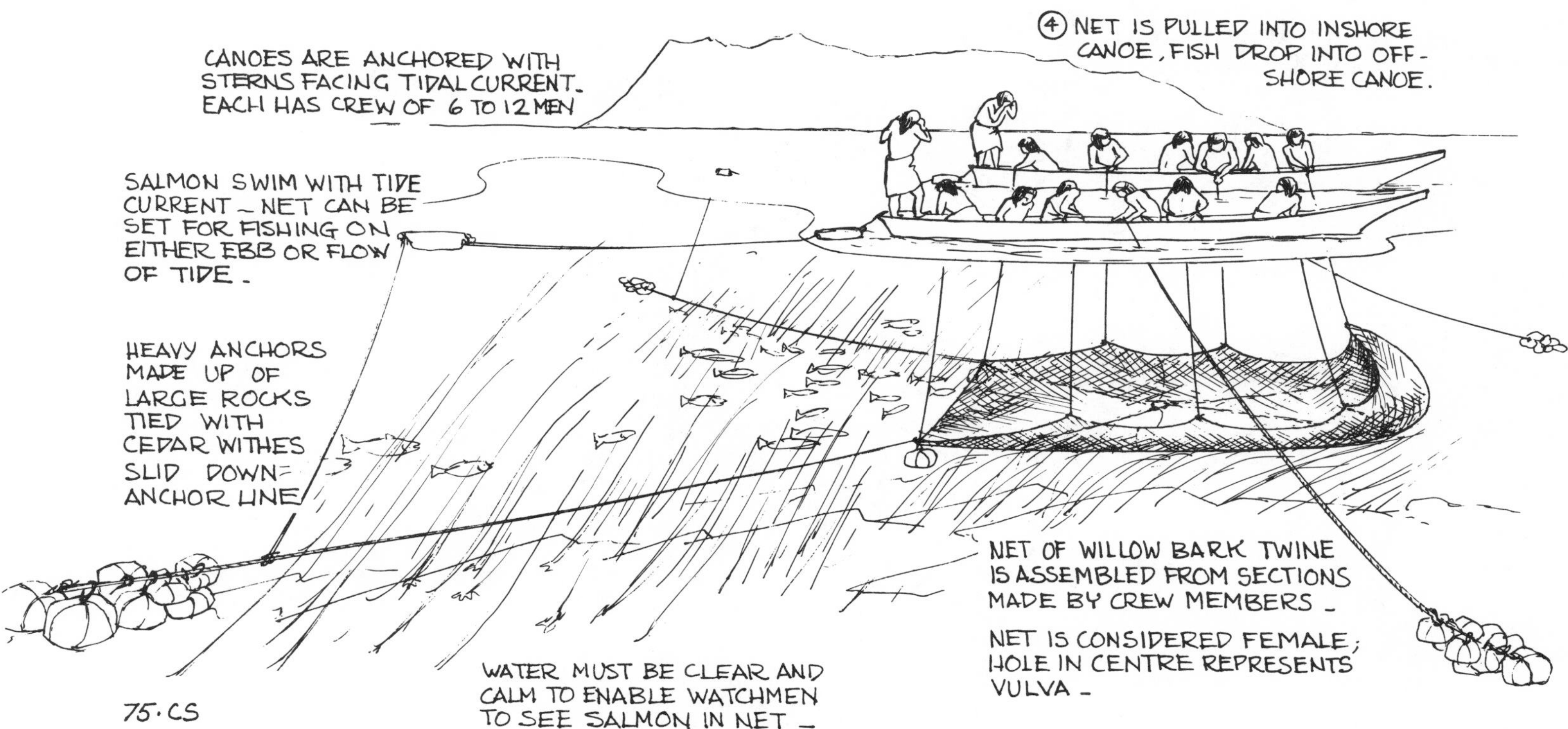

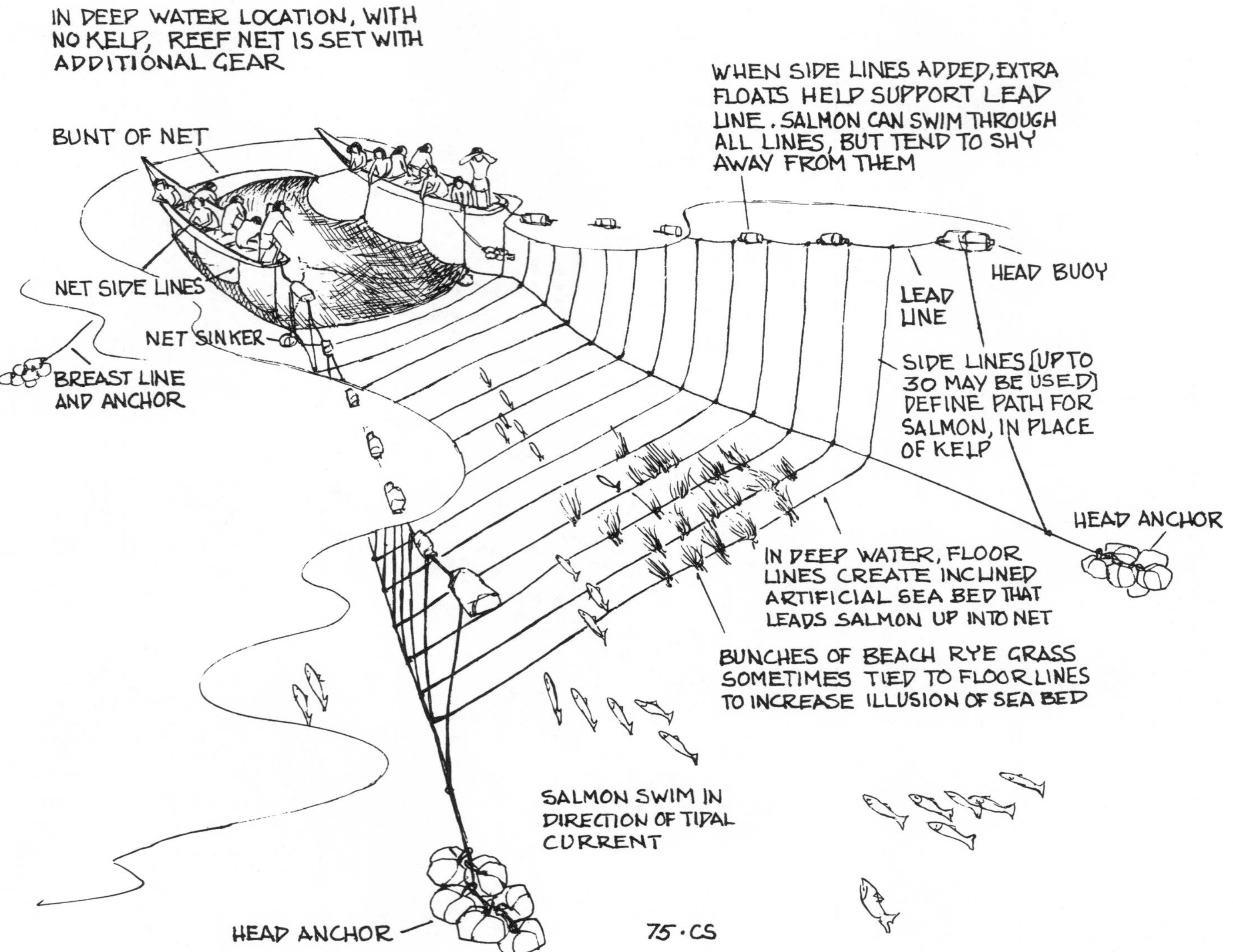
REEF NET, DEEP WATER
IN DEEP WATER LOCATION, WITH NO KELP, REEF NET IS SET WITH ADDITIONAL GEAR
BUNT OF NET
WHEN SIDE LINES ADDED, EXTRA FLOATS HELP SUPPORT LEAD LINE. SALMON CAN SWIM THROUGH ALL LINES, BUT TEND TO SHY AWAY FROM THEM
HEAD BUOY
LEAD LINE
NET SIDE LINES
NET SINKER
BREAST LINE AND ANCHOR
SIDE LINES [UP TO 30 MAY BE USED] DEFINE PATH FOR SALMON, IN PLACE OF KELP
HEAD ANCHOR
IN DEEP WATER, FLOOR LINES CREATE INCLINED ARTIFICIAL SEA BED THAT LEADS SALMON UP INTO NET
BUNCHES OF BEACH RYE GRASS SOMETIMES TIED TO FLOOR LINES TO INCREASE ILLUSION OF SEA BED
SALMON SWIM IN DIRECTION OF TIDAL CURRENT
HEAD ANCHOR
75 · CS

Eulachon Fishing

The contribution of the eulachon to the health and welfare of the Indian peoples makes it one of the important fish of the coast. The small, silvery fish, migrating in countless millions, were caught in enormous quantites. Some were eaten fresh and a great many dried, but the majority were rendered down for the rich oil they contained.

Often called "candlefish" (it is said you can light the tail of a dried fish and it will burn like a candle), the eulachon was also known as "salvation fish" since its arrival at the end of the winter meant so much to the food resources of the people. The Indian called it eulachon, a word pronounced with loose throat sounds difficult to spell with the English alphabet. In my research on this fish I have come across the following spellings, and there are probably more: eulachon, oolachon, eulachan, oolichan, hoolikan, hollikan, hollican, holligan, oligan, olachan, oulachon.

Eulachon spawn in a number of rivers on the mainland where the tides run strong. The migration lasts one or two weeks starting as early as the end of February in the north and continuing through to April in the south. Among the Tsimshian, the Nass and Skeena Rivers were major areas for catching the fish, as were the Kitimat River and the rivers of Knight Inlet for the Kwagiutl. The Bella Coola people fished the Bella Coola, Kimsquit and other rivers.

Most eulachon fishing was by net, and methods varied with different parts of the coast. At Fishery Bay, 14 miles inland from the mouth of the Nass, the river was still frozen over when the eulachon arrived and fishing was done through the ice. This ancient practice is still carried on today. People from the village of Greenville now

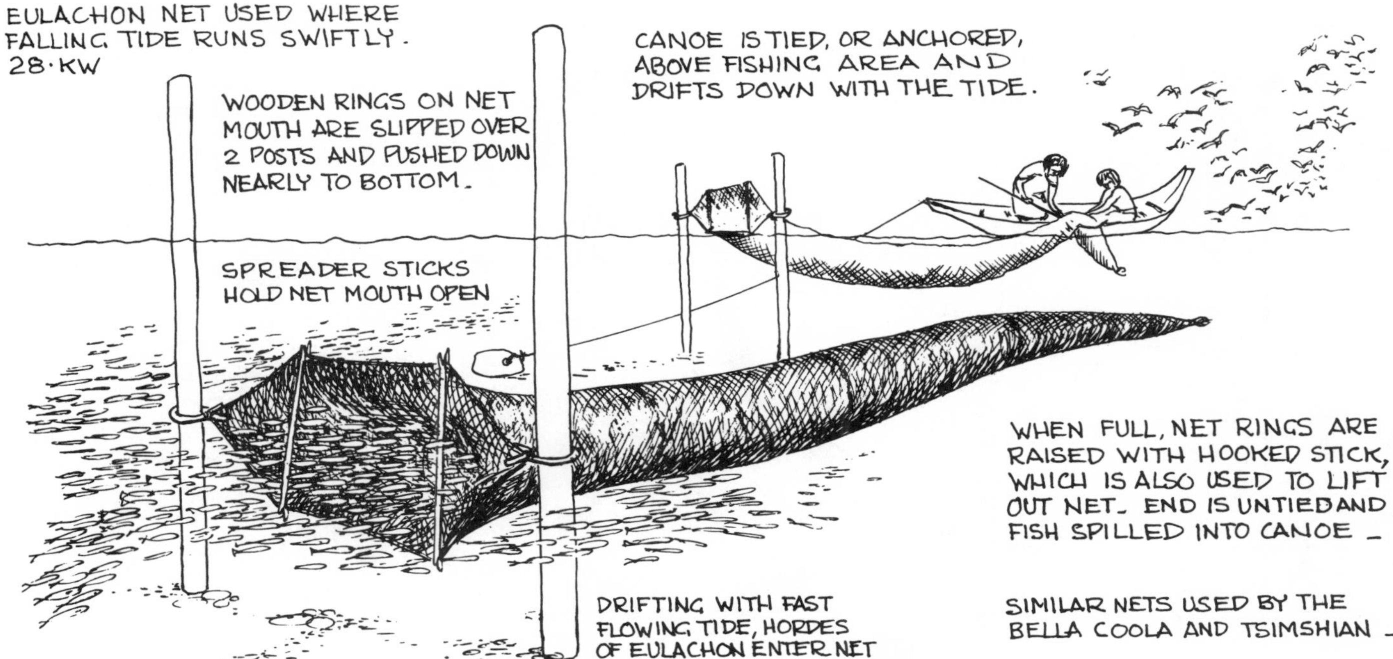

DIP NET OR BAG NET FOR EULACHON FISHING

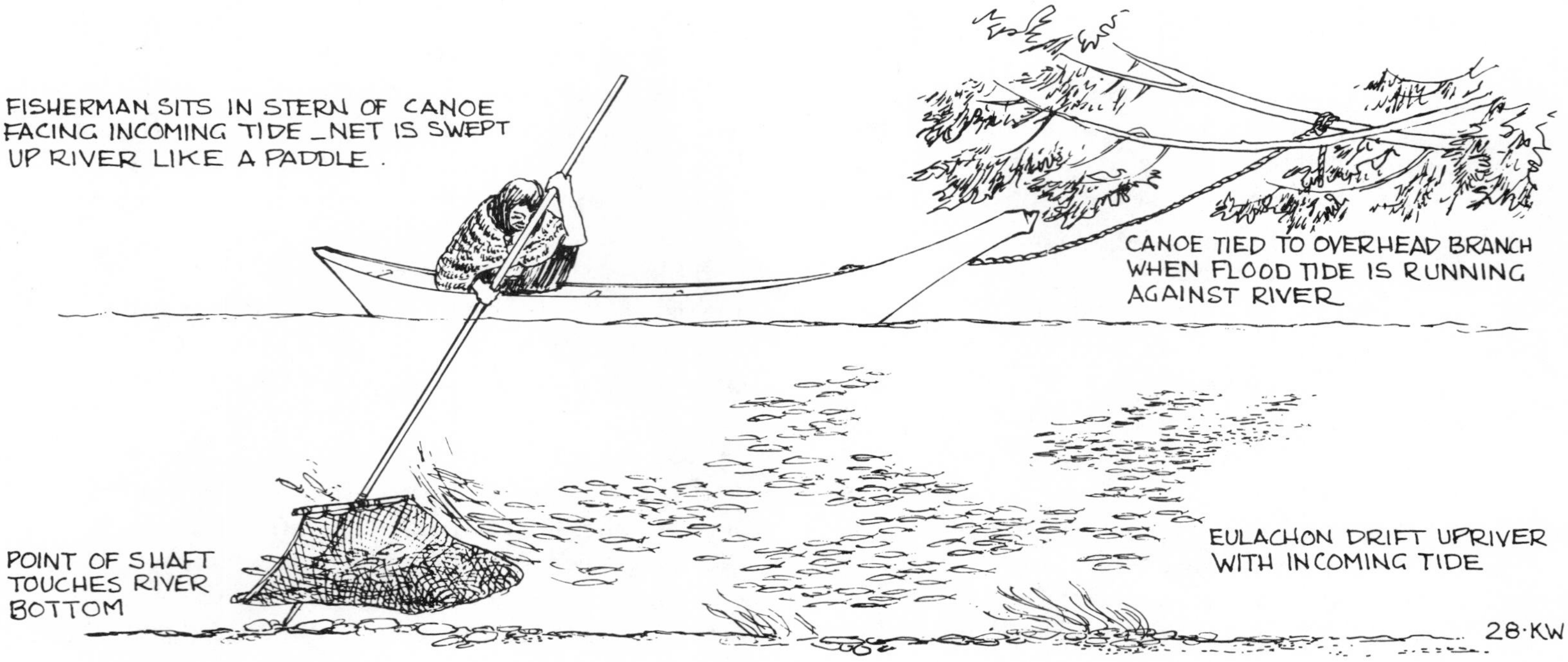
FISHERMAN SITS IN STERN OF CANOE FACING INCOMING TIDE _NET IS SWEPT UP RIVER LIKE A PADDLE.
CANOE TIED TO OVERHEAD BRANCH WHEN FLOOD TIDE IS RUNNING AGAINST RIVER
POINT OF SHAFT TOUCHES RIVER BOTTOM
EULACHON DRIFT UPRIVER WITH INCOMING TIDE
28·KW

BAG NET FOR EULACHON FISHING -
MAN STANDS IN BOW OF CANOE FACING STERN, LOWERS BAG NET ON RIGHT SIDE.
PUNTING POLE IS FOR HOLDING CANOE AGAINST CURRENT.
WOMAN SLAPS WATER WITH END OF PUNTING POLE THAT HAS CROSS PIECE ATTACHED. FISH ARE DRIVEN DOWN AND INTO NET.
CANOE FACES DOWNSTREAM
PRONGS OF BAG NET REST ON BOTTOM OF RIVER.
SUITABLE FOR SHALLOW RIVER
28·KW

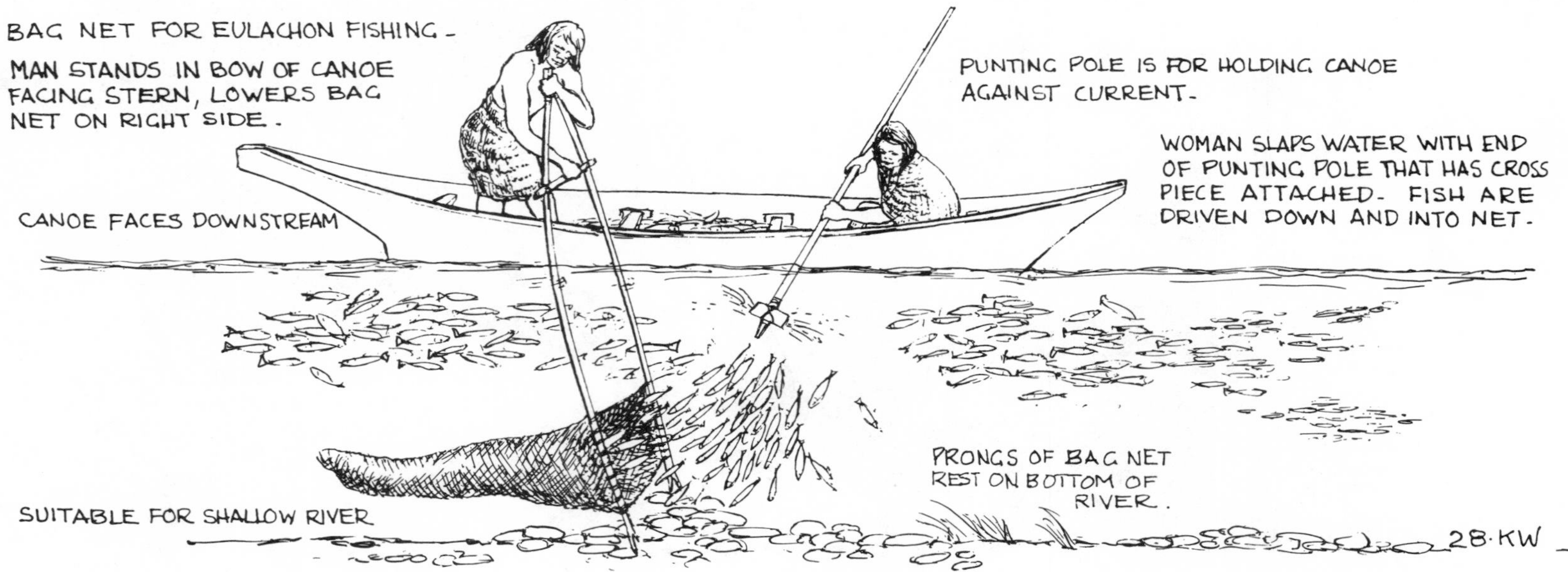

travel the five miles down river to reach their ancestral fishing village by horse and sleigh.

The first wave of the eulachon run—the females usually preceding the males—were eaten fresh as a welcome change of diet for a people relying most of the winter on dried smoked fish. As the run built up and peaked, great quantities were caught for both preserving and oil rendering.

The Indian was not the only one to await and welcome the eulachon's arrival. Sea lions, porpoises and whales followed the fish into the rivers; screaming hordes of seagulls filled the air, wheeling and diving to snatch at the glittering fish; bald eagles perched in trees along the river side, ready to swoop down and take their share. When the dead, spawned-out fish washed up on the river banks, the crows and ravens took the last of the feast.

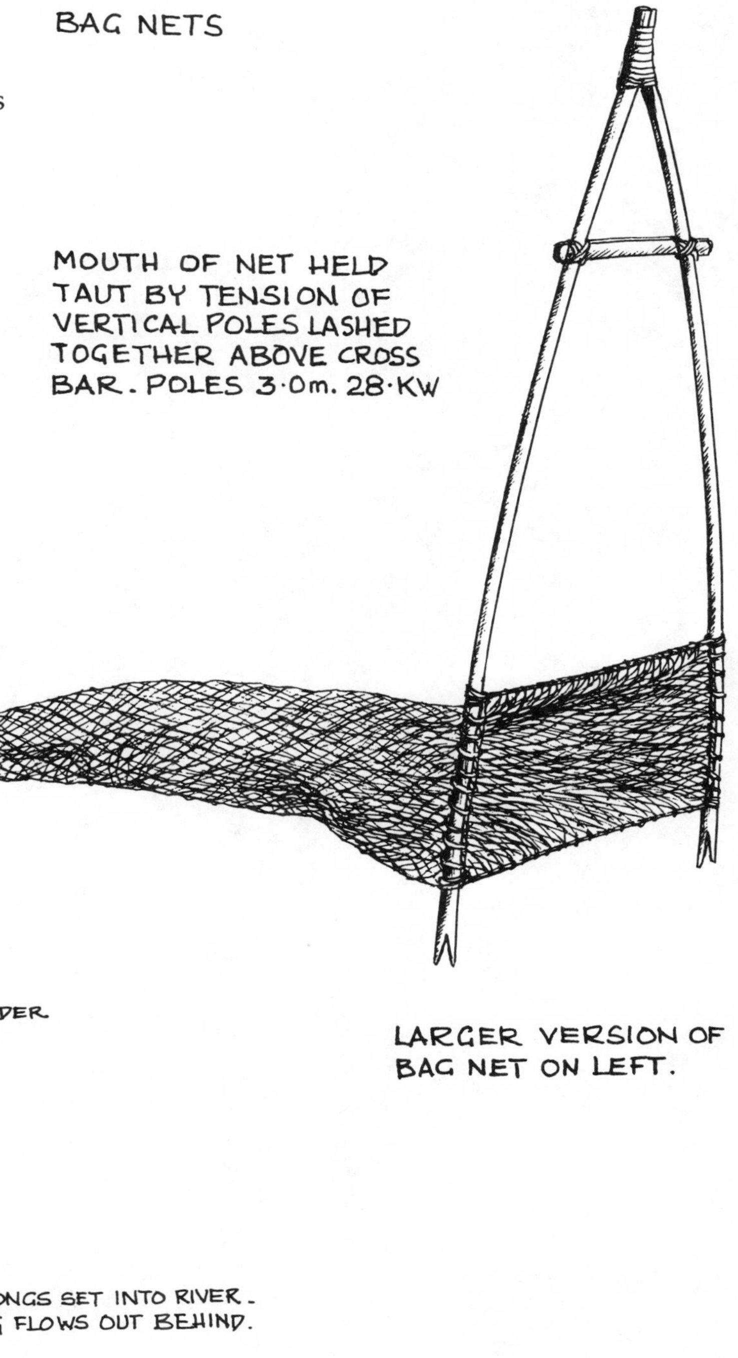

13.TS

Traps and Weirs

Probably the most productive of any of the fishing devices, the traps and weirs allowed large quantities of fish to be taken at a time when the salmon runs were at their peak.

Weirs—fences through which water flowed—were either built right across a shallow river or angled to guide the migrating fish into traps. The traps were either the removable type made with a basketry technique using sticks and lashing, or were structures built into the river bed.

Stone traps were basically wall-like rock alignments built singly or in a series, in a river, at its mouth, or in a bay drained at low tide. These would either function as a trap or funnel the fish towards the mouth of a trap.

Two basic principles were responsible for the success of almost all the weirs and traps. One was the relentless urge of the salmon to make its way upstream to its spawning grounds despite all obstacles; the other was governed by the ebb and flow of the tide. Many species of fish drift shoreward on the incoming tide, and recede again to deep water on the ebb tide. This especially applied to salmon congregated at the mouth of a river as they awaited melting snows or heavy rain to swell the creek. They swam over the traps on the flood tide and became trapped or stranded on the ebb.

Variations in trap devices depended on the species of fish, the type of environment, the building materials available, and the cultural background of the people. The wide variety of traps seems to underline the Indian's keen observation of marine life, and reflect his ingenuity in harvesting the resources of the sea.

Fish Weirs

Weirs were built in shallow estuaries, rivers and streams, either to block the upstream passage of salmon or to guide the fish into a trap—or towards the fisherman with waiting spear. Some fence weirs consisted of convenient-sized latticework sections lashed to the upstream side of a sturdy framework in the river. The lattice was put up for the fishing season and removed afterwards. The framework remained in the river all year and was repaired as necessary. Fir branches, vine maple saplings or other material could also form the fence.

Ownership rights to traps and weirs varied among the different cultures and bands, but usually a large weir across a major salmon river was owned by the whole village. Building the weir was a community effort—its very size made co-operation an advantage—and everyone shared in the catch. However, a weir across a small stream could be privately owned by a person of

Salmon weir on the Cowichan River, Vancouver Island, circa 1867. 11.CS

wealth or high rank. He would fish from it at night, when the run was at its best, and allow others to use it by day.

Downstream villagers owning weirs had first advantage in harvesting the run. When they had sufficient salmon, sections of the weir were removed to allow the fish to continue upriver, where they would encounter the weir of the next village. It is said that if the downstream people were tardy in opening the weir, their angry neighbours might launch a massive log into the fast flowing waters and smash it open.

It is still possible to find, in a stream or mud bank, or on the beach at the mouth of a stream, the remnants of a long since abandoned weir. Weather-worn stubs of wooden stakes stand in mute rows showing where the weir had once been. The truncated posts, continuing to defy years of spring flood and winter storm, testify to the strength of arms that once wielded a heavy piledriver to pound them into the river bed.

At the mouth of the Little Qualicum River, on the east coast of Vancouver Island, can be seen the posts that once were a part of a weir, and on the beach a two-metre-long post with steeply sharpened point lies partly buried, upended, in the gravel. Upriver is a modern government fish hatchery with artificial spawning grounds. Ten miles to the north, another river also holds the remnants of a fence weir on a beach that is now a trailer and campsite owned and operated by the Qualicum Indian Band. The rivers have seen changes!

PILE DRIVERS

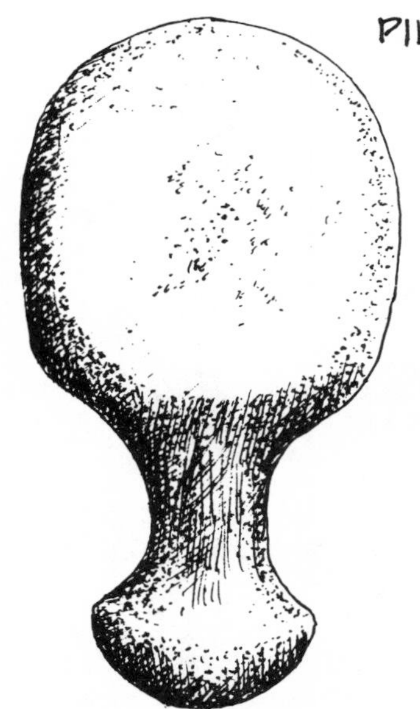

HANDLED PILE DRIVER OF SOUTHERN TRIBE, THE QUINAULT. 34.0cm. 34.CS

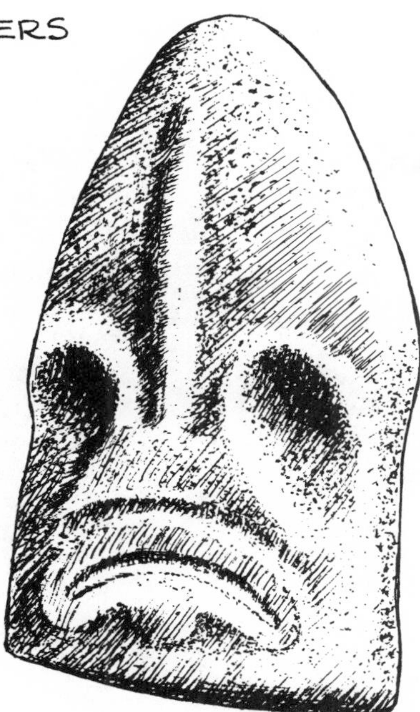

THUMB GROOVES FORM THE EYES OF DOGFISH HEAD DEPICTED ON PILE DRIVER

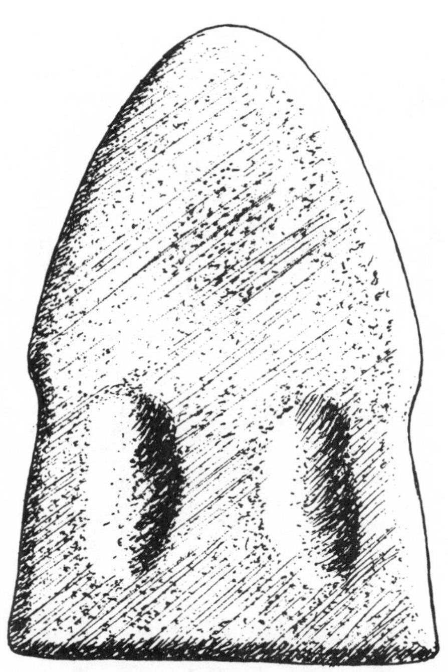

REVERSE SIDE HAS FINGER GROOVES. 39cm. 45.KW

USING PILEDRIVER TO POUND IN STAKES FOR FISH TRAP.

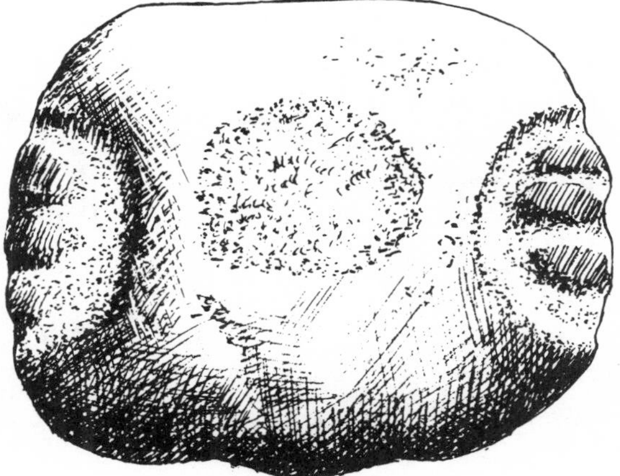

NATURALLY SHAPED BOULDER HAS SEPARATED FINGER GROOVES AND PITTED STRIKING SURFACE. THUMB GROOVES ON REVERSE. WEIGHT 32lbs. 31.2cm. 15.X

LATTICE FENCING

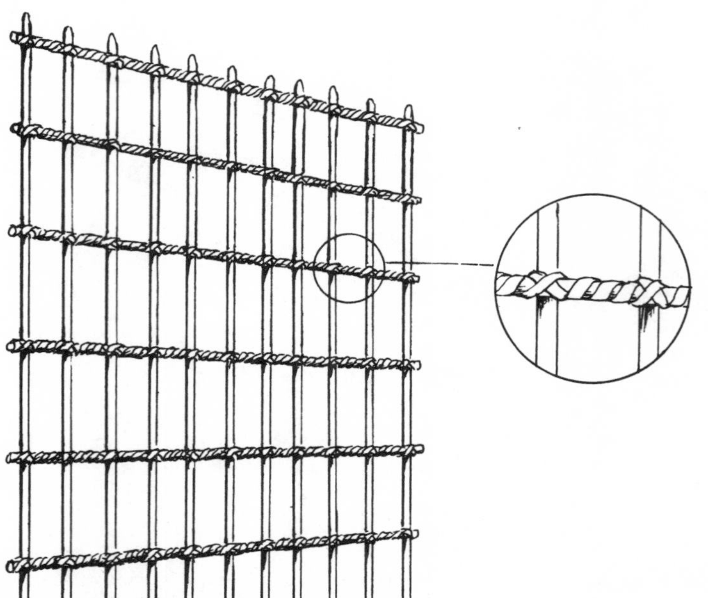

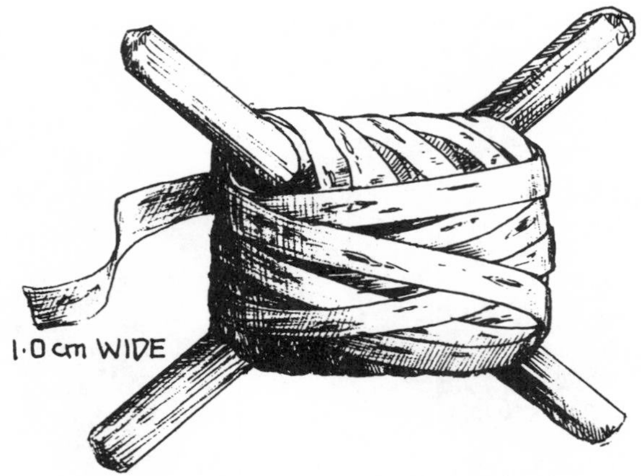

REEL OF WILD CHERRY BARK [PRUNUS EMARGINATA] — OUTER BARK IS FLAT, TOUGH AND RESISTS ROTTING — AN IDEAL MATERIAL FOR LASHING ON SPEAR AND HARPOON PRONGS, FOR ATTACHING HOOP OF DIPNET TO SHAFT.

THREE OTHER TYPES OF LATTICE FENCING FOR WEIRS -

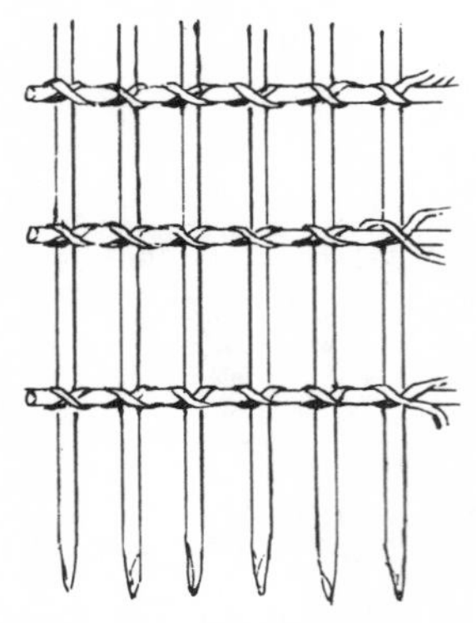

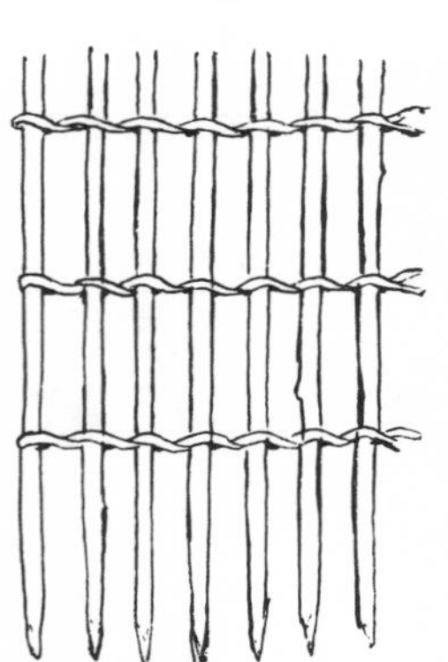

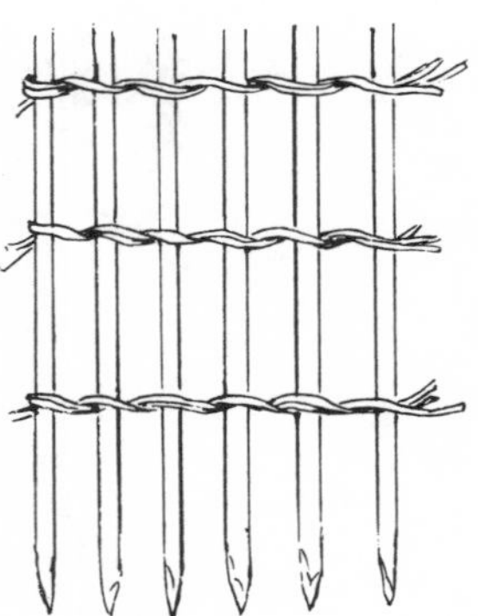

ONE TYPE OF LATTICE FOR MAKING FENCE WEIRS POINTED ENDS DUG INTO RIVER BED. 1·40m. 11·CS

SPLIT CEDAR STICKS LASHED WITH CEDAR WITHES. 32·CS

VERTICALS OF MAPLE OR HEMLOCK 42·CS

1 AND 2 STRAND TWINING WITH CEDAR WITHES _ 81·CS

FENCE WEIR FOR SALMON

ADAPTED FROM OLD PHOTO
OF COWICHAN RIVER 11·CS

FENCE WEIR WITH TRIPODS

FENCE WEIR WITH PLATFORMS, ACROSS SHALLOW RIVER OR STREAM – MIGRATING SALMON COLLECT AT FENCE UNABLE TO PROCEED UP RIVER, AND ARE TAKEN WITH DIPNETS. 32·CS

TIDAL FENCE TRAP

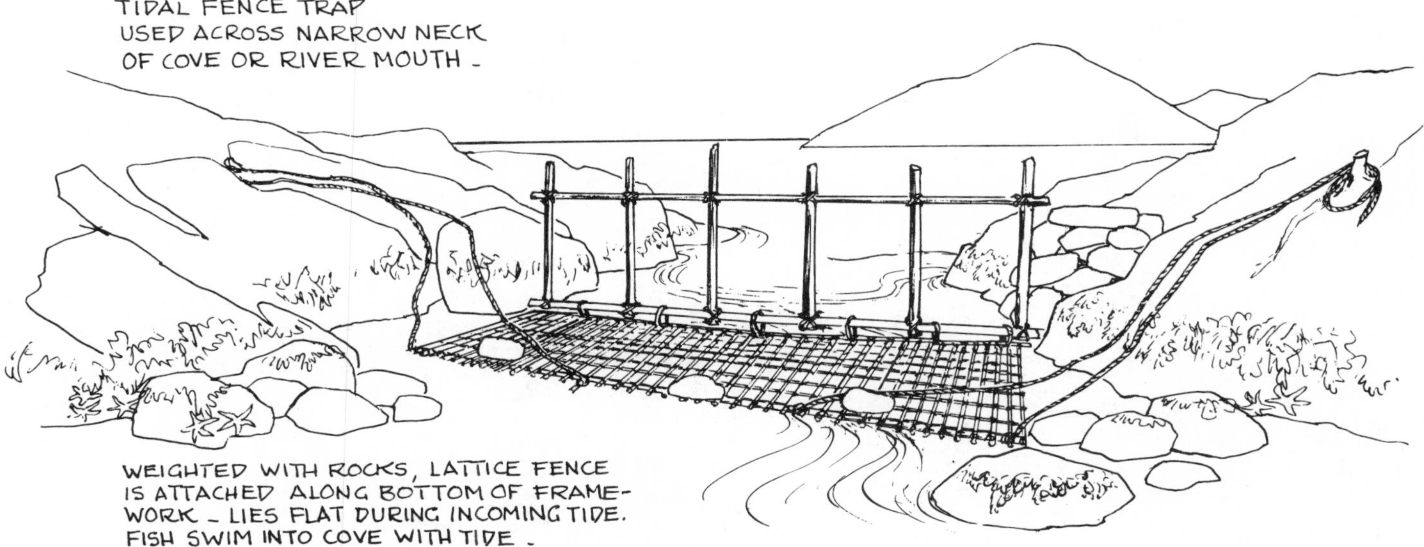

DOUBLE WEIR TRAP
TRAP USED IN SHALLOW RIVER:
FLEXIBLE BRANCHES ARE WOVEN
BETWEEN STAKES IN RIVER BED-
SALMON MIGRATING UPSTREAM LEAP
OVER FIRST FENCE, BECOME TRAPPED
BETWEEN THE TWO.
35. NORTHERN

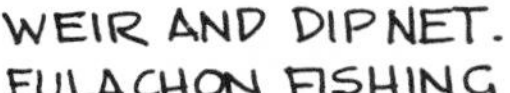

Canoes at Old Songhees, Vancouver Island. Canoe skids on beach facilitate hauling up canoes and protect hulls from scraping on stones. 11.CS

LOG. DAM TRAP
LOG DAM WITH OVERHANG PREVENTS SALMON FROM LEAPING OVER. FISH FALL INTO POOL BELOW OR SWIM BACK INTO STONE TRAP AND ARE SPEARED FROM EITHER PLACE.
28·KW

GRID TRAP FOR SWIFT WATER

IN SWIFTLY FLOWING STREAM, SALMON ENTER THROUGH FENCE OPENING. UNABLE TO PROCEED, THEY TURN BACK TO SEEK ALTERNATE ROUTE AND ARE SWEPT UP ONTO GRID, CAUGHT BETWEEN SLATS _ 32·CS

DAM AND FENCE TRAP

Basket Traps

Most basket traps worked in conjunction with a weir or blockade of some kind. Two converging weirs formed a V shape that funneled the migrating fish into the trap. Once inside, the fish became confused and were unable to find the small opening again to escape. Some traps were made very long and narrow so that the fish were unable to turn around to go back downstream in search of another route.

The Haida had names for their fish traps, and the Tlingit attached carved figures to the tops of the posts used in the structures. These beautifully wrought figures may have had special powers to attract the fish, or they may have been to indicate ownership.

Village of Bella Coola, possibly Kimsquit, 1863. Note row of basket traps behind visiting dignitaries. 13.BC

John Jewitt's narrative describes a large Nootka trap (which he calls a pot) and the method of its use:

"A pot of twenty feet in length, and from four to five feet in diameter at the mouth, is formed of a great number of pine* splinters, which are strongly secured, an inch and a half from each other, by means of hoops made of flexible twigs, and placed about eight inches apart. At the end it tapers almost to a point, near which is a small wicker door for the purpose of taking out the fish. This pot or waer [sic] is placed at the foot of a fall or rapid, where the water is not very deep, and the fish, driven from above with long poles, are intercepted and caught in the waer, from whence they are taken into the canoes. In this manner I have seen more than seven hundred salmon caught in the space of fifteen minutes. I have also sometimes known a few striped bass taken in this manner, but rarely."

Unfortunately very few of the various kinds of traps remain today. Large and cumbersome, they were not items for collection as were carvings and art objects, and so they eventually disintegrated outdoors. Traps can sometimes be spotted in the background of old photographs taken in more remote villages. Their construction was frequently complex, and most were made with the precision, care and fine finishing so often found in utilitarian items of the coast people.

*This wood was probably cedar.

BASKET TRAPS

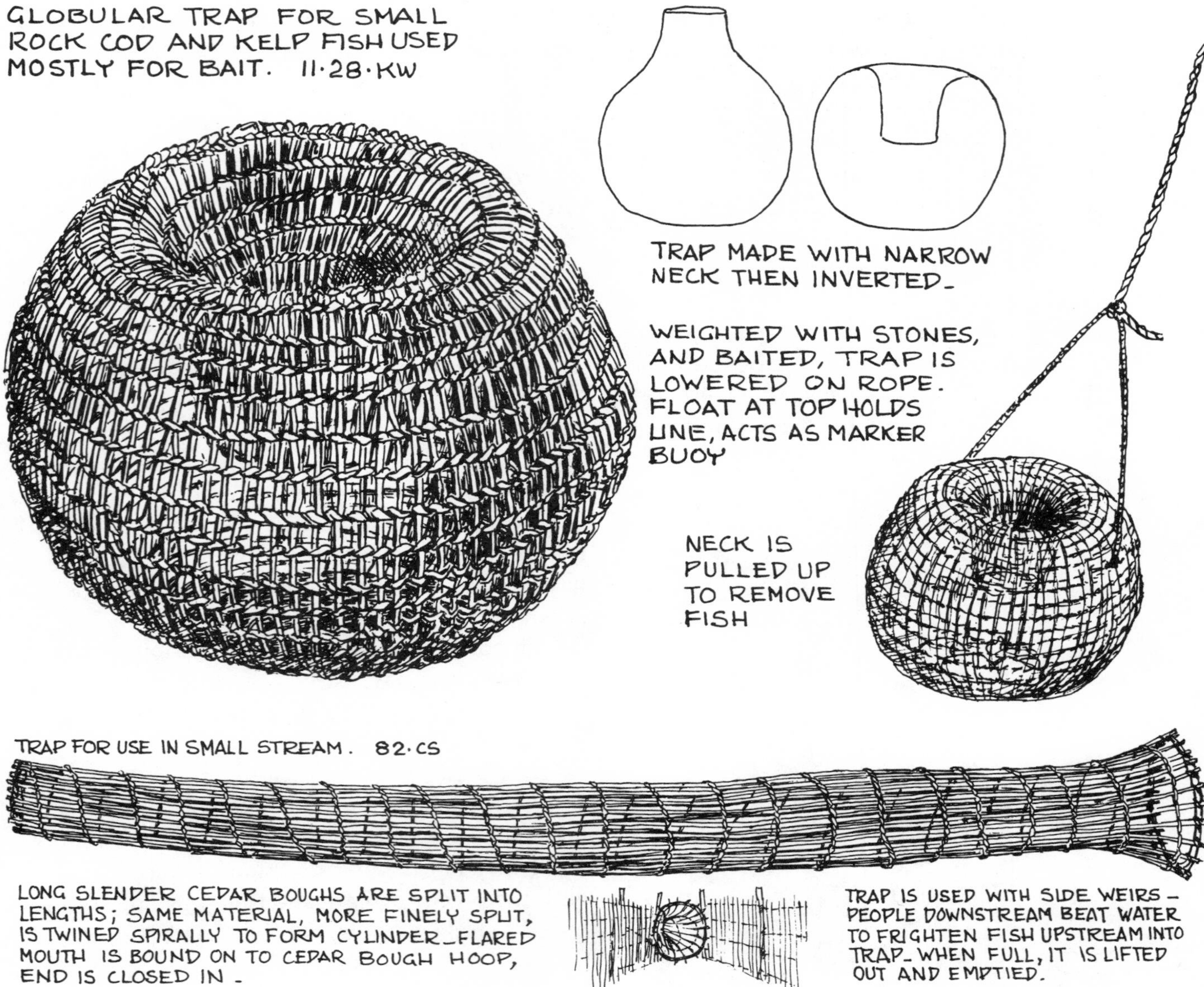

BASKET TRAP

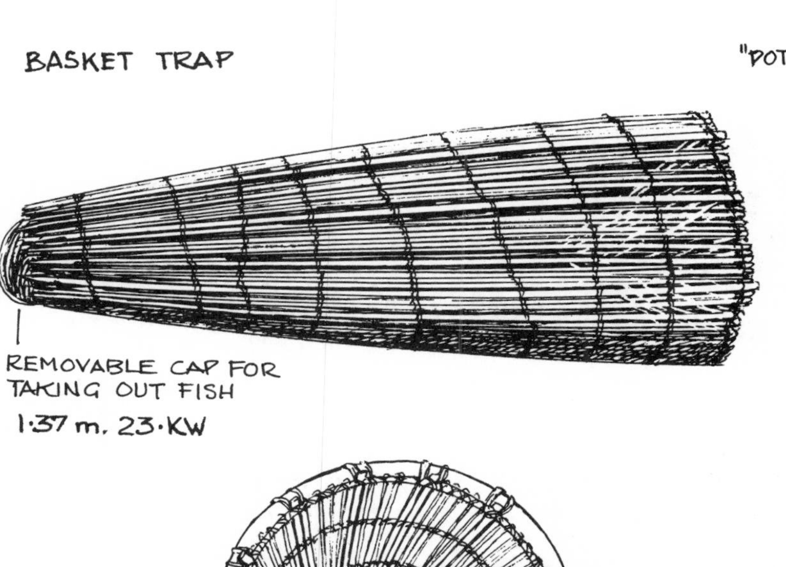

REMOVABLE CAP FOR TAKING OUT FISH

1.37 m. 23.KW

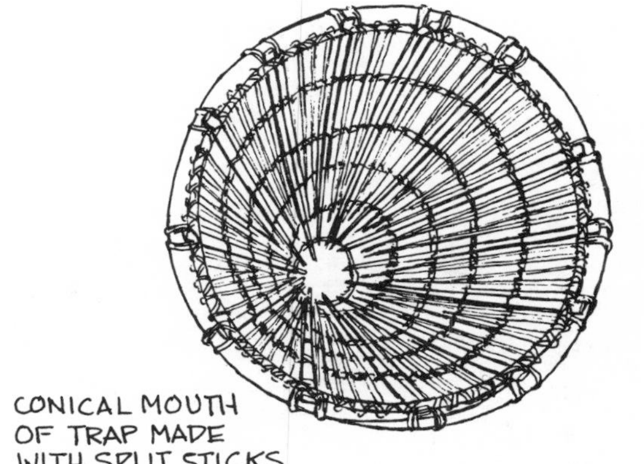

CONICAL MOUTH OF TRAP MADE WITH SPLIT STICKS

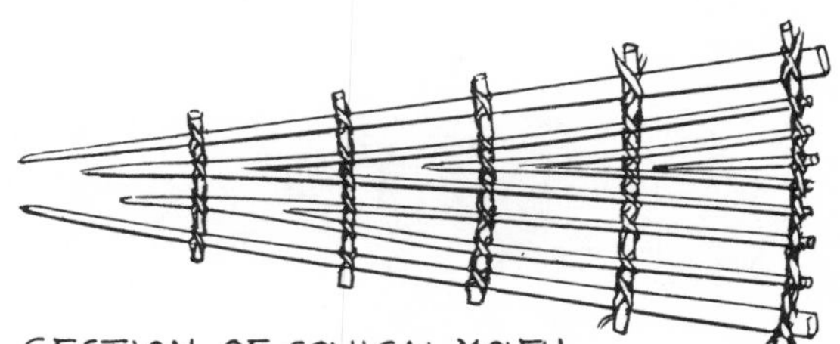

SECTION OF CONICAL MOUTH OF TRAP SHOWING SPLIT STICK ASSEMBLY — THIS AVOIDS CLUSTER OF TOO MANY STICKS AT NECK AND FACILITATES MAKING CONE SHAPE.

"POTHANGER" TRAP

TRAP FOR SALMON — JUST BELOW FALLS IN A RIVER, LATTICE IS ATTACHED TO FRAMEWORK. FISH FALLING BACK AFTER UNSUCCESSFUL LEAP ARE CAUGHT IN TRAP. 29.NK

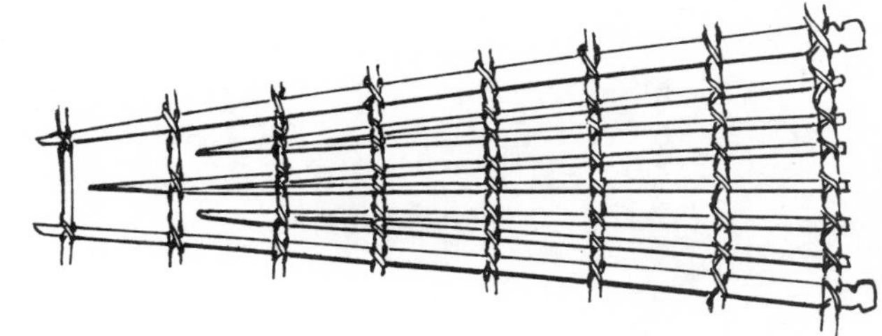

DIFFERENT SPLIT STICK ARRANGEMENT. DETAIL FROM A LARGER TRAP — 11.KW

BASKET TRAPS

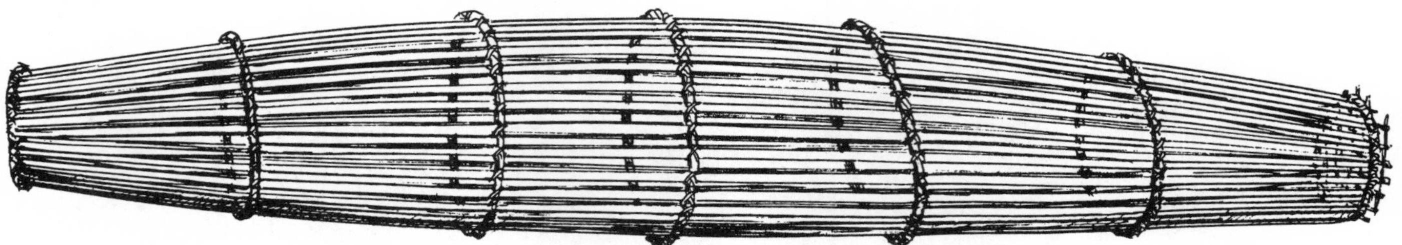

TYPE OF TRAP USED WITH FENCE WEIRS, OR PART OF LARGER TRAP COMPLEX _ DRAWN FROM EARLY PHOTO, LOCALE UNKNOWN. 27·X
APPROX. LENGTH 3 m

POSSIBLY USED THUS, WITH FENCE WEIRS _ 32·CS

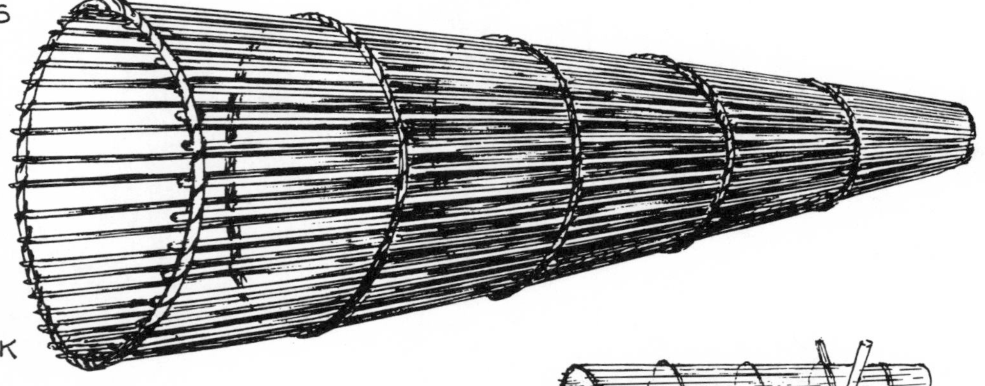

RIVER TRAP. 29·NK

TRAP USED IN SHALLOW, FAST FLOWING STREAM _ WHEN SALMON ARE MIGRATING, MEN UPSTREAM FRIGHTEN FISH BACK DOWN RIVER _ STRONG CURRENT DRIVES FISH UP INTO TRAP WHERE THEY ARE SPEARED.

MOUTH OF TRAP WEIGHTED WITH ROCKS. END RAISED UP ON SHEARS.

RIVER TRAPS

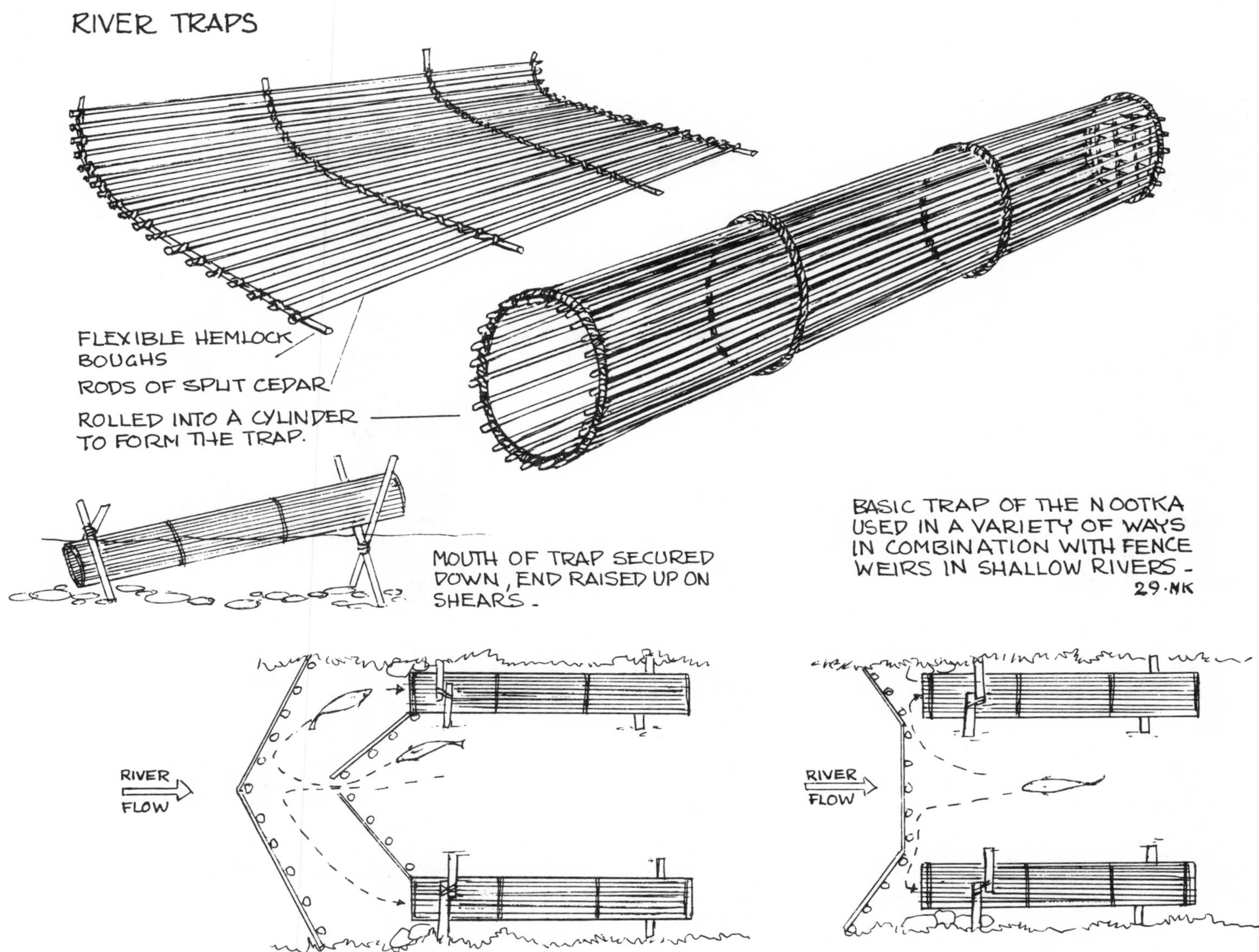
FLEXIBLE HEMLOCK BOUGHS
RODS OF SPLIT CEDAR
ROLLED INTO A CYLINDER TO FORM THE TRAP.
MOUTH OF TRAP SECURED DOWN, END RAISED UP ON SHEARS.
BASIC TRAP OF THE NOOTKA USED IN A VARIETY OF WAYS IN COMBINATION WITH FENCE WEIRS IN SHALLOW RIVERS.
29·NK
RIVER FLOW
RIVER FLOW

FISH TRAP FIGURES

RECORDED AS "TLINGIT MAN SITTING ON A BOULDER CARVED AS A BEAR WITH A 'KILLING STICK" 19-TL

SUCH FIGURES, ATTACHED TO STRUCTURES OF FISH TRAPS, ARE TO ATTRACT SALMON TO TRAP.

FIGURE INSIDE SALMON MAY REPRESENT BELIEF THAT SALMON ARE REALLY HUMANS IN FISH FORM. 95cm. 19.TL

HUMAN FIGURE SET UPRIGHT ON TRAP SAID TO INDICATE OWNERSHIP.
32.0cm 19-TL(?)

BASKET TRAPS

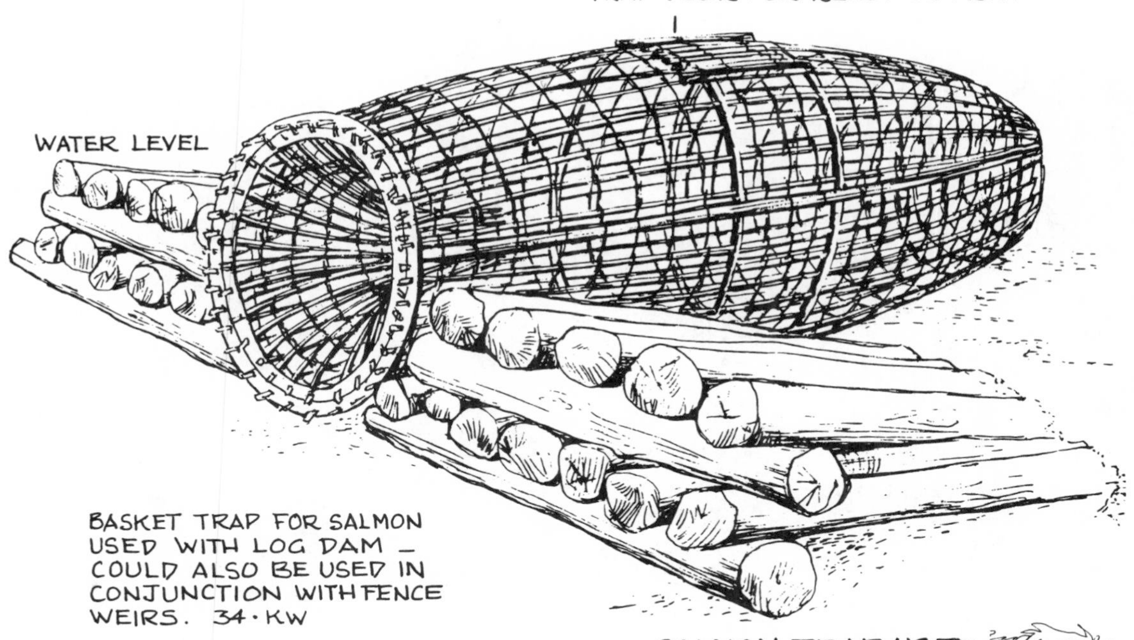

Remnants of old fish weir along beach near mouth of Little Qualicum River. 60. CS *Photograph by and courtesy of Don Abbott.*

SALMON TRAP USED IN NARROW STREAM.

TIDE WATER TRAP

LATTICE SECTIONS ARE LASHED TO POSTS SET INTO BEACH. TRAP IS BUILT ON TIDAL FLATS AT MOUTH OF RIVER WHERE SALMON CONGREGATE PRIOR TO MIGRATION UPSTREAM. HEIGHT ABOUT 2m. 29·NK

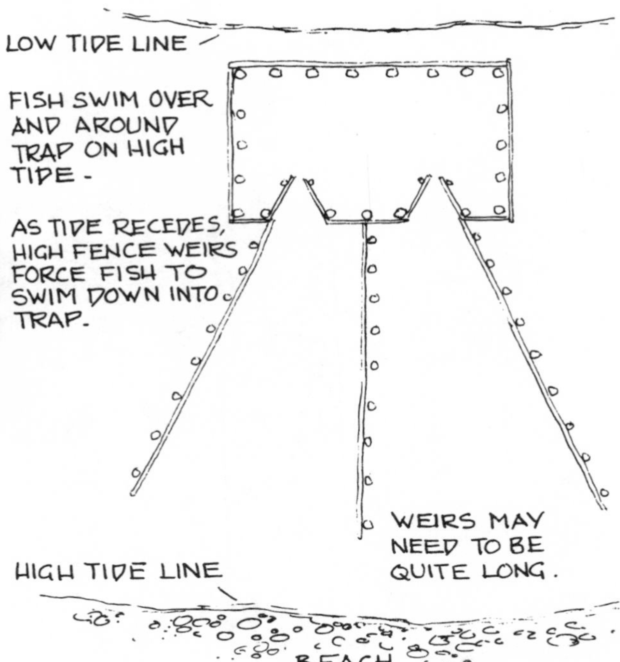

RIVER TRAP FOR SALMON

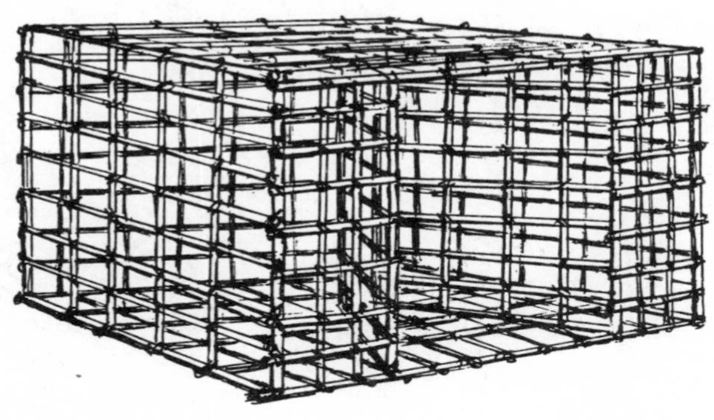

SIMILAR TO TIDEWATER TRAP BUT SMALLER AND PORTABLE _ USED WITH FENCE WEIRS _ LATER REMOVED TO ALLOW MIGRATION OF FISH UPRIVER. 29 NK

Stone Fish Traps

Stone traps were widespread along the whole coast, with the Kwagiutl people making the most extensive use of this effective method of catching fish. In their central coastal area, almost every creek or stream contained some kind of stone trap. Many and often elaborate were the stone-walled structures that relied on "tidal drift" for their success.

Salmon often congregate at the mouth of a stream or creek so that spring runoff or late summer rains may swell the river and make it deep enough for their passage upstream. As the tide rose, the waiting fish drifted shoreward with the flow of the water, swimming over the tops of the traps. As the tide receded they became trapped behind the stone walls, unable to retreat to deeper water.

So successful was this system that frequently a whole series of stone traps was built at one river mouth. Boulders reached a fair size, and the supply was not always close at hand. The large amount of labour involved in moving so many tons of rock into place, and the quantity of fish they would catch, suggest joint ownership and use by a whole village or groups of people. Smaller, single stone traps in suitable places would catch shiners and other small fish for bait.

An elderly and knowledgeable man of the Qualicum Band, Alfred Recalma, told me that there were once so many salmon in the sea at migration time that the traps did not have to be at the mouth of the river; traps along the beach anywhere in the vicinity would catch fish. "The salmon would go up the stream packed together so tight you'd swear there wasn't room for one more fish," he said. He blamed logging and the destruction of the watershed for the present-day lack of salmon. Heavy rains pour down the denuded mountain sides and swell the creeks to rushing torrents that sweep away the fertilized salmon eggs.

It is still possible to spot the remains of some of the stone fish traps in bays and inlets, even though many years of tidal action have torn apart walls that once stood much higher. On Mitelnatch Island (south of Cortes Island in Johnson Strait), in a large bay drained by the outgoing tide, is a fairly obvious V-shaped rock alignment. This is pointed out by a sign put up by the park naturalist on the island, and can be seen at low tide. Less obvious, though, is a series of small, half-circle rock wall remains, also within the bay. Their demarcation is helped by the fact that the oysters now growing there are concentrated on the outer side of the traps, but are sparse on the inner side. Often no more than one boulder high, the rocks of these old stone traps are usually larger than others in the immediate area, and fairly evenly placed in a straight or curved line.

Remains of stone fish traps are evident in Deep Bay on Vancouver Island, and are best seen when the tide is just high enough to allow the lines of the large boulders to appear above the water. Camping at Bajo Point, north of Friendly Cove on the outer west coast of the island, I found a large bay with the tide out and the remains of a series of small stone traps. Near our beach camp was the site of an ancient Indian village. Relatively young spruce trees marked out the rectangular areas where house floors had once been, each outlined by high mounds of earth now tall with wet grass. The rotted bow of a small dugout canoe, moss covered, silent, lay at the edge of the forest within sound of the sea.

STONE TRAPS

---- HIGH TIDE
—— LOW TIDE

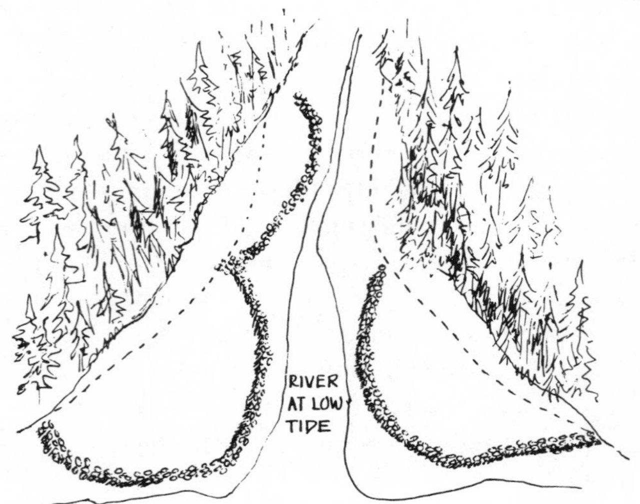

STONE TRAP AT MOUTH OF RIVER IN TIDAL WATER WHERE SALMON CONGREGATE PRIOR TO MIGRATION UPSTREAM. FISH DRIFT IN OVER ROCK WALL WITH INCOMING TIDE, ARE TRAPPED WHEN TIDE GOES OUT. 54·KW

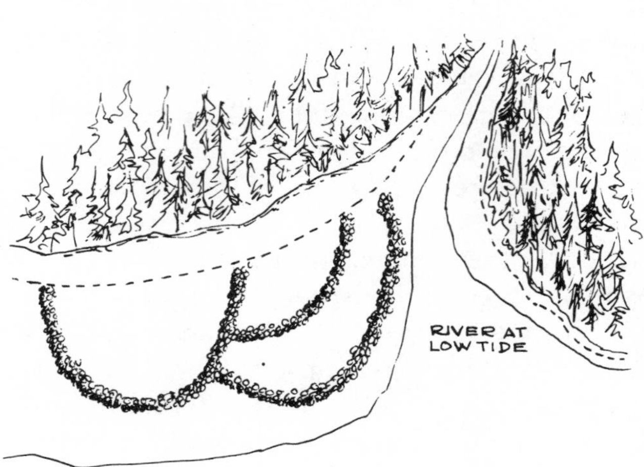

SERIES OF STONE TRAPS ON RIVER MOUTH BANK EXPOSED AT LOW TIDE. 54·KW

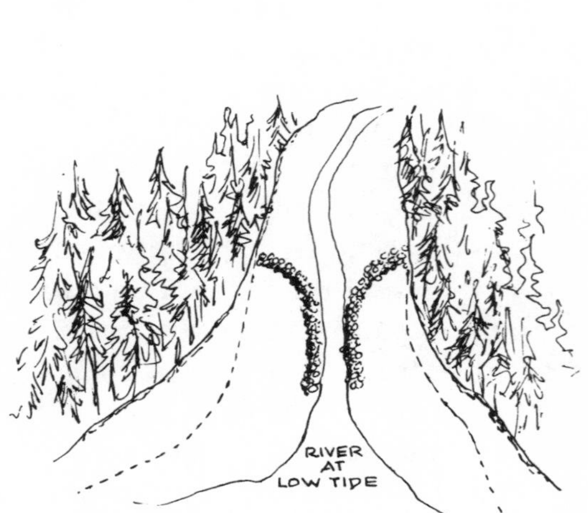

ROCK ALIGNMENT. QUITE LIKELY USED WITH BASKET TRAP AT NARROWED NECK 54·KW

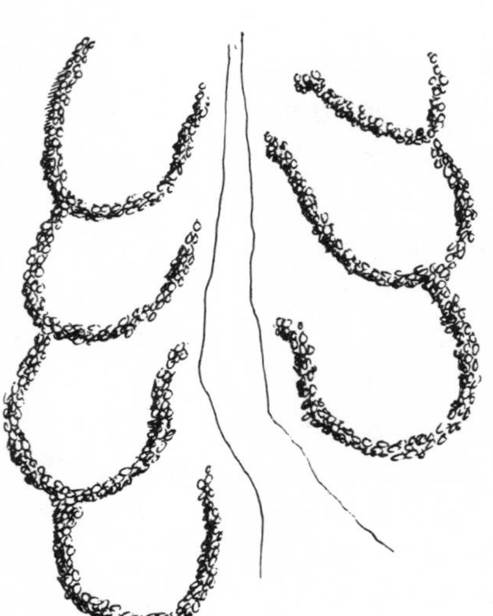

WING DAMS SOMETIMES BUILT IN MULTIPLE GROUPS ON RIVER BANKS 28·KW

APPROXIMATE LAYOUT OF TRAPS IN BAY ON MITELNATCH ISLAND. V NECK PROBABLY FUNNELLED FISH INTO BASKET TRAP. CS

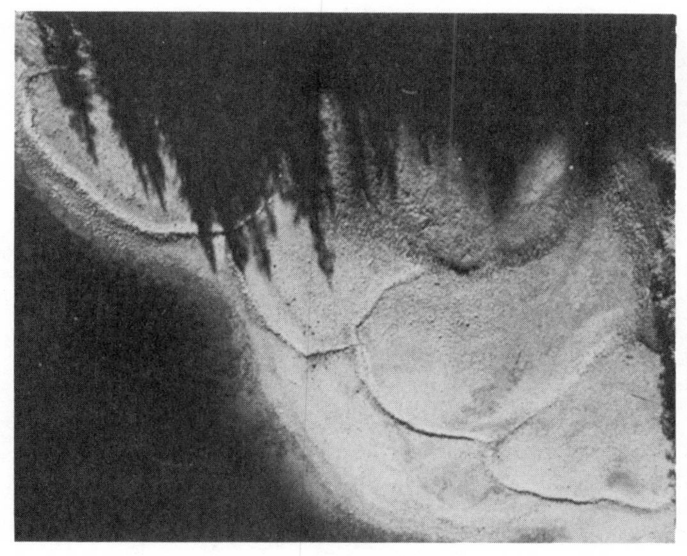

Complex intertidal stone traps at Evans Inlet.

Stone fish traps flank river mouth in Yeo Bay. Photos by and courtesy of Anthony Pomoroy. 54.KW

FISH DRIFTING INSHORE ON RISING TIDE SWIM OVER STONE WALL AND BECOME STRANDED WHEN WATER RECEDES – 38·BC

STONE TRAP FOR SLOUGH

STONE DAM AT MOUTH OF SLOUGH
TRAPS FISH AT LOW TIDE.

ADAPTED FROM EARLY PHOTO. 27-KW

Canoe runway, to give canoes safe access to beach, still shows up clearly at Deep Bay, Vancouver Island. Nearby are remains of stone fish traps.
60.CS

The Herring Spawn Harvest

Just as important as catching the herring was harvesting the eggs (spawn) of that fish, a delicacy much enjoyed by the coastal peoples of all areas.

Knowing that the herring run would start in early spring (March), and that the fish would congregate in certain bays and coves with quiet water to deposit their eggs on seaweed, the resourceful fisherman made use of this annual occurrence for his own benefit by careful manipulation.

Prior to the run he set out branches and other material in selected places, and the obliging herring took advantage of the ample supply of substance upon which to spawn. The fisherman, returning a few days later, carefully lifted the heavily laden branches out of the water, piled them in his canoe and returned home to the village.

Spawn-covered seaweed growing naturally was collected also, but the pre-set material was easier to harvest.

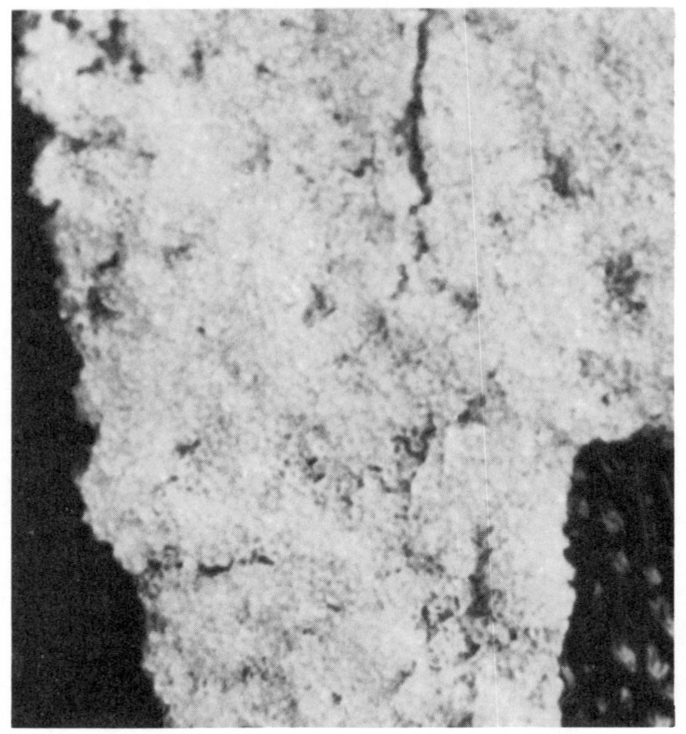

Herring spawn on kelp. 60.HA

Couple bring home skiff loaded with herring spawn on kelp. Skidegate Landing. 60.HA

HERRING SPAWN CULTURE.

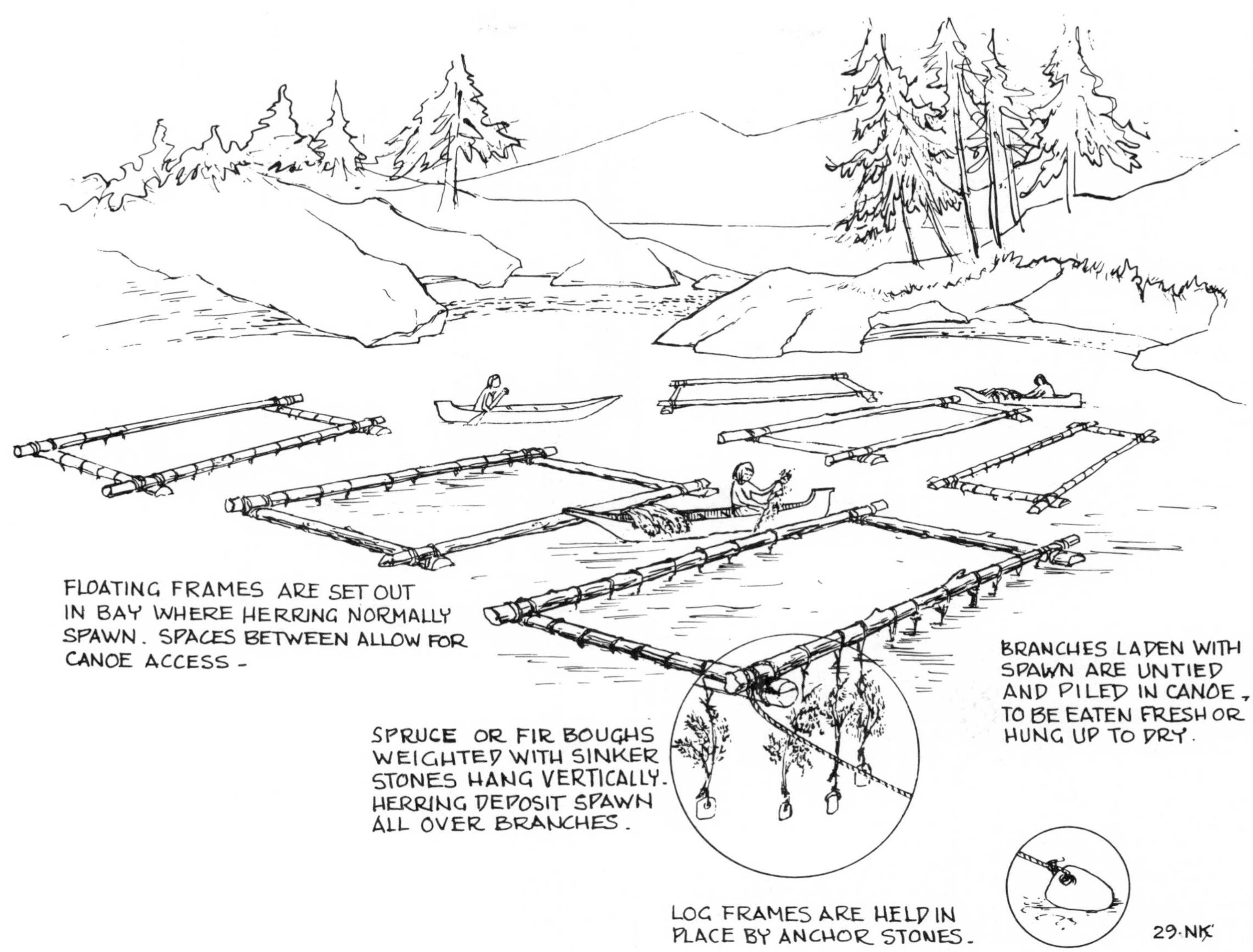

CATCHING SHINERS FOR BAIT 29·NK

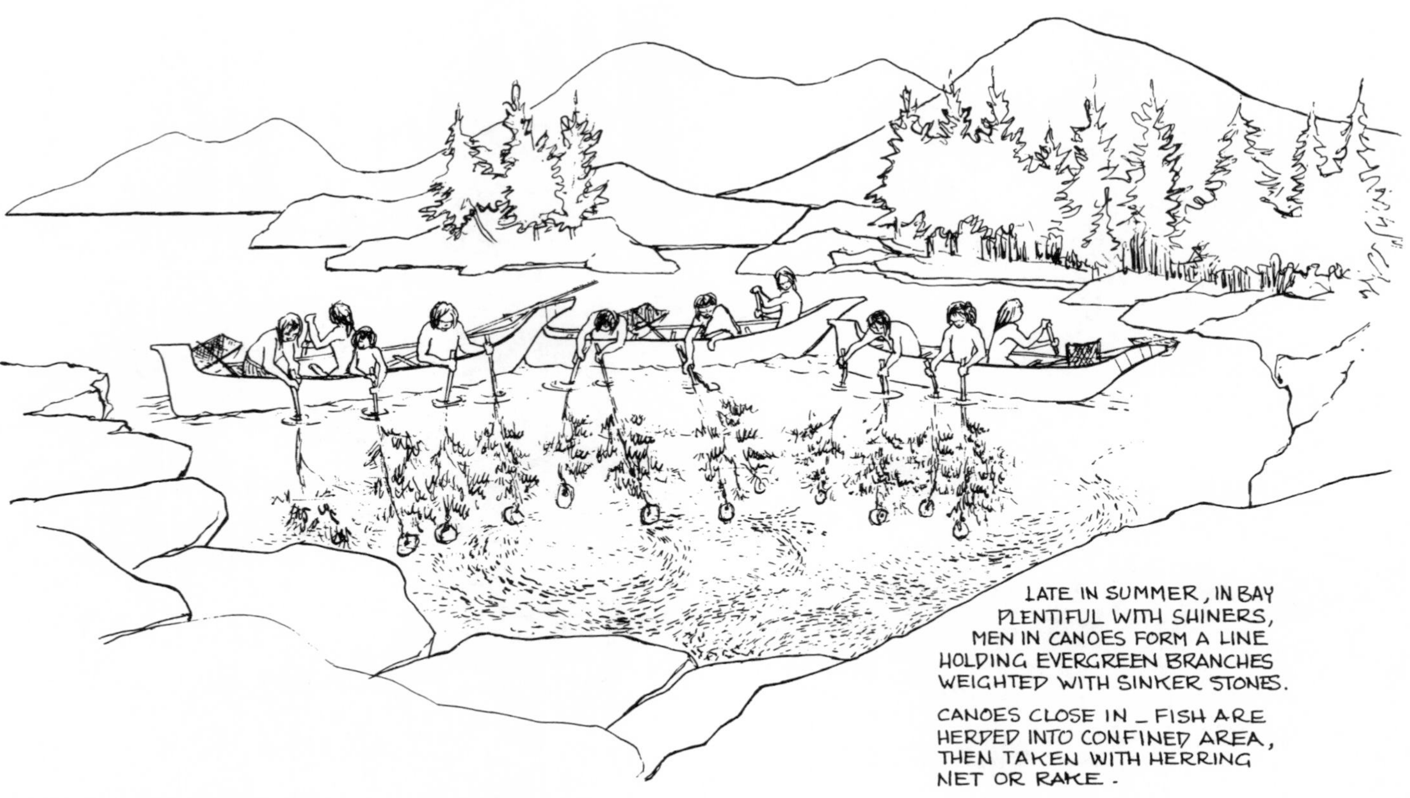

HARVESTING HERRING SPAWN

WEIGHTED FIR BRANCHES ARE SET AMONG EEL GRASS IN BAY WHERE HERRING ARE KNOWN TO SPAWN - EGG-COVERED BRANCHES ARE LIFTED OUT, HUNG TO DRY. 52·CS
SPRUCE OR HEMLOCK BOUGHS ALSO USED. 31·NK

ON LOW TIDE KELP IS PULLED IN WITH A GAFF HOOK. LOADED WITH HERRING SPAWN, BLADES OF SEAWEED ARE CUT OFF. 28·KW

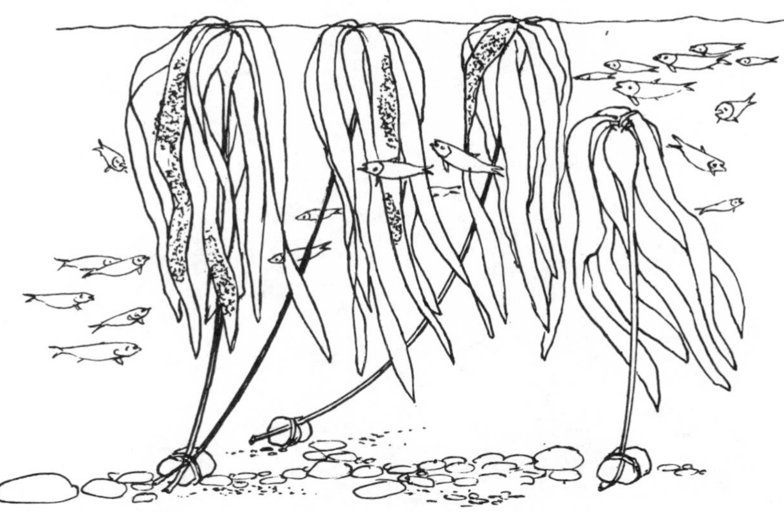

KELP IS BROUGHT INTO SPAWNING BAY AND ANCHORED; HERRING DEPOSIT SPAWN ON THE SEAWEED.

TWO METRE CEDAR OR HEMLOCK TREE IS ANCHORED IN SPAWNING BAY AND LEFT THREE DAYS - HERRING SPAWN ON BOTH SIDES OF FOLIAGE - SMALL BRANCHES ARE HUNG UP TO DRY. 40·CS

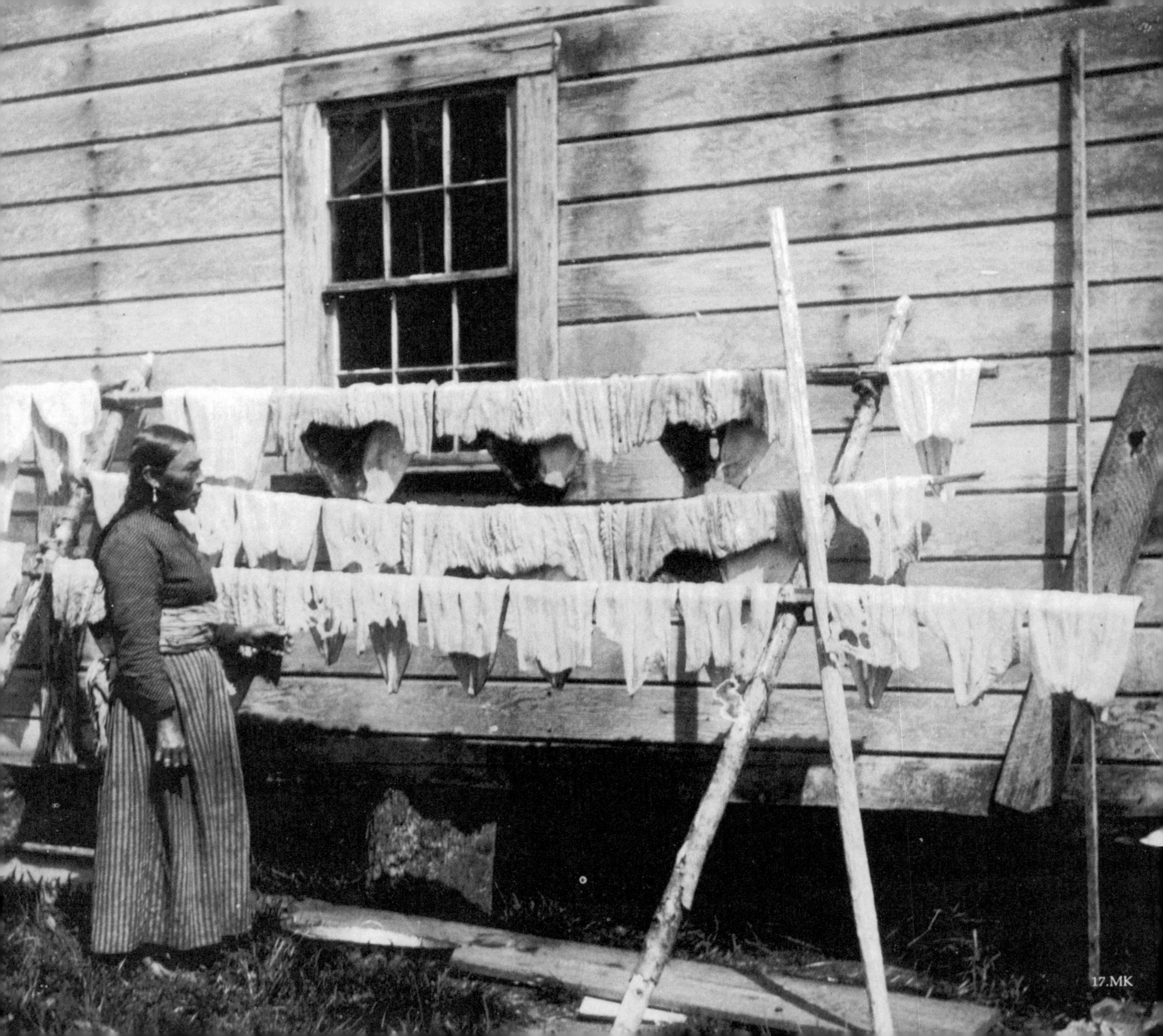
17.MK

Cooking and Preserving Fish

Cooking

Without any knowledge of pottery, coast Indian peoples boiled, simmered, steamed, baked, toasted and roasted most of their food. Box, basket, earth pit, rock oven, hot ashes, and roasting tongs and sticks, all in conjunction with fire, were the ways used for cooking. Not all peoples used all methods, although boiling, steaming, and roasting were common to all and most generally used, especially for fish.

Pieces of dried fish could be toasted over the fire until hot and crisp. To be boiled, dried fish required soaking overnight. For roasting, the fish had to be freshly caught, and a hot, smokeless bed of coals was needed.

Anyone who attended the annual inter-tribal canoe races of the Coast Salish people will have had the opportunity to taste salmon roasted over an alder fire. Cut into individual steaks, the fish is skewered on a stick of iron wood *(Holodiscus discolor)*, four to a stick. A continuous row of these sticks leans towards the fire, each carefully watched and turned at just the right moment. For many years before his death at the age of 87, Chief Dominick Charlie was in charge of the salmon roast at all the canoe races held on the North Vancouver shore of Burrard Inlet.

"The Inside of a Habitation in Nootka Sound," well-known engraving from Captain Cook's Third Voyage Around the World *published in 1784, shows quantities of fish hanging from drying racks, dried fish piled up in corner, and fish on sticks roasting over fire.* 62.NK

While camping on a remote wilderness beach on the west coast of Vancouver Island, and feasting off the fish and intertidal abundance of the environment, we discovered the gourmet flavour of salmon roasted over an alder wood fire. Using cooking tongs and split cedar sticks to hold the split fish open, we let the long slow cooking preserve the juices and the wood fire enhance the flavour. Eaten with wild beach peas growing in profusion near our camp, and sun dried dulse gathered from a small offshore island, this succulent salmon feast ended with a clam shell full of assorted wild berries and a bowl of spruce leaf tea.

On another day at our beach camp we caught a small ling cod and chose to cook it in a steam pit, together with a few clams. We dug a pit, filled it with wood, put rocks on the top and set the wood on fire. When the fire died down we put fresh seaweed on the hot rocks, a layer of large leaves over the seaweed and then the fish pieces and the clams; more leaves and more seaweed until the pit was full. Water was added and the pit was covered over. The flavour of both fish and clams was delicious, and the steam pit had the advantage of not having to be watched; it kept the food hot until we returned from berry picking.

In the Indian village of the coast all cooking was done by the women. They were conversant with many different species of fish, and with a variety of parts of those fish, not just fillets and steaks. When a chief gave a great potlatch it was the women who cooked and prepared the huge quantity of food to feed the many guests who stayed for days, sometimes weeks.

Boiling and cooking was done in the cooking

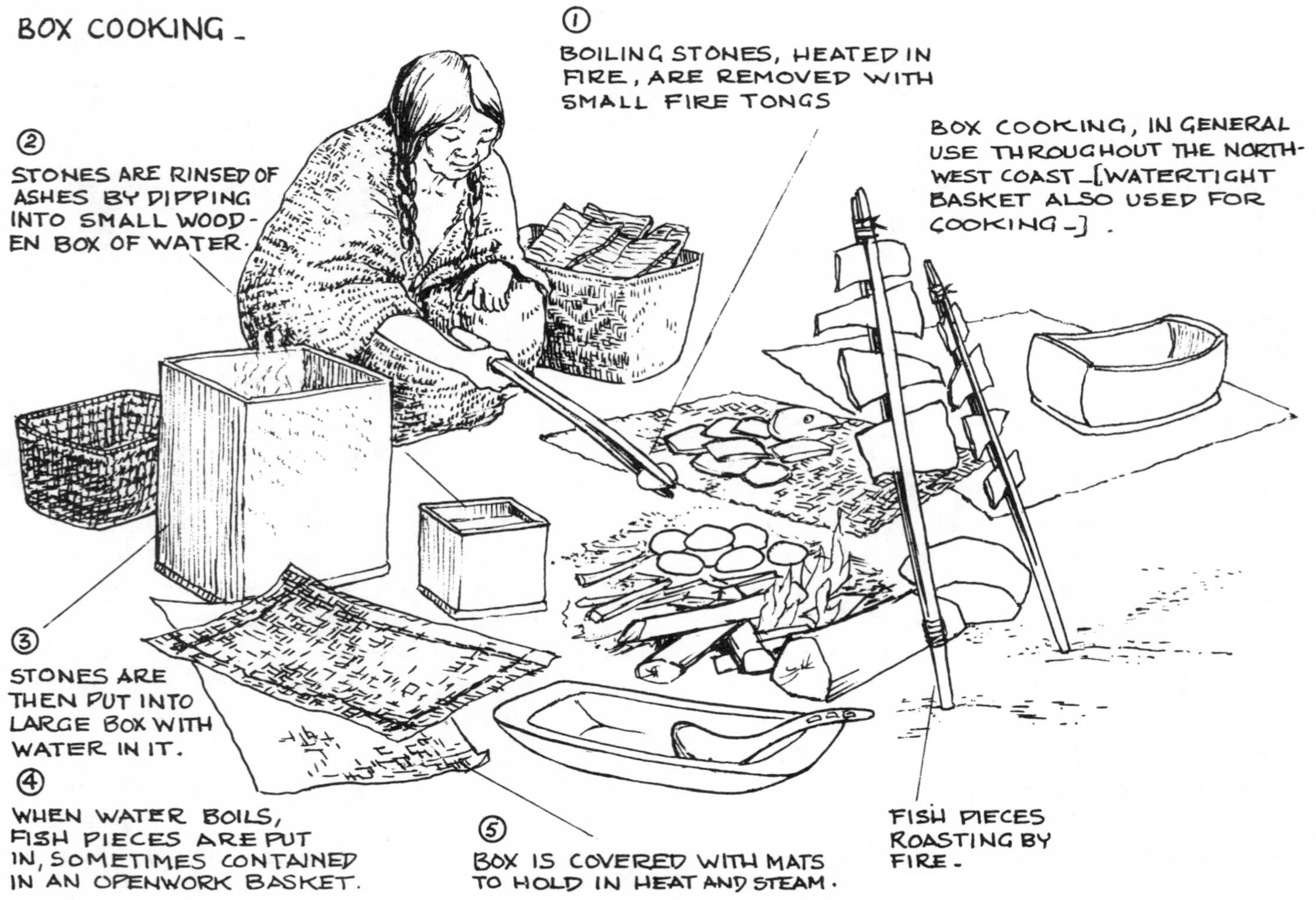

box, or sometimes a waterproof basket, that was set near the fire. Heated rocks, picked up with tongs, were dipped into a small box of water to rinse off the ashes, then put into the bentwood box partially filled with water. When the water came to a boil, the food was added and the lid put on the box. Prolonged cooking or simmering was maintained by replacing the cooled rocks with freshly heated ones. Other ingredients could be added to the box to make stew. When ready, the food was either ladled out, or lifted out with a strainer.

Every part of the salmon was cooked; and even tails, quite meaty on one end, were used. These were held in the tongs and roasted over the fire until they blackened, then removed and set just above the fire to keep warm. The owner of the house could then help himself to a few as a snack when he became hungry. Dried backbones, too, butchered so as to have a lot of meat left on, were broken into pieces and toasted over the fire for snacks.

The rock "oven" was an ancient method of baking fish, and remains of these are found in archaeological excavations, as well as circles of stones indicating where fire hearths once were. At the 1971 excavation of the Katz site, on the bank of the Fraser River downstream from Hope, we found both, together with many fragments of ground slate knives used for butchering fish. Only a stone's throw away, an elderly Indian woman daily tended her gill net in the river, butchered the fish, and hung it up on a fish rack to dry in the warm winds. It was no coincidence that she was at the same spot on the river as the people who had used the slate knives and rock ovens, the people who had a village there for hundreds of years.

STEAM PIT COOKING

(1) PIT DUG IN THE EARTH IS FILLED WITH WOOD, SET ALIGHT AND STONES ADDED.

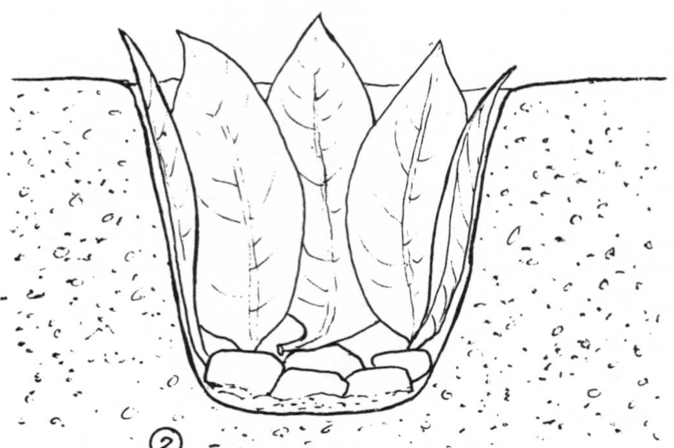

(2) WHEN FIRE BURNS DOWN, SIDES OF PIT ARE LINED WITH SKUNK CABBAGE LEAVES. [OTHER LARGE LEAVES ALSO USED]

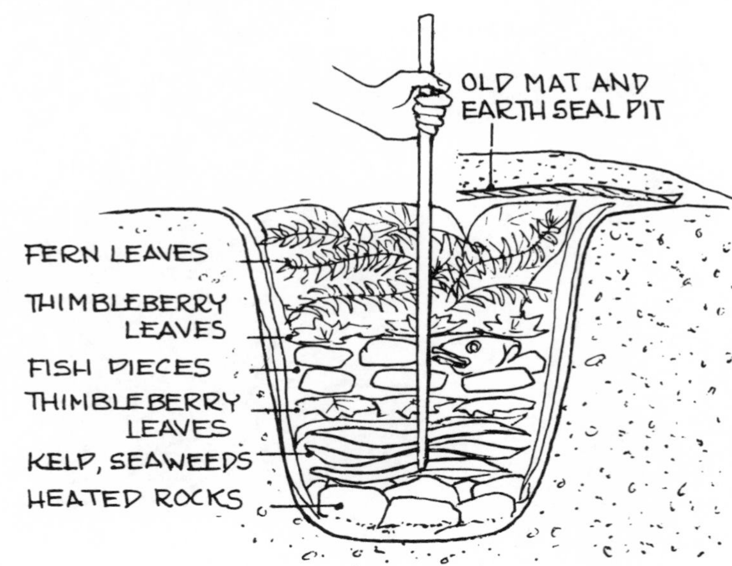

(3) PIT IS FILLED AS ABOVE. STICK INSERTED AND WITHDRAWN, THEN WATER POURED DOWN HOLE ONTO HOT ROCKS. (4) PIT IS SEALED, STEAM BUILDS UP AND COOKS FOOD. THIS METHOD ALSO GOOD FOR SHELLFISH, ROOTS, BULBS.

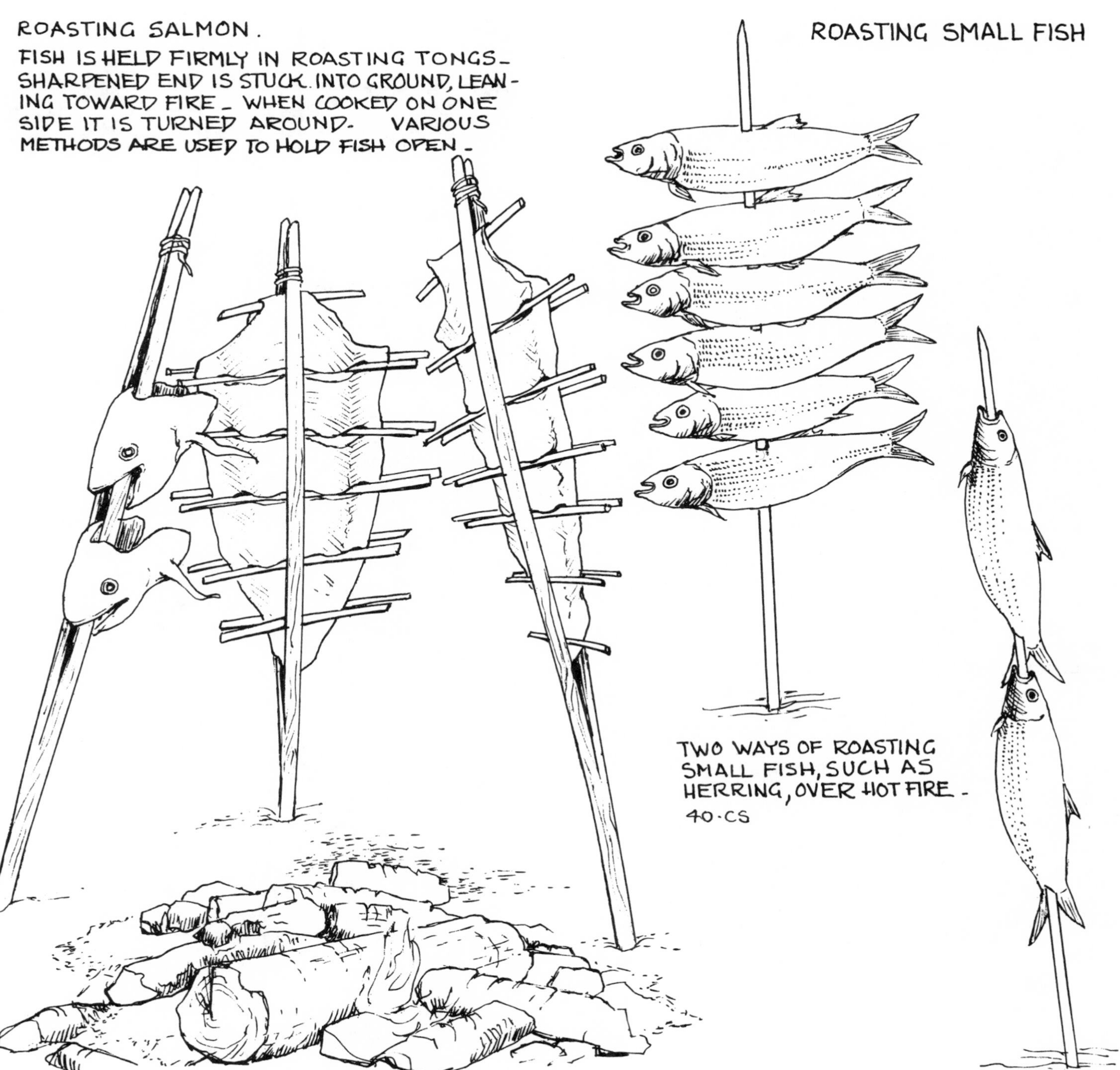
ROASTING SALMON.
FISH IS HELD FIRMLY IN ROASTING TONGS-
SHARPENED END IS STUCK INTO GROUND, LEANING TOWARD FIRE - WHEN COOKED ON ONE
SIDE IT IS TURNED AROUND- VARIOUS
METHODS ARE USED TO HOLD FISH OPEN -
ROASTING SMALL FISH
TWO WAYS OF ROASTING
SMALL FISH, SUCH AS
HERRING, OVER HOT FIRE -
40-CS

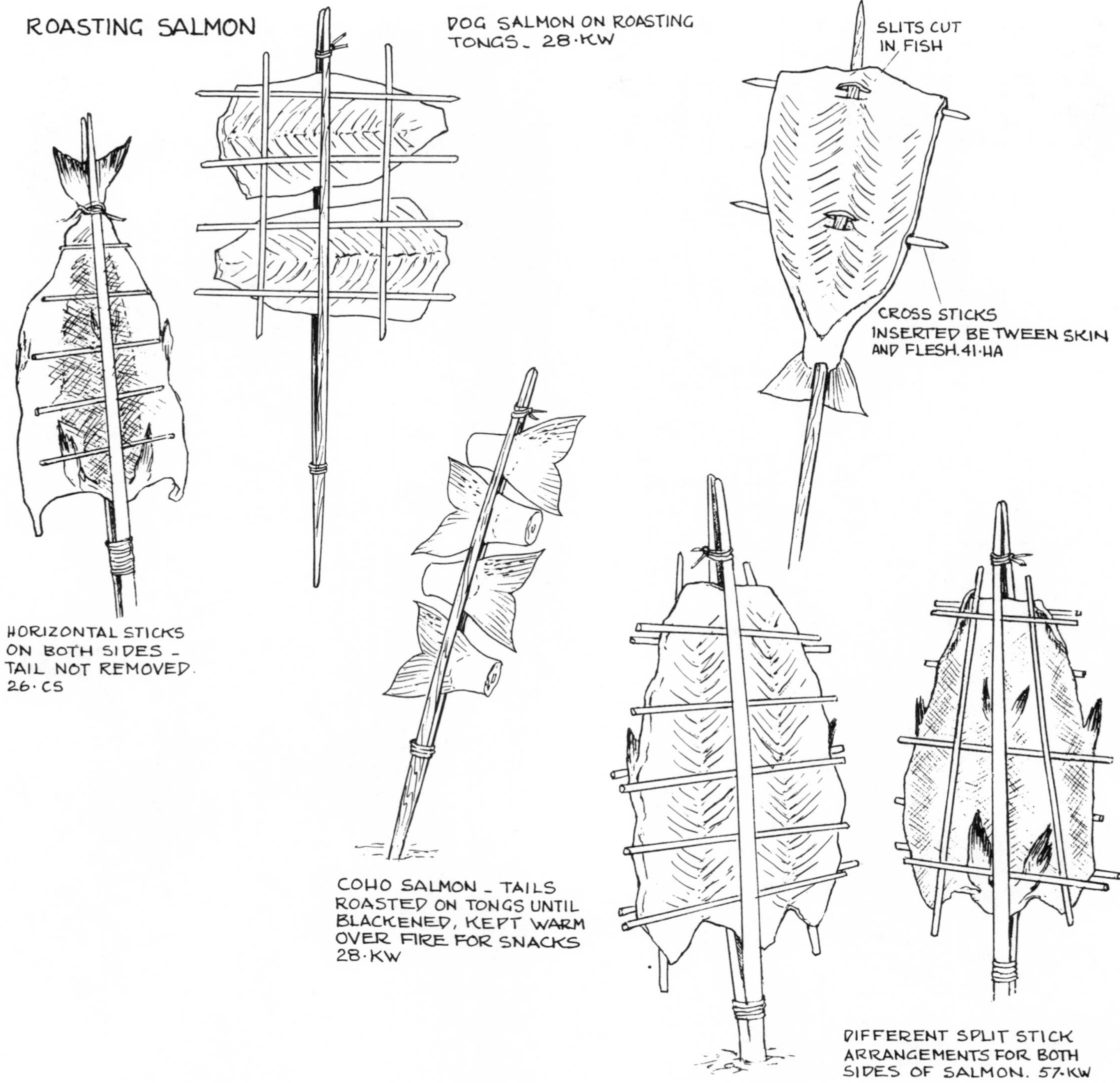
ROASTING SALMON
DOG SALMON ON ROASTING
TONGS _ 28·KW
SLITS CUT
IN FISH
CROSS STICKS
INSERTED BETWEEN SKIN
AND FLESH. 41·HA
HORIZONTAL STICKS
ON BOTH SIDES -
TAIL NOT REMOVED.
26·CS
COHO SALMON _ TAILS
ROASTED ON TONGS UNTIL
BLACKENED, KEPT WARM
OVER FIRE FOR SNACKS
28·KW
DIFFERENT SPLIT STICK
ARRANGEMENTS FOR BOTH
SIDES OF SALMON. 57·KW

Preserving Fish

There were almost as many ways of butchering and preserving fish as there were of catching them. The various methods differed with the species of fish, the season, the climate of the area, and tribal or local tradition. The result, whatever the method, was dehydration of the fish so that it could be kept for a considerable period of time. It was this skill in preservation that enabled a large population to thrive along the coast, for the ability to catch a great quantity of nutritious food at any one time would have been of no use without the ability to preserve it for a future time of need.

If the salmon run failed or was poor, there could be hunger or even starvation in a village. But if the run was abundant, bad weather could be equally disastrous. In bad weather as much as possible of the butchered fish would be taken into the houses to dry, but the limited space would not allow for the drying of sufficient fish to last the winter.

Improperly dried fish turned mouldy and spoiled, and even well-dried fish was subject to attack by insects unless frequently inspected and carefully watched. Thus the preservation of the catch was as important as the quantity.

The two basic ways of preserving fish were by drying and smoking, or by sun and wind drying. In the drier areas along the Fraser River, where the weather could be relied on with greater certainty, the age-old method was the outdoor drying rack roofed over with planks or branches as protection against direct sunlight and possible showers. Opened flanks of salmon, backbones, roe, and even heads were carefully tended to ensure even drying, with the flesh sliced in a special way to facilitate the process. Large spring salmon caught late in the season, when the weather was unstable, were cut thinner to promote faster drying.

Salmon drying rack perched on rocky knoll in Fraser Canyon, high above river. Fir boughs keep sun off fish, warm winds dry it for preservation. 60.CS

Just beyond Yale on the Fraser River, where hot August winds funneled through the canyon, drying racks were poised high on rocky outcrops. Here salmon hanging from the poles dried in a few days. Layers of the flat dried fish were stacked between branches of green alder boughs to keep them in good condition and away from wasps until they were taken back to the village. The racks are still there and are still used, but as numbers of salmon diminish and government regulations tighten, they are no longer filled to capacity as I have seen them in years past.

Most other coast peoples had to contend with the rain and damp of unpredictable Pacific weather. They relied on drying and smoking to preserve their fish, and enjoyed the added flavour that smoking gave. Smoke houses, some quite large, were a vital part of the fish camp. Built of cedar planks over a sturdy post and beam frame,

Whole salmon specially butchered to facilitate complete drying by warm winds blowing through Fraser Canyon; an ancient method of preserving salmon still in use today. 60.CS

the building often had a second storey with a notched log ladder for access, and this was sometimes used for storage. Inside, rows of long slender poles held the fish high as the smoke permeated the fish before making its escape through the open hole in the roof and the cracks between the planks. Some smoke houses had a low bench-like rack around the walls where dried salmon were stacked in such a way as to permit air circulation. From pegs in walls hung strips of roe and pairs of backbones, while fish heads (the cheeks were a delicacy) were skewered on sticks for smoking.

Salmon could be half smoked for eating right away; then it was left soft. Fully smoked fish became hard as it was completely dehydrated for storage. Some people pounded the fish frequently during the smoking process in order to keep it soft.

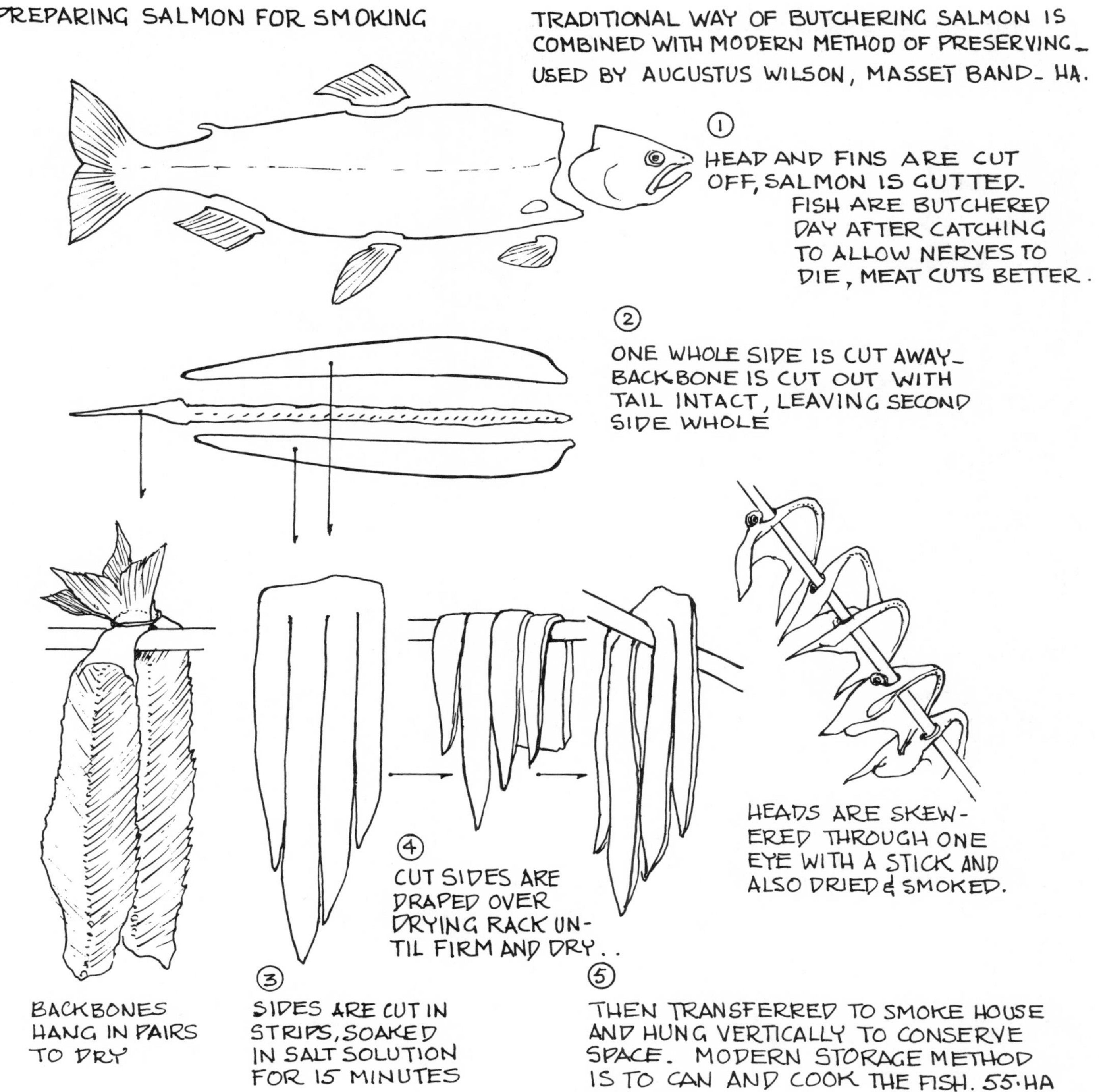
PREPARING SALMON FOR SMOKING
TRADITIONAL WAY OF BUTCHERING SALMON IS COMBINED WITH MODERN METHOD OF PRESERVING_ USED BY AUGUSTUS WILSON, MASSET BAND_ HA.
①
HEAD AND FINS ARE CUT OFF, SALMON IS GUTTED.
FISH ARE BUTCHERED DAY AFTER CATCHING TO ALLOW NERVES TO DIE, MEAT CUTS BETTER.
②
ONE WHOLE SIDE IS CUT AWAY_ BACKBONE IS CUT OUT WITH TAIL INTACT, LEAVING SECOND SIDE WHOLE
HEADS ARE SKEWERED THROUGH ONE EYE WITH A STICK AND ALSO DRIED & SMOKED.
④
CUT SIDES ARE DRAPED OVER DRYING RACK UNTIL FIRM AND DRY . .
③
⑤
BACKBONES HANG IN PAIRS TO DRY
SIDES ARE CUT IN STRIPS, SOAKED IN SALT SOLUTION FOR 15 MINUTES
THEN TRANSFERRED TO SMOKE HOUSE AND HUNG VERTICALLY TO CONSERVE SPACE. MODERN STORAGE METHOD IS TO CAN AND COOK THE FISH. 55·HA

CUTTING SALMON FOR SMOKING

SALMON FLESH IS SPLIT TO PROMOTE FASTER DRYING, LEFT ON RACK UNTIL PARTIALLY DRY, THEN HUNG OVER FIRE TO SMOKE –

Racks for hanging fish inside smoke house. 60.TS

PRESERVING SALMON

LARGE SPRING SALMON CAUGHT LATE IN THE SEASON WITH LESS DEPENDABLE DRYING WEATHER ARE CUT THINNER FOR EASIER DRYING.

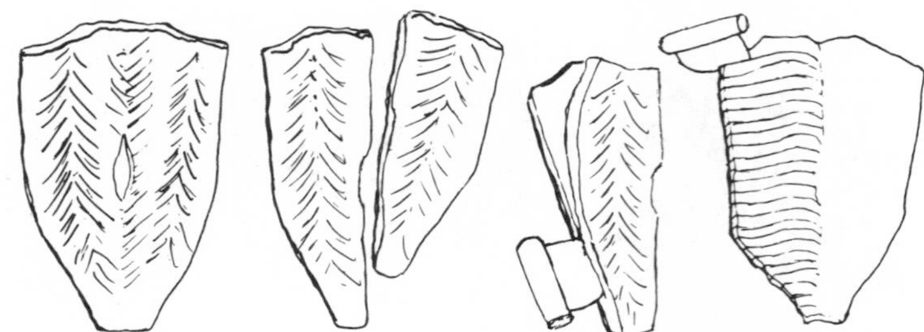

FISH IS OPENED OUT AS USUAL . . . CUT IN HALF . . . EACH HALF IS SPLIT OPEN . . . SIDE WITH SKIN IS SLIT. 37·CS

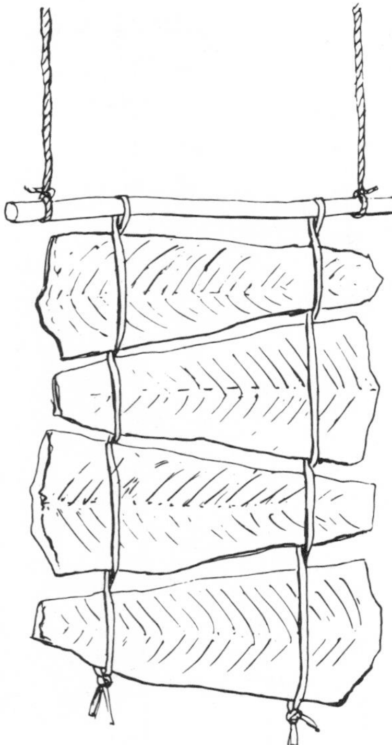

DOG SALMON – SIDE FLANKS ARE HUNG ON RACK TO PARTIALLY DRY [TO BECOME FIRM] THEN HUNG BETWEEN SPLIT CEDAR BARK STRANDS UNTIL DRYING IS COMPLETE. FISH IS STORED IN BASKETS INDOORS. 28·KW

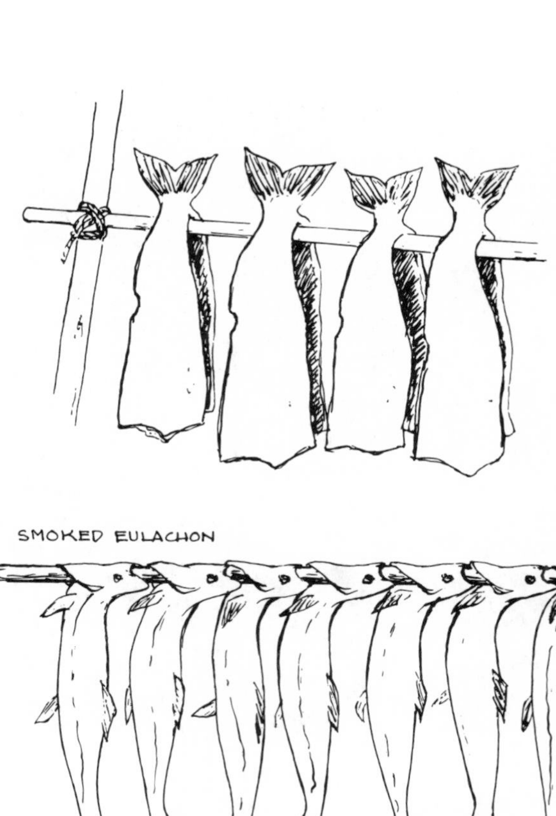

'OLD SALMON', I.E. FROM FAR UP RIVER, IS SLIT IN HALF AND HUNG TO DRY. 28·KW

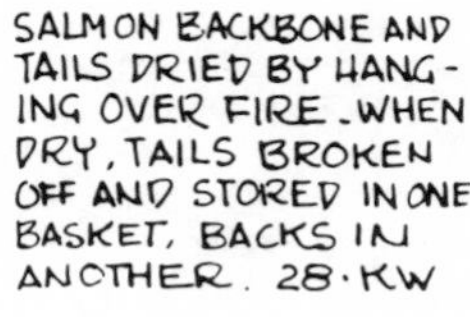

SALMON BACKBONE AND TAILS DRIED BY HANGING OVER FIRE. WHEN DRY, TAILS BROKEN OFF AND STORED IN ONE BASKET, BACKS IN ANOTHER. 28·KW

SMOKED EULACHON

EULACHON, THREADED THROUGH GILL AND MOUTH ON STICKS 1·20 m. LONG, HANG ON DRYING RACK ROOFED OVER WITH BOUGHS _ IN GOOD WEATHER, WIND AND SMOKE OF ALDER WOOD FIRE CURE FISH IN FIVE DAYS _ 37·CS

DRIED EULACHON ON STICK 41·TS

EULACHON HANGING IN PAIRS TO DRY AND SMOKE _ ONE FISH IS PULLED THROUGH MOUTH AND GILL OF THE OTHER. 41·TS

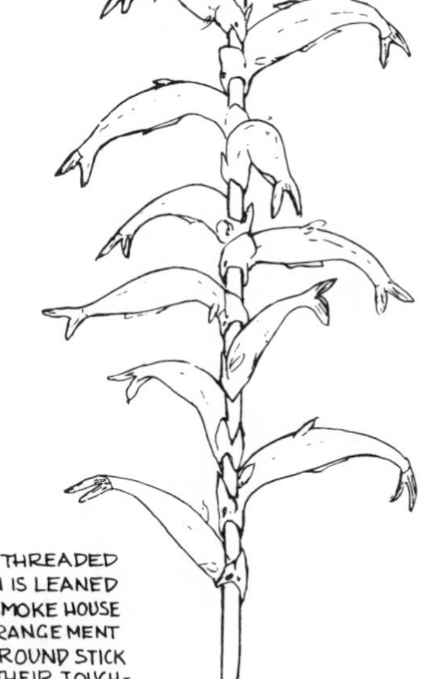

STICK OF THREADED EULACHON IS LEANED AGAINST SMOKE HOUSE WALL _ ARRANGEMENT OF FISH AROUND STICK PREVENTS THEIR TOUCHING. 40·KW

EULACHON STRUNG ON SLENDER CEDAR OR HEMLOCK BOUGHS TIED TO FORM A LOOP ARE HUNG UP IN SMOKE HOUSE 40·KW

Haida Dog Salmon. Polymer argillite casting by Grace Miller, from the original silver engraving by Bill Reid. 60

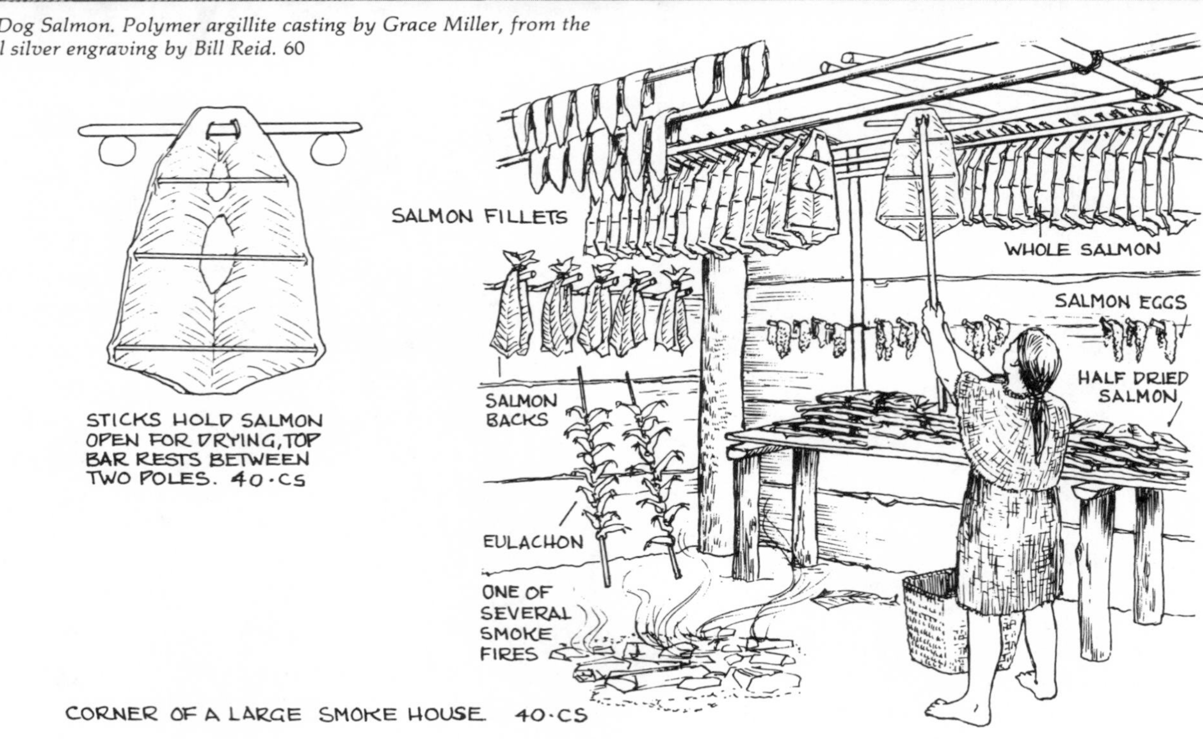

Well worn notched log ladder leads to second storey of smoke house. 60.TS

As well as in the smoke house, fish were often dried in the bighouse close to the fire or hanging from poles under the roof where they would be flavoured by the smoke of the fires spiralling up to the smoke hole.

In early June one year when I was canoeing with friends in the Queen Charlottes we paddled into the sheltered mouth of the Ain River, in Masset Inlet. Well constructed cabins straggled along the grassy bank and between the trees, some built on similar lines to the old-style plank houses but having a corrugated iron roof. At the far end of the fish camp an old disused smoke house was leaning under the weight of great age and weathering. Its beams and posts were mostly hand-adzed. Another smoke house, not as old, served the present needs of the fish camp, and looking inside I saw the ashes and charcoal of four fire hearths on the dirt floor, evenly spaced in the four quarters of the interior. The vertical cedar plank walls and the racks were blackened from the smoke of many years.

Rights to fish the Ain River traditionally belong to the Haida of Masset, and many of them still make the long trip by boat (the only way to reach it) to net the salmon that annually migrate up the river to spawn. The fishing season had just ended and the camp was deserted, but in the smoke house the delicious aroma of smoked salmon still lingered.

More recently, I visited another of this band's fish camps, at the mouth of the Yakoun River on the opposite (south) side of Masset Inlet. Here the cabins perched on the brink of the river bank on both sides, and wooden ladders provided access down the steep bank to the river when the tide was low. Drying racks stood close by the smoke houses and vivid red fillets of sockeye salmon contrasted sharply with the dull grey of the overcast sky. I watched expert hands butchering and processing the fish, and went out with the fishermen to check the nets periodically. Powerful outboard motors had long replaced the tedious process of poling the canoe upriver against the current, but the problem of seals coming into the river to take bites from the fish caught in the nets remained the same.

Fish camp on the Yakoun River, Queen Charlotte Islands, 1975. 60.HA

Cabin, smoke house, pile of alder wood and fish drying rack — some of essential ingredients for a fish camp. Yakoun River, Queen Charlotte Islands. 60.HA

Augustus Wilson, from Masset, butchers salmon in the traditional way. Yakoun River fish camp. 60.HA

Augustus Wilson checks salmon on rack. When dry and firm, fish will be hung in smoke house. 60.HA

Cleaning halibut on the beach at Neah Bay, early in the century. 17.MK

PRESERVING HALIBUT

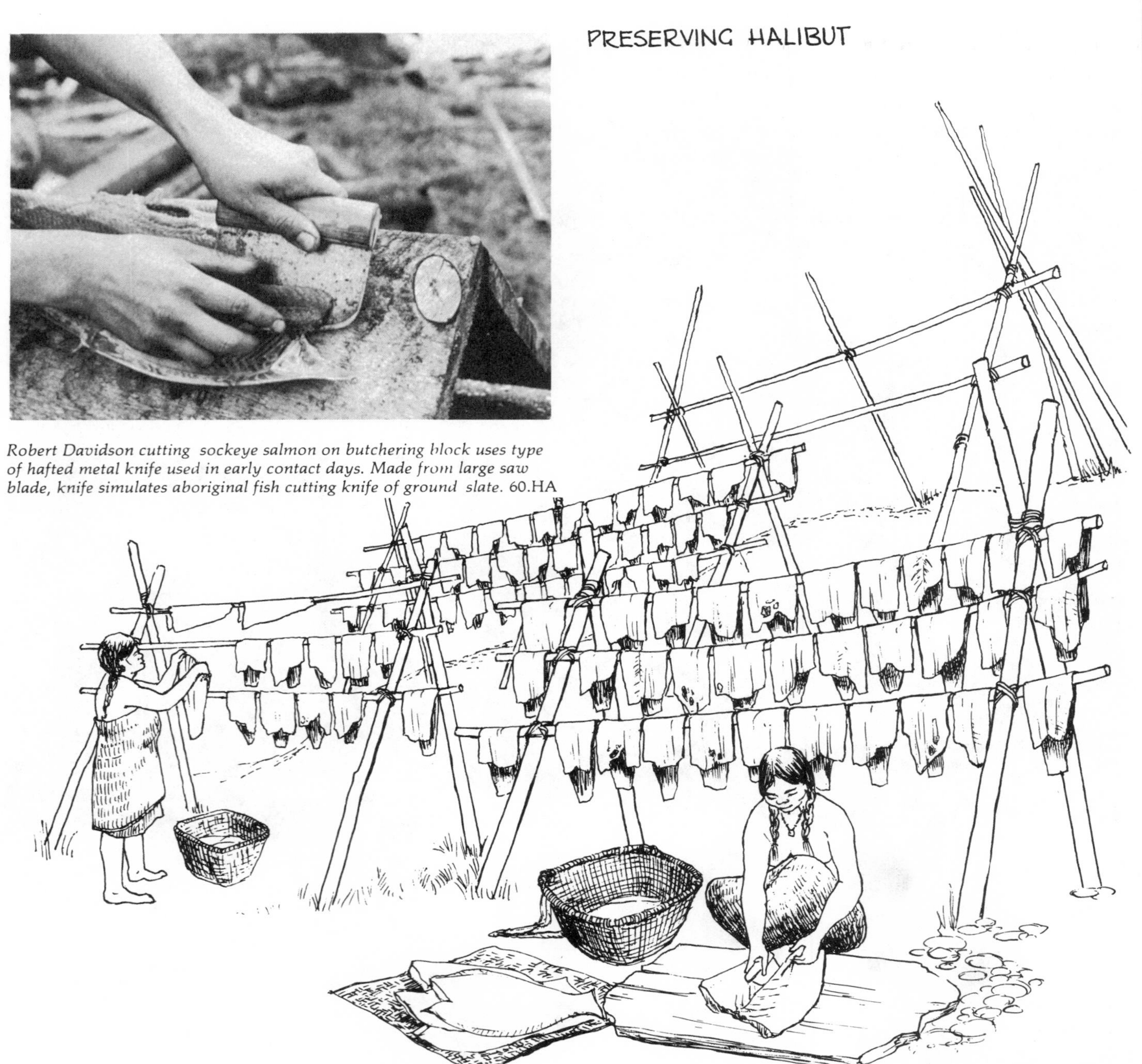

Robert Davidson cutting sockeye salmon on butchering block uses type of hafted metal knife used in early contact days. Made from large saw blade, knife simulates aboriginal fish cutting knife of ground slate. 60.HA

Salmon from the smoke houses was eventually canned and cooked in a large metal container on an outdoor fire. Now the bentwood boxes of smoked and dried fish of the old days have been replaced with rows of shiny cans stored away in kitchen cupboards. But the love of the salmon is the same, and the pursuit of it brings families back to the fish camps year after year.

Not having rivers teeming with hordes of salmon as in most areas, the Makah, Haida, and Tlingit were more reliant on halibut for their winter supplies. The flesh of the large fish, sliced as thinly as possible, was draped over the drying rack like pieces of fabric, after much of the moisture was first pressed out with weights. When it had been sufficiently smoked, the white meat turned a golden tan colour. Black cod, also, was dried and smoked for storage, but it did not keep as long as halibut.

Having a good supply of food put away for the winter must have been comforting, but it was not achieved without a great deal of effort by the whole community. During the salmon runs especially, because of the sudden influx of such a huge quantity of fish, long hours of work were required to catch, transport, butcher, clean, fillet, dry, smoke and then finally store away the catch. Men often fished all through the night when the run was at its best, for it was men's work to catch the fish. They were the skilled harpooners, the spear throwers and the netters; it was men who pounded stakes into river beds to construct traps and weirs, and who hauled heavy rocks to build up the stone dams. While a woman paddled a canoe, a man swept the herring rake through the water and filled the craft to the gunwales with the glittering fish.

But the credit for providing a winter supply of food did not rest solely with the men. All the great catches of fish and all the abundance of food from the sea would have been useless without the skilled hands and hard work of the women. It was the women who laboured long and tediously to clean and butcher the catch. A trap might take a hundred salmon at a time, but the fish had to be cleaned and cut individually, one at a time. It was the women who hung up the butchered fish, tended the drying racks, watched over the fires in the smoke house, turned the fish at the right time, and took it all down when experience told them it was fully cured. Women stacked up the dried flesh, loaded the baskets and boxes, filled the caches, and kept a constant check on the stored food to ensure that it did not spoil.

And when evenings shortened and darker nights turned fall into winter and north winds blew; when the feasting and potlatching began, and when bowls of eulachon oil were set beside dishes of smoked salmon or halibut; or when large feast bowls were brim full of fish soup and the big house was filled with guests and the aroma of good food, then the weeks of work by both men and women—and youngsters too—were rewarded in many different ways.

PRESERVING SALMON ROE -

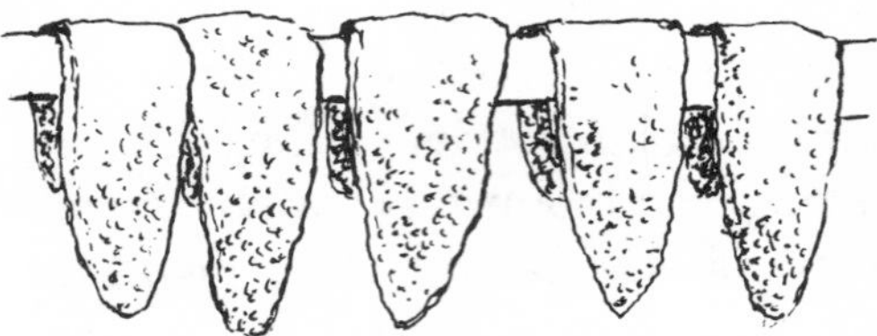

STRIPS OF SALMON ROE HUNG ON RACKS TO DRY - A WIDESPREAD METHOD OF PRESERVATION -

DEER STOMACH HALF FILLED WITH SALMON EGGS, HUNG IN SMOKE HOUSE - BAG KNEADED DAILY - MOISTURE EVAPORATES, TURNING EGGS INTO CHEESE-LIKE CONSISTENCY IN DRY SHRUNKEN BAG - 40·CS

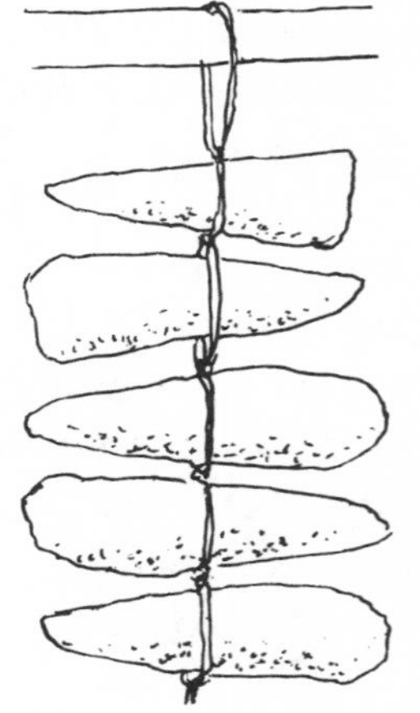

DRIED & SMOKED ROE HUNG UP FOR STORAGE. 40·CS

ROE OF HUMPBACK OR CHUM SALMON BURIED IN EARTH PIT 1m. DEEP. PIT IS LINED THICKLY WITH MAPLE LEAVES, HOLES PUNCTURED IN LEAVES AT BOTTOM ALLOW OIL TO DRAIN OFF. IN TWO MONTHS EGGS HAVE CONSISTENCY OF CHEESE. EATEN RAW OR BOILED WITH WATER FOR SOUP. 37·CS

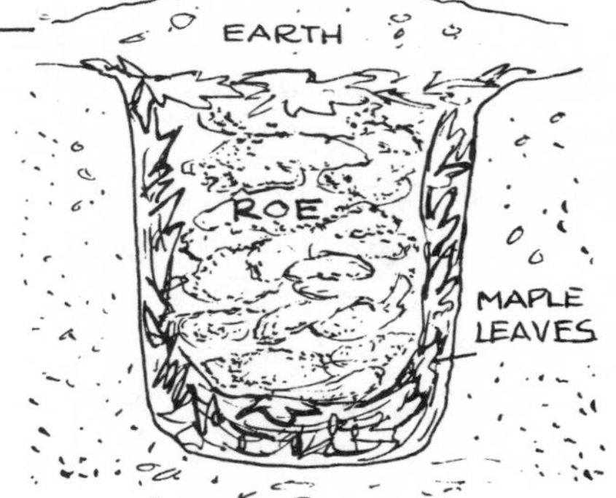

SALMON ROE BURIED IN BOXES BELOW HIGH WATER MARK, LEFT TO DECOMPOSE BEFORE BEING EATEN 53·HA

Dried Herring Spawn

Herring spawn on kelp hanging up to dry on porch of house at Skidegate Landing, Queen Charlotte Islands, May, 1975. During this bumper year for spawn, local hardware store owner said he sold out entire stock of clothespins in two weeks. 60.HA

A favourite food of the past, herring spawn is still gathered, dried and enjoyed by many Indian peoples today. I was in the Queen Charlotte Islands in the early spring of 1975, a year that experienced an exceptionally heavy run of herring. Standing on the dock at Skidegate Landing I watched a small boat being rowed in. The craft was laden with piled-up lengths of spawn-covered kelp draped over the seats and in the bow. The young couple in the boat had gone out early to be at the kelp beds at low tide, when it was easier to reach the seaweed.

In the village of Skidegate long lengths of seaweed, creamy amber with spawn, hung from nearly every porch and sun deck; racks and clothes lines in gardens and carports were festooned with it. Some of the kelp was draped over the lines, but much of it hung down full length, held at the top with clothes pins, blowing freely in the breeze. The owner of the large hardware store in Charlotte City said he hadn't a clothes pin left in the place.

In the old days, spawn-covered branchlets were hung in the sun on racks or lines, or spread out on mats and turned frequently to ensure complete drying all over. In some areas the branches were taken down and the spawn wiped off and scattered on mats to finish drying. Put in a lidded box, the crisp, dried egg masses were stored for winter use.

Spawn-laden kelp was always hung for drying, and the long edible fronds waved in the winds to dry along with the spawn. When hard and brittle they were tied in bundles of ten and put away in a lidded box.

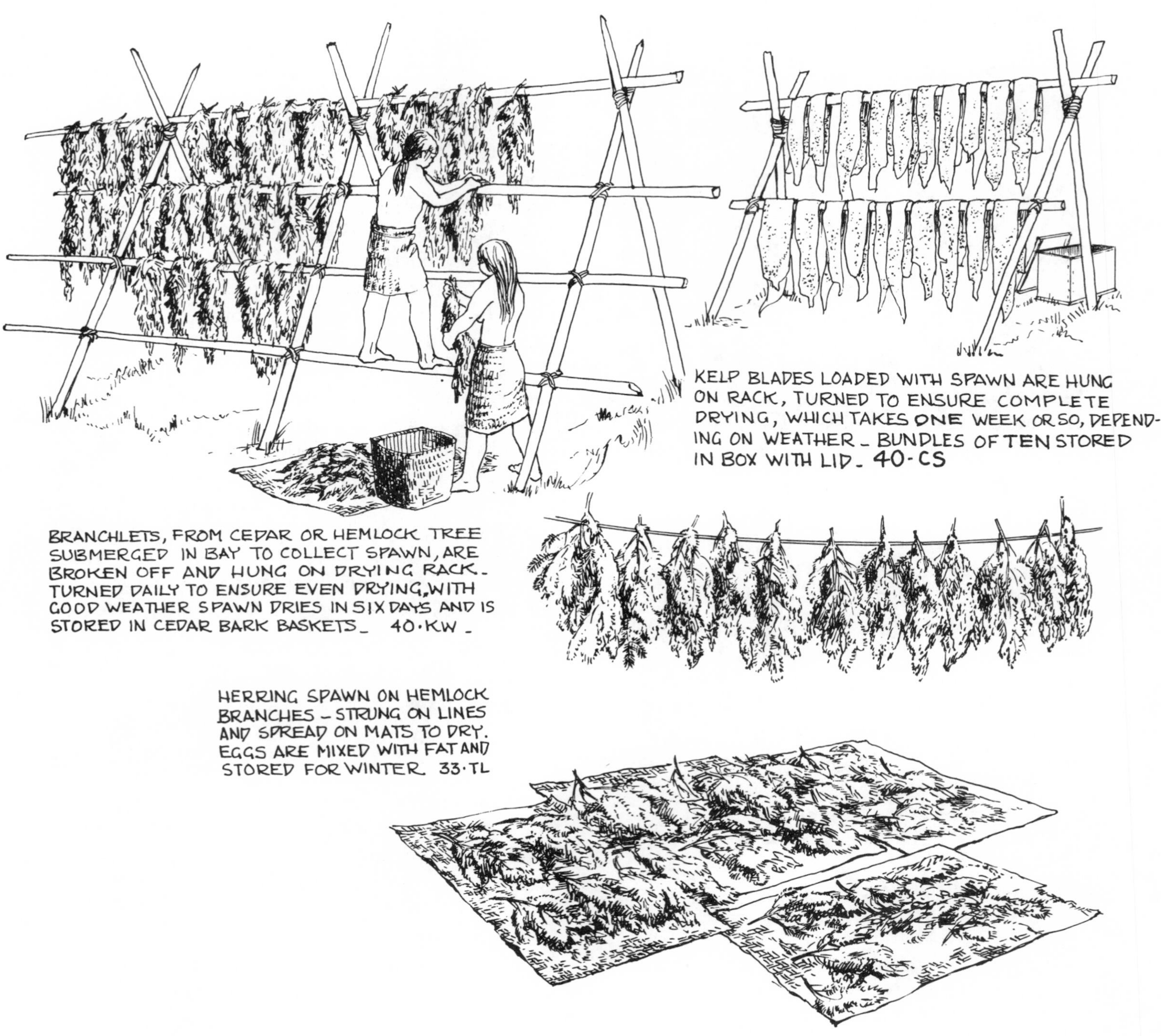
KELP BLADES LOADED WITH SPAWN ARE HUNG ON RACK, TURNED TO ENSURE COMPLETE DRYING, WHICH TAKES ONE WEEK OR SO, DEPENDING ON WEATHER _ BUNDLES OF TEN STORED IN BOX WITH LID _ 40-CS
BRANCHLETS, FROM CEDAR OR HEMLOCK TREE SUBMERGED IN BAY TO COLLECT SPAWN, ARE BROKEN OFF AND HUNG ON DRYING RACK _ TURNED DAILY TO ENSURE EVEN DRYING, WITH GOOD WEATHER SPAWN DRIES IN SIX DAYS AND IS STORED IN CEDAR BARK BASKETS _ 40·KW _
HERRING SPAWN ON HEMLOCK BRANCHES _ STRUNG ON LINES AND SPREAD ON MATS TO DRY. EGGS ARE MIXED WITH FAT AND STORED FOR WINTER 33·TL

Eulachon Oil

Tons of eulachon in large wooden pits left to "ripen" prior to being rendered for oil. In background, strings of fish hang to dry. Fishery Bay, Nass River. Maynard photo. 1884. 11.TS

The arrival of the eulachon in spring meant far more than a change of diet, welcome though the fresh fish were. The purpose of catching the fish in such great quantities was for the extraction of their rich and nutritious oil, often referred to as grease.

Villages having hereditary rights to rivers with eulachon runs were able to render large amounts of oil not only for their own consumption but also for trading purposes. Those in villages some distance from such rivers bought temporary rights to fish and render the oil. They encamped by the river until the processing was complete, then returned home with the valuable oil. The Haida, Tlingit and Nootka on Vancouver Island had neither eulachon rivers nor rights to the fish; consequently they, and others, came long distances to trade for the oil with those who had a surplus.

So much sought-after was the oil that it was traded great distances eastward through the mountains to tribes in the interior. Recent research on obsidian trade routes, conducted by British Columbia archaeologist Dr. Roy Carlson, led to a three-man expedition through the coast mountains to the sea. Evidence from their findings proved that when explorer Alexander Mackenzie made his famous journey overland to the Pacific ocean, he followed one of several ancient trade routes to the coast. Eulachon oil carried along these and other routes has given rise to the name "grease trails."

The rendering of the oil was a family or community affair; in early spring, camps on the river banks resembled a massive processing plant. Methods of doing some things varied among the different peoples, but in general the process was much the same.

A large pit dug in the ground was filled with eulachon and covered over with logs; the fish were then left to "ripen" for ten days to three weeks, depending on the weather. The warmer the weather, the quicker the disintegration of the flesh that would allow the oil to be released readily. In a large bentwood box, fire-heated rocks were added to water to bring it to a boil, then the rotted fish was put in. As the rocks cooled they were removed, rinsed of fish bits, and returned to the fire for reheating. Fresh hot rocks were then added to maintain simmering, while continual stirring and agitating helped to free the oil from the fish.

After several hours the mixture was allowed to stand. The sediment and liquid sank to the bottom, while the purified oil rose to the top to be skimmed off or ladled out in small boxes with lids.

The canoe that brought in the fish could also become the vessel for rendering the oil. Partly buried in the sand or ground, and supported at the sides with stakes, it served very conveniently as a large container.

With the top oil removed, the residue of mush was scooped up into pliable baskets of woven spruce root. Remaining oil was pressed out with a lever device or by trampling on the baskets in the canoe. Further boiling finally rendered out the very last of the oil.

A three-man canoe filled with eulachon would yield between five and six gallons of oil; a fisherman might catch eight to twelve canoe loads of the fish.

As can be imagined, the odour from processing the oil was excessively strong, almost intolerable for unaccustomed nostrils, and the oil had a flavour to match! The late Chief August Jack Khahtsahlano once declared the oil "good medicine": when it was two weeks old it had a mild flavour, at one month it was strong; at two months it was "very strong." The Rev. C. M. Tait, an itinerant minister earlier in this century, recalled an instance when he arrived very late one night at an Indian fishing village:

". . . I was immediately ushered into the chief's house, and his wife began to prepare food for me. A fresh lot of halibut had just come in and she began to cook. Out came her oolichan box, and the big horn spoon, a sort of great ladle made, I think, from the horn of the big-horn sheep. Of course the more grease—they value it—the greater the honour to the guest. I protested that I was unworthy of so much grease, but without avail. To my chagrin she was lavish, and simply showered her esteem on me by smothering the halibut with grease. I never acquired a taste for it. I am without hope that I ever shall."

Indian peoples relished the flavour and used the oil extensively with their meals. Dried fish, roasted roots, and many other foods were dipped into it, and guests were served the oil in individual bowls, often handsomely carved. Dried berries were mixed with the grease and stored for winter, but even fresh berries were enjoyed with this added ingredient. To eat berries without oil was considered a sign of poverty. Containing iodine and many necessary vitamins, eulachon oil was an important part of the diet.

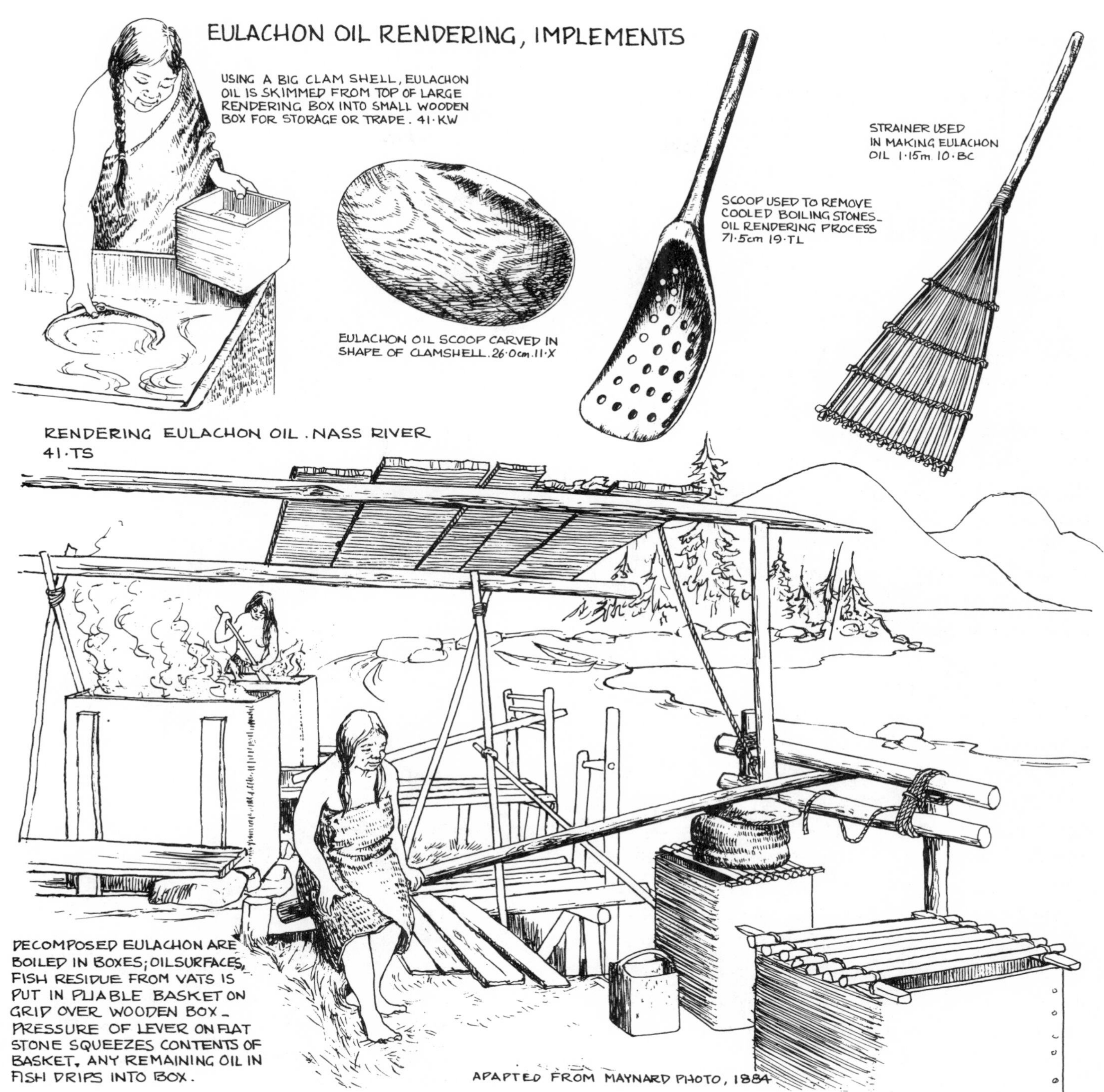
EULACHON OIL RENDERING, IMPLEMENTS
USING A BIG CLAM SHELL, EULACHON OIL IS SKIMMED FROM TOP OF LARGE RENDERING BOX INTO SMALL WOODEN BOX FOR STORAGE OR TRADE. 41·KW
EULACHON OIL SCOOP CARVED IN SHAPE OF CLAMSHELL. 26·0cm. 11·X
SCOOP USED TO REMOVE COOLED BOILING STONES_ OIL RENDERING PROCESS 71·5cm 19·TL
STRAINER USED IN MAKING EULACHON OIL 1·15m. 10·BC
RENDERING EULACHON OIL . NASS RIVER 41·TS
DECOMPOSED EULACHON ARE BOILED IN BOXES; OILSURFACES, FISH RESIDUE FROM VATS IS PUT IN PLIABLE BASKET ON GRID OVER WOODEN BOX _ PRESSURE OF LEVER ON FLAT STONE SQUEEZES CONTENTS OF BASKET. ANY REMAINING OIL IN FISH DRIPS INTO BOX.
ADAPTED FROM MAYNARD PHOTO, 1884

RENDERING EULACHON OIL
ADAPTED FROM EARLY PHOTO
COVERED PIT FOR EULACHON TO DECOMPOSE
BASKETS FOR PRESSING OUT OIL FROM RESIDUE
CANOE PARTLY BURIED IN SAND TO HELP STABILIZE IT. STAKES & CORD HOLD IT SECURE.
CANOE FILLED WITH FISH, WATER
[CENTRE] COOLED STONES PUT ON RACK OVER CANOE. OIL AND FISH BITS RINSED OFF BEFORE REHEATING.
LADLING OIL
REMOVING COOLED STONES
LADLES
STRIP OF CEDAR BARK FOR DRAWING FLOATING OIL TO BOW OF CANOE WHERE IT IS LADLED INTO LARGE BOX.
TONGS TO PICK UP HOT STONES WHICH ARE PUT INTO CANOE TO MAINTAIN BOILING
STONES BEING HEATED
33 · TL

Stopping off at Hot Springs Island, in the Queen Charlottes, I once had an unexpected opportunity of tasting eulachon oil. A Haida family were staying in their summer cabin close to the springs and graciously offered us the use of the bath house they had built incorporating the hot mineral water—a luxury for us after weeks of boating and beach camping. They also invited us to lunch and for the first time I tried steamed mussels and discovered how delicious they were. On the table was a jar of what, in our ignorance, we thought to be honey with its whitish, semi-crystalline appearance. Fortunately our hostess did not allow us to use it as honey, for it was eulachon oil. She did give us the opportunity of experiencing the taste but, like the good reverend, I am without hope that I could ever get to like it.

Oil rendering was not a process exclusive to the eulachon, although eulachon excelled as a source. The Haida, who were without this oil unless they traded at the Nass River for it, boiled quantities of black cod and skimmed the oil that came to the surface. On the Fraser River, the Coast Salish extracted oil from salmon by putting whole fish in wooden troughs which were left in the sun. When the fish decomposed the oil seeped to the bottom.

The dogfish, with its large, oil-rich liver, was also rendered for its oil content, though not aboriginally. In the early days of sawmilling in Vancouver, Indians caught dogfish off Point Grey, extracted the oil in big kettles on Deadman Island (just inside the present harbour), and sold it to the sawmills. Similarly, the Nootka had a small industry going in the 1880s. They sold the oil to logging outfits, who used it as a lubricant on the timbers over which logs were skidded to bring them out of the woods.

Still manufactured by several families with access and rights to eulachon fishing, the oil continues to find a market up and down the coast. It is now sold by the gallon and the price is high, testifying to its continued demand. In 1968, in the Charlottes, it was $25.00 per gallon; some years later it was selling for $35.00. The price on Vancouver Island in 1976 for oil from Alert Bay reached $50.00 per gallon, but to those who still treasure this important and nutritious food supplement, it is worth it.

Kelp Bottles for Eulachon Oil

A lightweight storage container for eulachon oil was made from the long kelp stems that grow best in a strong current. These were harvested in the fall on a low tide when they were most accessible. With the leaves of the seaweed cut off, the stipe (stem) was scraped with a section of cockle shell cut to fit its curvature. Dried on a rack over the fire for two days, the stipes were carefully tended to ensure even shrinkage.

To test for airtightness, the stems were inflated and the open end plugged with a wooden stopper and lashed tightly into place. Those that did not leak air were further dried and bleached before being deflated and stropped around a stake to soften them.

A funnel made by cutting the top off a kelp bulb was used for filling the long stems with eulachon oil. Kelp bottles of oil were coiled up into a box or hung on the wall for storage.

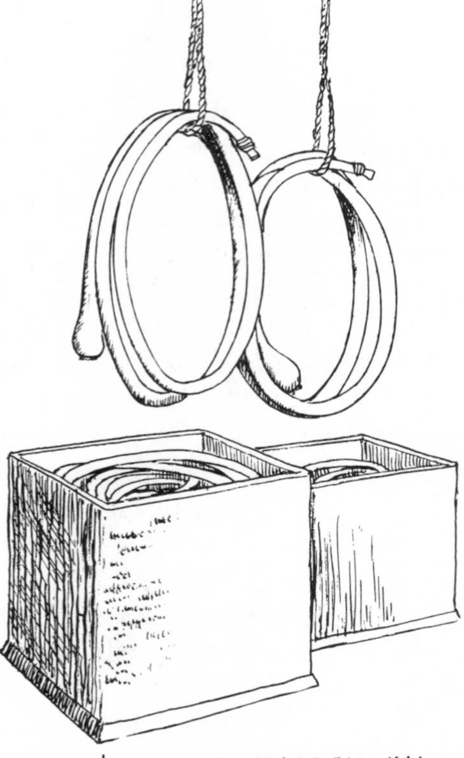

'BOTTLES' OF OIL ARE HUNG ON WALL OR COILED IN BOXES FOR STORAGE.

KELP BULB

CUT FOR FUNNEL

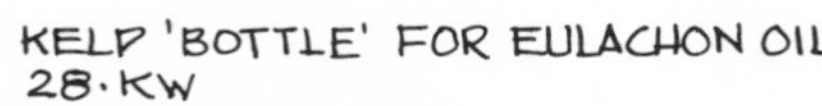

HOLLOW LENGTHS OF GIANT KELP ARE SPECIALLY PREPARED TO SERVE AS STORAGE CONTAINERS. OIL IS POURED THROUGH FUNNEL [CUT KELP BULB] WITH LADLE OR SHELL TO FILL TUBE. OPEN END IS PLUGGED AND TIED.

Fish Knives

Fish knives made by the author; hafted ground slate knife and herring knife made from ulna bone of deer. 60.

The implement most used for cutting up fish was a thin-bladed knife made of ground slate, bevelled on the edge and hafted at the top. The wafer-like quality of many of these knives is astounding. Some from the Marpole site in Vancouver, excavated by Dr. Charles Borden, are only two and three millimetres thick, and some, interestingly, bear a strong resemblance to the Eskimo ulu, or woman's knife. The oldest known ground slate knives date back about 5,000 years; they were used at a site on the Fraser River near Yale.

From the Katz dig, near Hope on the same river, an almost complete ground slate knife was found. So that he could experience the value of this implement, the dig director, Gordon Hanson, used it on one of the salmon an Indian lady living close by had taken in her net. After the fish had been cut open with a heavier stone knife, the ground slate knife easily cut deep scores through the flesh to open it for drying. To see the knife again cutting salmon on the bank of the river brought home the continuity of Indian habitation in the valley.

The Nootka, on the west coast of Vancouver Island, traditionally used only a shell knife for fish, made from the large sea mussel *(Mytilus californianus)* so abundant on the outer coast. With the edge ground on a sandstone abrader the knife was amazingly sharp. The Nootka felt that the sea shell was a fitting material with which to cut the much respected salmon, and long after metal knives became available to them, they could not bring themselves to put the steel blade into the flesh of the fish. To do so would have been an insult to the salmon.

I was intrigued to find in two museums small copper implements shaped like a mussel shell. There were no data on these, but I speculated that they might represent early attempts to make fish knives from metal. The material used was a break with tradition, but at least the appearance of the shell shape was maintained—perhaps out of respect for the salmon.

Another useful knife was one easily made from a deer's ulna bone, a lower foreleg bone. The shape of the bone lent itself naturally to edge sharpening, and while it is usually referred to as a herring knife, used for splitting open herring, I feel sure it had many other uses around the house. I made one of these and found it would cut nettle fibre string and cedar bark as well as split herring.

Eventually, when iron and steel began to replace more and more of the natural materials used for tools and implements, the ground slate fish knife fell into disuse. It was replaced with a knife made from part of the blade of a hand saw, though this knife was used the same way and given the traditional shape with the same hafting. Ultimately it too was replaced by the modern, long-bladed knife bought from the store.

In the renewal of Indian people's interest in their old ways, and in the search to better understand how things were done, the saw blade knife is back at work. Robert Davidson, renowned Haida artist, carver and jewellery maker working in the Lower Fraser Valley, returns to the Queen Charlotte Islands annually at the time of the salmon run to fish and preserve the much loved sockeye. At the fish camp on the Yakoun River I found him butchering the red meat in the old way, using the traditional shaped knife on the triangular wooden cutting block.

FISH KNIVES

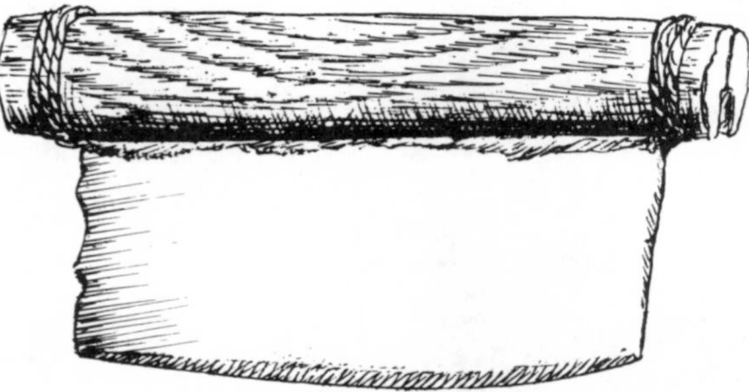

GROUND SLATE KNIFE FOR BUTCHERING FISH.

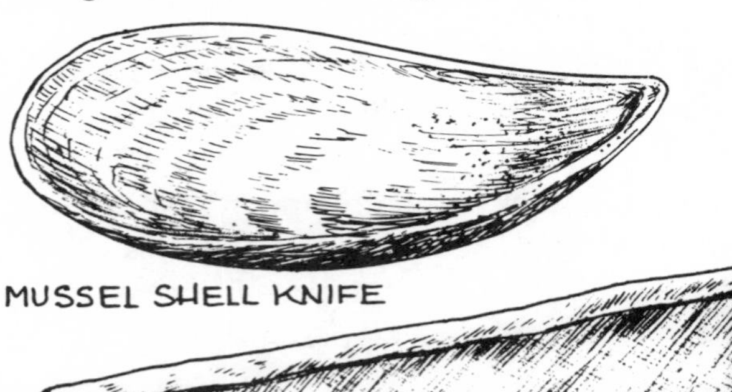

MUSSEL SHELL KNIFE

COPPER KNIFE RESEMBLES SHAPE OF MUSSEL SHELL KNIFE. POSSIBLY USED FOR FISH. 12 cm. 19·TL

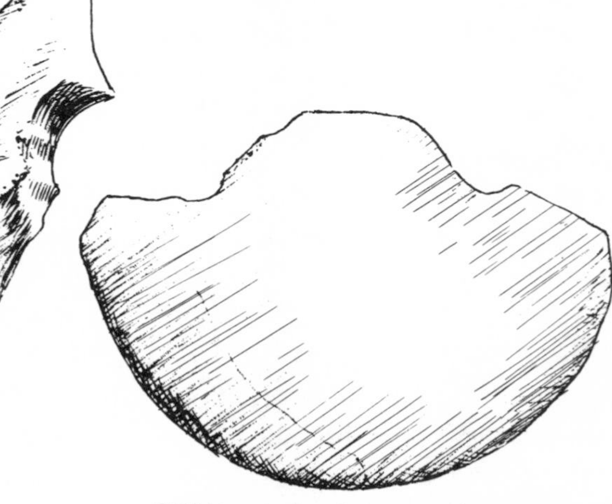

SEMI-LUNAR GROUND SLATE KNIFE. TOP PROJECTION FOR HAFT ATTACHMENT 14·5 cm. 12·CS

SHARP EDGE

HERRING SPLITTING KNIFE MADE FROM ULNA BONE OF DEER. EDGE IS SHARPENED BY GRINDING ON ABRADER STONE. 12·0 cm. 13·CS

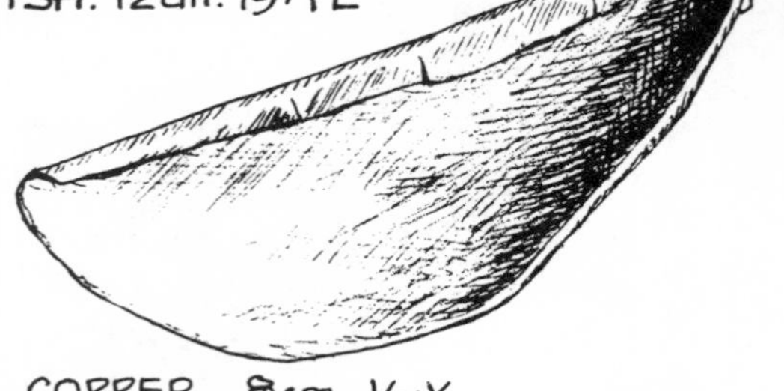

COPPER. 8 cm. 16·X

IMPLEMENTS

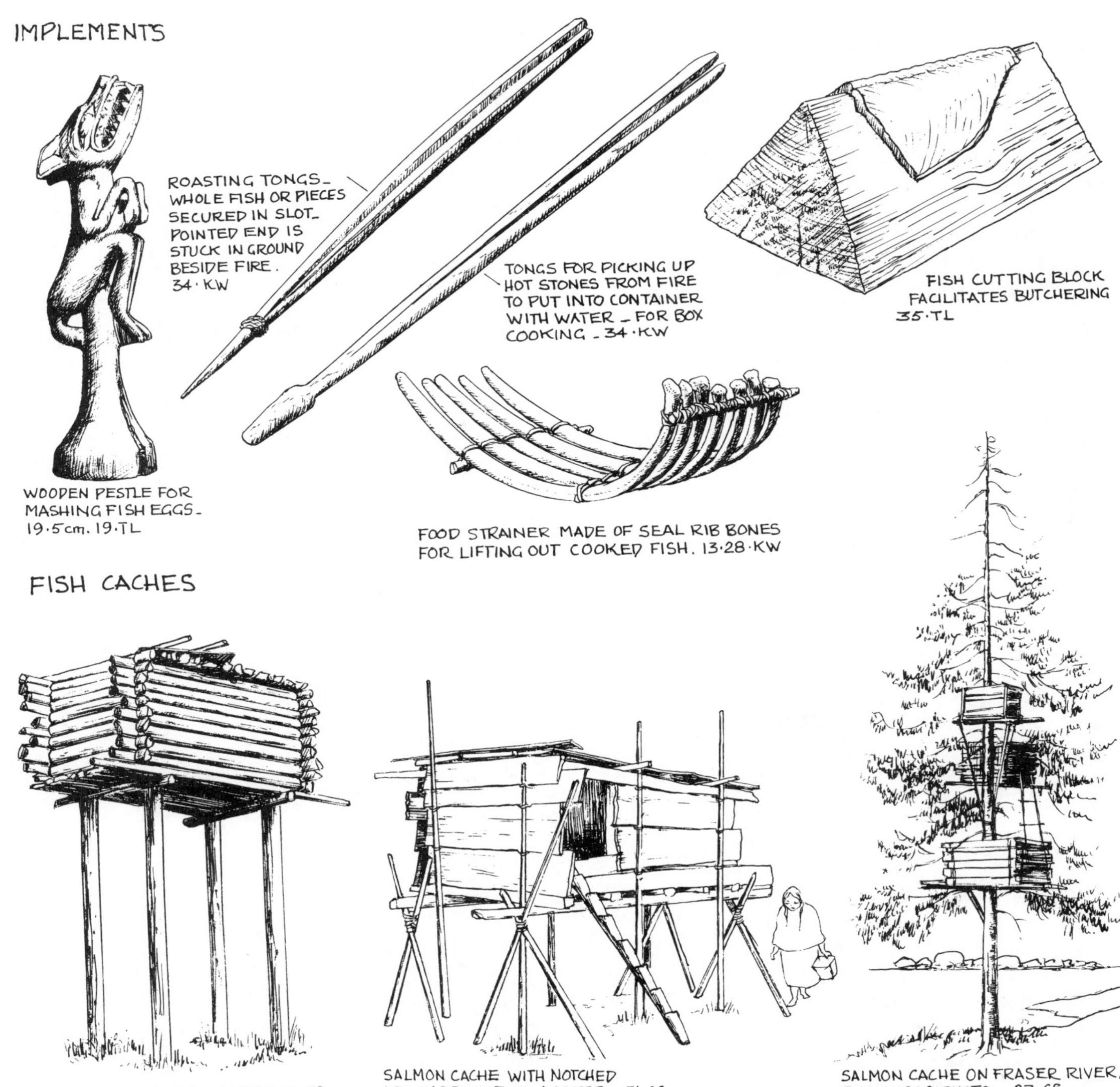
ROASTING TONGS_ WHOLE FISH OR PIECES SECURED IN SLOT_ POINTED END IS STUCK IN GROUND BESIDE FIRE. 34·KW
TONGS FOR PICKING UP HOT STONES FROM FIRE TO PUT INTO CONTAINER WITH WATER _ FOR BOX COOKING _ 34·KW
FISH CUTTING BLOCK FACILITATES BUTCHERING 35·TL
WOODEN PESTLE FOR MASHING FISH EGGS_ 19·5cm. 19·TL
FOOD STRAINER MADE OF SEAL RIB BONES FOR LIFTING OUT COOKED FISH. 13·28·KW
FISH CACHES
NASS RIVER SALMON CACHE, 51·TS
SALMON CACHE WITH NOTCHED LOG LADDER FOR ACCESS_ 51·CS
SALMON CACHE ON FRASER RIVER, FROM 1868 PHOTO. 27·CS

Spoons, Ladles and Bowls

Some of the most superb carvings of the Northwest Coast were to be found among the eating and serving utensils of a household. Artists carved bowls, spoons and ladles with pure flowing lines in simple statement, or elaborately embellished. Family status and wealth were reflected through the splendour of great feast dishes, the elegance of individual bowls for oil and the complex intricacies of goat and sheep horn spoons and ladles. But the care and attention focused on the eating utensils might well have also been a tribute to that vital and life-sustaining creature: the fish.

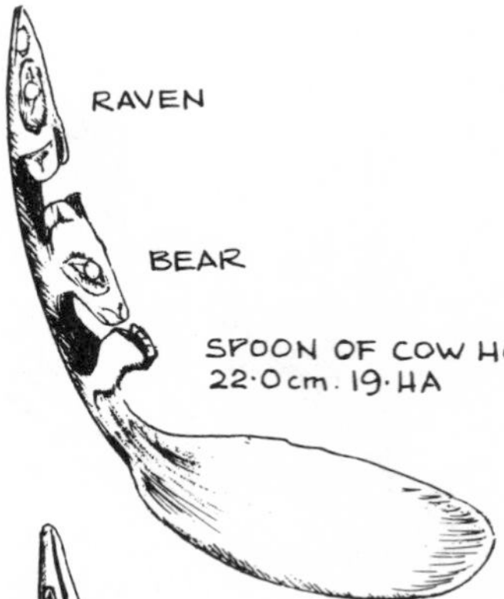

RAVEN

BEAR

SPOON OF COW HORN 22·0cm. 19·HA

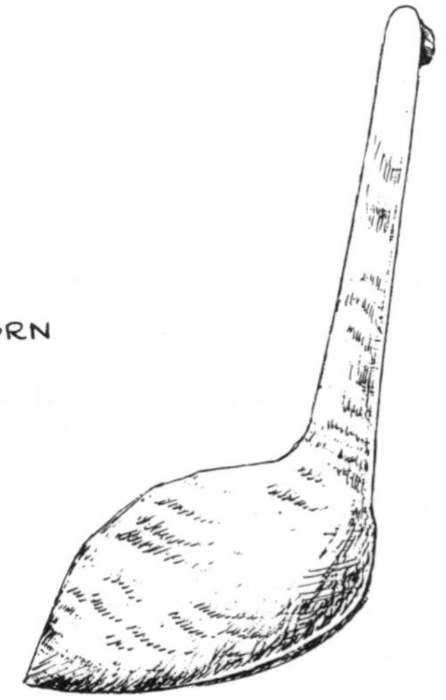

WOOD LADLE 38·0cm 43·12·CS

SHEEP HORN LADLE 43·2cm.46·X

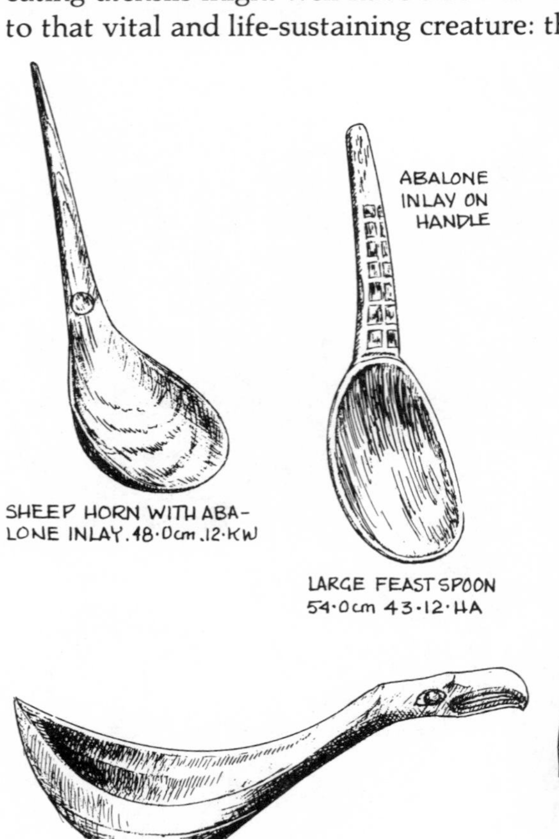

SHEEP HORN WITH ABALONE INLAY. 48·0cm .12·KW

LARGE FEAST SPOON 54·0cm 43·12·HA

GOAT HORN SPOON WITH ANTLER HANDLE . 18·0cm.19·TS

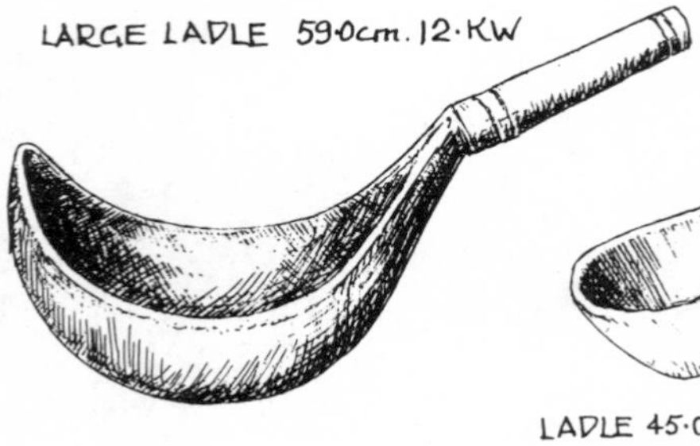

LARGE LADLE 59·0cm. 12·KW

LARGE FEAST LADLE 77·0cm 43·12·KW

LADLE 45·0cm 12·KW

LARGE FEAST LADLE WITH RAVEN HANDLE 1·20m. 43·12·KW

Etiquette and Feasting

Just as our society requires good table manners and eating habits from those said to be "well brought up," so did the Indian cultures have standards of mealtime behaviour and etiquette among people of high class.

The seating arrangement was of prime importance, particularly when guests were invited. People were seated according to rank and social status and the highest ranking people received the most desirable portions of the food. Good manners required that small bites be taken with only partially opened mouth, the food be eaten slowly, and the chewing and swallowing done discreetly. It was not good manners to talk about food while eating. Solid food was eaten with the fingers, and water was provided before and after a meal to cleanse the hands, with shredded cedar bark for hand towels.

For special guests and at feasts, the "best dishes" were brought out and used. These would be the beautifully carved feast dishes, the handsome individual oil bowls, often inlaid with operculum, the carved sheep horn ladles and bowls, and goat horn spoons.

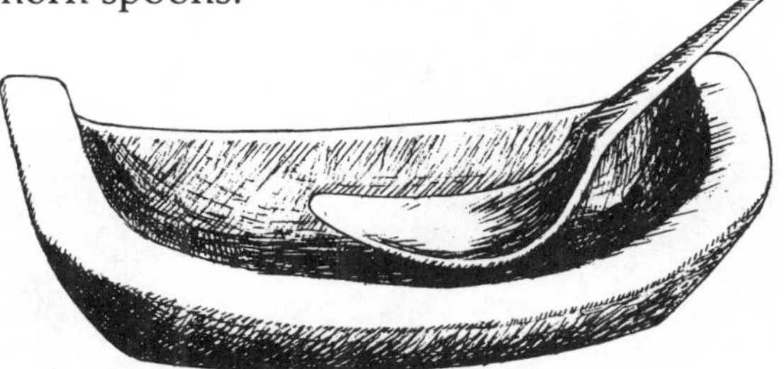

DISH 28·0cm. SPOON 7·5cm 48·12·KW

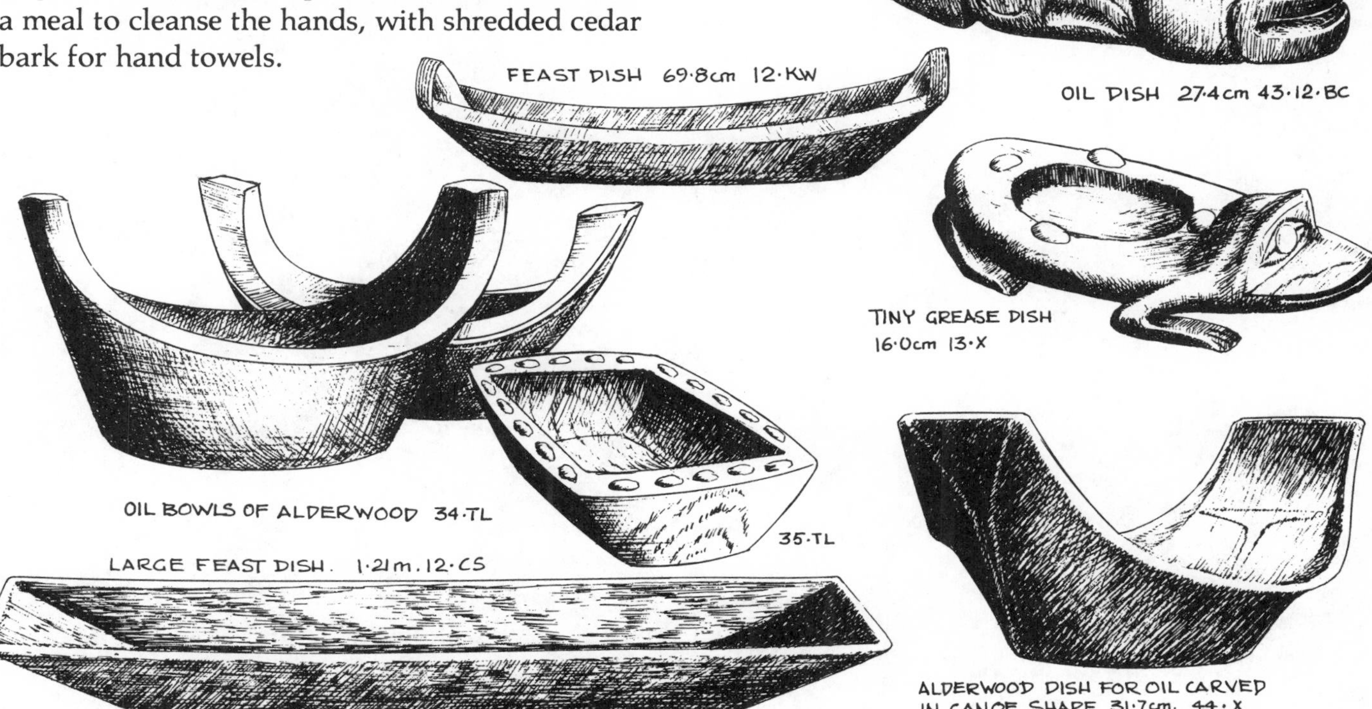

60.19.TL

Spiritual Realms

Prayers and Ceremonies

The Indians of the Northwest Coast showed much reverence and caring for the natural resources that were important to their cultures. They recognized that all living things—plant, animal, bird or creature of the sea—were endowed with a conscious spirit and therefore could present themselves in abundance or not at all.

There would have been years when the salmon came in extraordinary numbers and years when the run was poor or there was no run at all; years when the eulachon teemed up the rivers at a regular time and years when they came late; years when berries failed to mature and the picking was lean and years when the branches bent under the weight of the fruit. Most years migrating waterfowl would arrive in great flocks, but occasionally they would not. Since they saw the creatures' coming as voluntary, the Indians reasoned that in a year of scarcity taboos had been broken or disrespect shown.

Writing in 1905 of the interior Indians of the Lillooet area, Charles Hill-Tout says:

"Nothing that the Indian of this region eats is regarded by him as mere food and nothing more. Not a single plant, animal or fish, or other object upon which he feeds, is looked upon in this light, or as something he has secured for himself by his own wit or skill.

Canoe loaded to the gunwales with cod and other fish, circa 1900.
17.MK(?)

"He regards it as something which has been voluntarily and compassionately placed in his hands by the good will and consent of the 'spirit' of the object itself, or by the intercession and magic of his culture heroes, to be retained and used by him only upon the fulfilment of certain conditions."

Much the same attitude seems to have been prevalent among coast Indians. The "certain conditions" to be fulfilled were taboos, customs, and ceremonies that made an appeal to the spirit of the plant or creature to be harvested or caught. The ceremony might be simply a prayer—a supplication for success and abundance— and it showed humility, gratitude, and respect on the part of the human.

A prayer was said to the spirit of the great cedar tree before felling it, that it might fall in the desired direction. A prayer was said before the bark of the standing tree was stripped off, explaining what it was to be used for. It was a courteous apology as well as a prayer of thankfulness and recognition of so useful a material. The prayer was a gesture of reverence and a way of caring.

The fisherman used many different prayers and songs to communicate with the spirit of the fish and achieve success in fishing; these might be spontaneous, or acquired through spiritual experiences or in dreams. Those favoured with supernatural help guarded their songs and prayers with secrecy and became exceptionally good at fishing. Sometimes these individuals specialized in one particular kind of fish, earning an enviable reputation.

The Haida people of Skidegate said a prayer to the spirit of the mountain from which ran the salmon stream called Claig-a-doo, meaning "land of plenty." If, at the end of September when the salmon came, the water was too low for their migration, the prayer beseeched the mountain spirit to make it rain and fill the level of the water so the fish could make their way upstream. 64.HA.

Head-dress ornament (wood, with abalone shell inlay) represents bear holding salmon. Photo by Lisa Little. 20.TS

Sustenance for most of the people of the Northwest Coast was dependent on the return of the migrating species of salmon, and there were prayers said on the occasion of catching the first of the season, or of the run. The "First Salmon Ceremony" was a ritual of reverence and respect expressed in many different ways. Some people had a ceremony for the first of each species to be caught, some for just the first of the season; with some it was a family ceremony, with others the whole village participated. There were a ritual and prayers for catching the first load of eulachon.

Part of "Cannibal Society" ceremonial dress. Carved elements, which include thunderbird and fish, were originally attached to cedar bark shirt; from Tsawdi, Knight Inlet. Photo taken at St. Louis Lousiana Purchase Exposition, 1904. 25.KW

In each case the fishing season was not "open" until the ceremony had been performed.

The First Salmon Ceremony was also a celebration, a time of joy and renewal that brought cohesion to the village. It reminded the people of the rhythmic cycles in nature and the interdependence of all beings. It was a time to perpetuate the ancient customs and reinforce the regulating taboos. It was a time of thankfulness—for making it through to another year and for the return of the life-giving fish. The people looked forward to the start of the salmon run with great eagerness, for the dried fish of winter storage could be replaced with succulent red meat, fresh from the water.

Early running species of salmon will congregate at the mouth of a shallow creek before the spring runoff has swelled it sufficiently to allow them to proceed up to the spawning grounds. At this time, if a fisherman paddling a canoe in the vicinity saw a salmon jumping, he at once prayed to it:

"Haya! Haya! Come up again, Swimmer,
that I may say Haya, according to your wishes,
for you wish us to say so, when you jump,
Swimmer,
as you are speaking kindly to me when you jump,
Swimmer." 66.KW

Also:

"Welcome, friend Swimmer,
we have met again in good health.
Welcome, Supernatural One,
you, Long-Life-Maker,
for you come to set me right again
as is always done by you.
Now pray take my sickness
and take it back to your rich country
at the other side of the world,
Supernatural One."

The man answered for the fish and said "Ha, I will do so." 66.KW

The form of the First Salmon Ceremony was based on the normal activities associated with the fish—the handling, butchering, cooking, serving and eating—but it was embellished and made more affirmative, sometimes even dramatized. The method of taking the salmon up the beach to the house was often an elaborate one, testifying to the special occasion, and a new mat was made to lay the honoured guest upon.

When a Kwagiutl fisherman trolling with hook and line for sockeye salmon caught the first nine fish, he clubbed them only once so that they were not quite dead. With a long twisted cedar withe he strung them through gill and mouth, tying both ends of the cedar to form a hoop. Holding each side of the hoop in his hands he prayed:

"O, Swimmers, this is the dream given by you,
to be the way of my late grandfathers
when they first caught you
at your playground in this river.
Now you will be the same way, Swimmers.
I do not club you twice, for I do not wish
to club to death your souls so that you may go home
to the place where you came from, Supernatural Ones, you,
Givers-of-Heavy-Weight.
I mean this, Swimmers, why should I not go
to the end of the dream given by you?
Now I shall wear you as a neck ring going to my house,
Supernatural Ones, you, Swimmers." 66.KW

The fisherman put the hoop over his head and it formed a ring similar to the cedar bark neck ring of the winter dances. He wore the ring of fish as he walked up the beach to his house and then, lifting it off, he held it in his hands and prayed:

"O, Swimmers, now I come and take you into my house.
Now I will go and lay you down on this mat
which is spread on the floor for you, Swimmers.
This is your own saying when you came
and gave a dream to my late grandfathers.
Now you will go." 66.KW

The ring of fish was placed on a new mat of cedar bark strips made especially for the occasion. The fisherman's wife sat beside the mat, holding a fish with her left hand and a ground slate knife in her right. She prayed:

"Thank you Swimmers, you Supernatural Ones,
that you have come to save our lives,
mine and my husband's,
that we may not die of hunger,
you Long-Life-Maker.
Only protect us that nothing evil may befall us,
you, Rich-Maker-Woman,
and this also, that we may meet again next year,
good, great Supernatural Ones." 66.KW

And she cut the fish with the slate knife in the accepted manner.

Another prayer for the first salmon of the season caught by hook was:

"Swimmer, I thank you
because I am still alive at this season,
when you come to our good place,
for the reason why you came
is that we may play together
with my fishing tackle, Swimmer.
Now, go home and tell your friends
that you had good luck on account of coming here,
and that they shall come with their wealth bringer,
that I may get some of your wealth, Swimmer,
also take away my sickness, friend,
Supernatural One, Swimmer. 66.KW

At the mouth of the river where the congregating salmon were plentiful and the water clear, the first fish was often speared from the bow of the canoe. Clubbing it once, and holding it in his hands, the fisherman prayed to it:

"We have come to meet alive, Swimmer,
do not feel wrong about what I have done to you,
friend Swimmer,
for that is the reason why you came,
that I may spear you,
that I may eat you,
Supernatural One, you, Long-Life-Giver, you,
Swimmer.
Now protect us, me and my wife,
that we may keep well,
that nothing may be difficult for us
that we wish to get from you,
Rich-Maker-Woman.
Now call after you your father and your mother,
and uncles and aunts
and elder brothers and sisters
to come to me also, you Swimmers,
you Satiater." 66.KW

When the first four silver salmon (coho) were caught by trolling, the fisherman's wife met her husband's canoe at the beach and said a prayer of welcome to the fish. She brought them up to the house and butchered them according to custom, leaving the heads and tails still attached to the backbones. These she set in the roasting tongs to cook by the fire. When the eyes of the fish were blackened, the family group was assembled in the house, and they sat behind the fire. The tongs with the roasted fish were laid on new mats spread before the people, who were given water to drink. The one of highest rank then prayed to

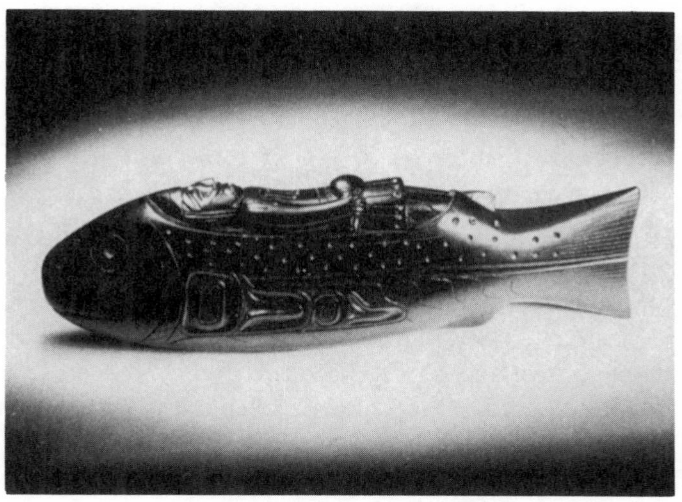

Argillite carving depicts shaman within salmon. 16cm (6¼ inches). 60.13.HA

the food before it was eaten:

"O friends! thank you that we meet alive.
We have lived until this time when you came
this year.
Now we pray you, Supernatural Ones, to protect
us from danger,
that nothing evil may happen to us when we
eat you,
Supernatural Ones!
For that is the reason why you came here,
that we may catch you for food.
We know that only your bodies are dead here,
but your souls come to watch over us
when we are going to eat
what you have given us to eat now."
"Indeed!" 66.KW

After eating, the family wiped their hands on shredded cedar bark, but did not wash them. The wife gathered up the bones and all that was not eaten into the mat, and threw it into the sea, including the mat, thus ensuring that the salmon would become whole again and return to the land of the Salmon People. Others of their species seeing them knew they had been treated with due respect and honour, and so they too would follow up the river. It seems the custom of all the tribes to return the bones to the water, with the exception of the Tsimshian, who burned them in the fire.

The pattern for the Tsimshian First Salmon Ceremony was laid down in a myth, as were many of the codes of behaviour that governed certain aspects of life, and from this it is not difficult to envision the solemnity and joy of the celebration of the return of the salmon.

When the first salmon of the season were caught, four elderly shamans were called down to the fishing platform at the water's edge from which the fish had been caught. They brought with them a cedar bark mat, freshly made for the occasion; eagle down, symbol of peace and friendship, and red ochre. One of the shamans put on the garment worn by the man who had caught the fish, and painted his face with the ochre. In his right hand he held his ceremonial rattle, and in his left an eagle tail, the long black feathers tipped with white.

The four shamans carefully placed the salmon on the new mat, and holding it by the four corners carried it up to the chief's house, the place where special guests were always taken. The shaman wearing the fisherman's raiment led the procession, shaking his rattle and swinging the eagle tail, eagle down on his head floating to the ground. Eventually they reached the big plank house of the chief, where young people having recent contact with birth and puberty (the ritually unclean who might offend the salmon), were required to leave.

Old people led the procession into the house,

Button shirt. Grey dogfish on red with mother-of-pearl buttons. 99cm (40 inches). 60.19.TL

and they were followed by all the shamans of the village dressed in colourful ceremonial regalia.

Amid the continued singing of special songs, the honoured fish was placed on a cedar board, and four times the shamans encircled it, rattling their beautifully carved rattles and swinging the eagle tails. The singers finished the songs and seated themselves in the proper place around the house. The fire crackled, making light and shadow patterns along the roof beams and the sturdy walls.

All was hushed. The shaman wearing the fisherman's garment called upon two old women

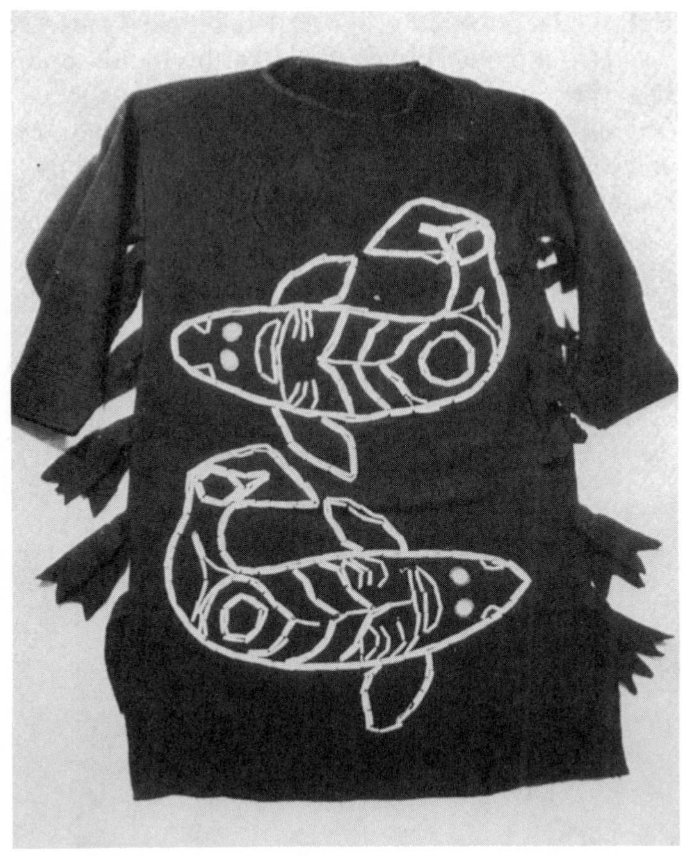

Red wool shirt with dogfish designs in dentalia, or tusk shell. Each fish approximately 51cm (20 inches) across. 60.19X

shamans to cut the fish, for butchering fish was traditionally women's work. With a mussel shell knife the salmon head was first severed, then the tail, followed by a cut along the ventral side to remove the inner parts. All the people assembled maintained silence, and as the fish was being cut, the women shamans called the salmon by honorary names of great significance: "Chief Spring Salmon . . . Quartz Nose . . . Two Gills On Back . . . Lightening Follow One Another . . . Three Jumps." 68.TS

The giving of names bestowed high social privileges, and the first salmon of the season was thus being honoured. Finally the fish was cooked in the prescribed manner and shared among the guests. When they had finished, all the bones, entrails and any uneaten parts were gathered up carefully into a clean mat and ceremonially put into the fire. This ensured the fish's revival and return to its home in the Spring Salmon village out in the sea. Since it had been well treated and duly honoured, the other salmon would follow up the river.

With the ceremony concluded, the catching of great quantities of the fish could then proceed.

Among the Comox people of the Coast Salish, the First Salmon Ceremony for sockeye involved the Ritualist (a shaman) who stood on a platform singing a secret spiritual song, shaking his ceremonial rattle. His face was painted with red ochre and there was eagle down in his hair, symbol of peace and welcome. He then took his canoe out and harpooned several sockeye, putting to one side the first one he caught.

Everyone was on the beach anticipating his return. He carried the first salmon gently up to his house, where his immediate family gathered, and they too had eagle down on their heads as a symbol of welcome to the fish. The Ritualist sang special songs while he shook his rattle, and honoured the fish by sprinkling eagle down over it. When the salmon had been boiled, everyone in the family shared the meal, including the children.

The following day all the villagers were invited to the Ritualist's house for a feast, and they ate the remainder of the salmon that had been harpooned. With the ceremony over, all the families were then entitled to go out fishing.

The Saanich, to the south of the Comox, practised a variation of the ceremony when the

Ritualist, with helpers, caught several sockeye with the reef net. When they returned to the beach, the people had formed an avenue from the water's edge up to the cooking fires. Children, with red ochre painted faces and white eagle down in their shining black hair, each carried up a salmon by holding the dorsal fin in their teeth. They stroked and soothed the fish as they went in procession up the avenue, with the Ritualist singing songs to the fish and shaking his rattle. At the fire, his wife was directed by him on how to cut and roast the fish, which were cooked over alder fires in trenches. The salmon, served on long planks of split cedar, had to be handled so that the heads always pointed inland or upstream, the direction the run was to go. At the conclusion of the meal, all the bones were gathered up and returned to the sea. 69.CS

Across the water from the Saanich were the Squamish on the mainland (also Coast Salish), who had a different custom involving the children. Anthropologists describe how the youngsters there carried the salmon up the beach from the canoe in small slings they had made of flexible cedar branches, one for the head and one for the tail of each fish. After conveying the fish to the Ritualist's house, they returned to the beach and shouted up river, "We're going to break its head off!" 69.CS (I can't help feeling that something has been lost in the translation here!)

Among the Haida and Tlingit people there was no salmon ceremony. For them the fish was less abundant, and they were not dependent upon it since they were able to catch in great quantity the great halibut, a fish that could also be preserved and stored for winter.

The Kwagiutl halibut fisherman prayed when putting tackle into the water. Once in the canoe with all his gear he set out on the incoming tide. But first he drew alongside a rock, plucked seaweed from it and rubbed it all over his hands, and held them underwater. This was to remove the human scent before handling the hook and bait, since he knew the fish had a sense of smell. While cleansing his hands he prayed to the halibut, using the customary term "Old Woman" and other nicknames, and referring to the hook as "younger brother."

"O Old Woman! Look at my work on your behalf.
Now this is clean, my younger brother,
with which I am going to catch you . . . yes, yes.

After he attached the bait to the hooks, and set the lines, the sinkers and the bladder floats, he further beseeched the halibut:

Mortuary and totemic pole with halibut crest, from Cumshewa, Queen Charlotte Islands. 25.HA

"Top bladder, go on, Old Woman!
Crawl up to it. Now it is well prepared.
This is your sweet food,
You, Wrinkled-In-The-Mouth!
You, Squint-Eye! Go on, go on,
else I may be stiff when I leave this place,
Old Woman!"

Before long Old Woman took the sweet food and as he hauled in the long line the fisherman prayed to Younger Brother, the hook, not to lose the catch:

"This is what I was wishing, Old Woman,
not to wait long on the water for you.
Now hold this my younger brother.
Don't let go this my younger brother."

With all the gear and the halibut stowed safely into the canoe, he took his fish club in one hand and prayed to the fish:

"Now come, Old Woman!
Now you have enough to eat,
now you have tasted your sweet food.
Now I shall give you this sweet food
as your second course." 28.KW

And the halibut was killed with a blow on the head. Another prayer beseeching the halibut to take the bait was:

"Now go to it, Scenting Woman.
do not play at your sweet tasting meat.
Take it at once, Born-To-Be-Giver.
Go ahead Old Woman, take your sweet tasting food.
Do not let me wait long on the water.
Go ahead, come on,
my younger brothers are dressed with your sweet tasting food,
O Flabby-Skin-In-The-Mouth." 66.KW

There was also a prayer addressed to the hook while it was being made:

"O Younger Brother, pay attention.
Now Younger Brother, your dress has been put on.
You will go to the village of Scenting Woman,
Born-To-Be-Giver-Of-The-House,
Old Woman, Flabby-Skin-In-The-Mouth.
Now clean and purify yourself, Younger Brother,
Do not let go of Old Woman . . .
when she takes hold of you, good Younger Brother.
I shall blacken you, Younger Brother,
with these spruce branches, that you may smell good,
that you may be smelled by Scenting Woman
when I first put you in the water." 66.KW

A simple ceremony marking the catch of the first halibut of the season was observed by the Kwagiutl. There were no doubt many variations of this, but one demanded that the fish be butchered and cooked without delay, following a specific procedure.

The flanks were removed for drying, and all the rest steamed in a pit with eel grass, broadleaved grass and hot rocks. The fins were roasted over the fire in a grid of split cedar sticks. Guests, invited in to share the meal, put all the bones and other uneaten parts on a new mat placed before them. After the meal all the scraps, and the guts also, were gathered up into the mat, the contents tossed back into the sea and the mat washed.

Were the fisherman not to observe this ritual, he would not get another bite. 28.KW

Eulachon, so important for the rendered oil, was also recognized with a ritual when the run began. A chief, with the privilege of catching the first of the eulachon, went in his canoe to a special place in the river, tying the canoe up to a particular overhanging branch. It was always the same place. Taking up his dip net, he addressed it in prayer that it might be successful:

"Go on, friend,
on account of the reason why you came,
placed in the hands of my late ancestors
by our Chief Above, our Father,
and go and gather in yourself the fish,
that you may be full when you come back,
friend.
Now go into the water where you may stay,
friend." 66.KW

He then partially lowered the dip net three times, and pushed it right down for the fourth. When it was hauled up he prayed to the shimmering mass of fish writhing in the net:

"Now come, fish, you who have come
being sent by our Chief Above, our Praised One,
and you come trying to come to me.
Now call the fish to come and follow your magic
power that they may come to me." 66.KW

The chief then poured the hundreds of slender, silver fish from the net into the canoe. Four times over he did this to complete the ceremony, and then returned home. All fishermen were then allowed to start harvesting the oil-rich fish that came in millions every year. When each man pulled up the first in his dip net, he offered a prayer of gratitude to the eulachon. There were different ways of saying it, but a common prayer was:

"Thank you, Grandchildren, that you have come
to me
to make me rich as it is done by you, fish,
you Dancers. You will protect me
that I may see you again next year, Grandchildren.
Thank you that you do not disdain trying to
come to me,
Supernatural Ones." 66.KW

Another prayer was:

"Now you have come, Grandfather, you fish,
that you may not ill-treat me,
that you may only bring good luck by your
coming to me,
Supernatural Ones, you Dancers, I pray you,
Supernatural Ones, that we may meet again
next year,
and please, protect me, friends, you fish." 66.KW

Tons of eulachon were rendered for their oil each year, but great quantities were also strung up to dry, and a prayer of welcome was said to the first to be strung:

"Now welcome, fish, you who have come,
brought by the Chief of the World-Above,
that I see you again,
that I come to exert my privilege
of being the first to string you, fish.
I mean this, that you may have mercy on me
that I may see you again next year

when you come back to this happy place, fish." 66.KW

There were many ways of greeting and honouring the different kinds of fish, and a great variety in the prayers offered to both the fishing gear and the species of fish. These tributes were far more profound than they might appear; they were deeply significant to a people who based their way of life on the natural rhythms of their environment, a people who had a close spiritual relationship with the plant and animal kingdoms of their coastal world.

The significance of the prayers and ceremonies cannot be fully understood by those of us who were not a part of the culture, but they nevertheless convey a message as meaningful today as it was a thousand years ago. It is a legacy of wisdom: that to honour and respect the resources of the sea and river is to ensure their continuous abundance for all time.

Basket of split root painted in red and black to represent dogfish. 10cm (4 inches) high. 60.13.X

Beliefs, Customs and Taboos

Because the fish of the river and sea were life itself to the coast Indian peoples, rules (customs and taboos) arose to regulate the activities connected with fish and fishing, and beliefs gradually surrounded the mystique of a never-ending supply of food from the waters. Because the five species of salmon were, for the majority of the coast cultures, the most important of all the fish, there were more beliefs and customs about salmon than about any other fish.

Some of these beliefs have about them a certain charm, while many touch on the attitude of caring for the fish as people, and of reverence for their role in life. Some are fearful, and some seem difficult for us to equate with present day society and our knowledge of biology. But these were the thoughts of a people living intimately with the river and sea, a people with their own way of understanding the intricacies of biology. For them it worked, and it worked unimpaired for thousands of years.

While many beliefs, with variations, were widespread and shared by many different cultures of the coast, others would be more localized, belonging to a region, a band, or perhaps a single village.

Without attempting to analyse the reasoning, here is a sampling of various beliefs and customs I have come across and found worth remembering.

- It was a general belief along much of the southern coast that the salmon were really people who lived in villages in a magical place under the sea, at the edge of the horizon. Five villages housed the five tribes of Salmon People, each with its own habits and breeding places. At specific times of the year these people transformed themselves into fish and swam up the rivers after journeying through the sea. Some fishermen believed the fish were led by their chief, who would then be the first one caught, and therefore must be accorded such honour as befits a chief. But others believed they sent scouts out ahead, and if the scouts were not treated with courtesy and respect when caught, then other salmon would not follow to ascend the river.

Shamans could tell when the salmon would arrive. In visions they could see them as they headed across the open sea or up the inlets to the rivers. 68.TS

Twins had great rapport with salmon, and many varying customs grew out of this general and fairly widespread belief.

Twin children would be sent down to the river bank, or out into the stream if it was shallow, to call the salmon, singing special songs and shaking rattles to entice the fish into the traps. 69.KW

Rubbing of fish petroglyph on boulder 1.5m x 2.1m (5 feet x 7 feet), originally on end of long, narrow point jutting into Nanaimo Harbour, now at Nanaimo City Museum, Vancouver Island. Such petroglyphs, often associated with rivers and streams, were probably to welcome salmon or entice them up river. Petroglyph rubbing by Beth Hill. 78.CS

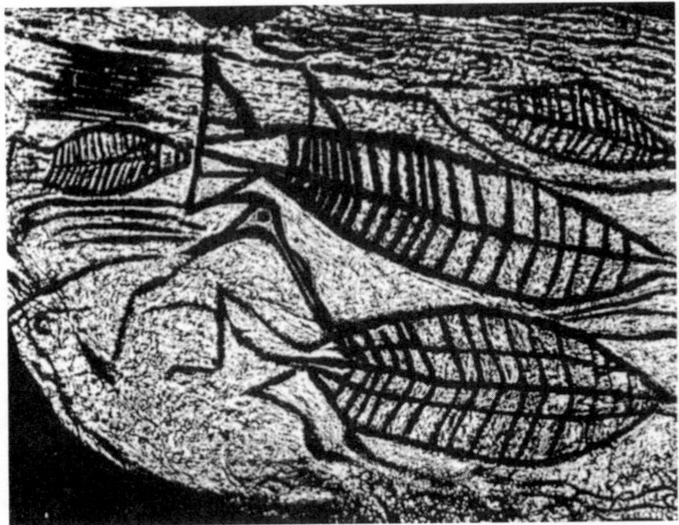

Twins had the power to call the eulachon as well as salmon. 69.TS

The father of twins held special powers in the salmon world. During fishing season he would spend a great deal of his time and energy in singing and performing secret rituals to ensure a maximum salmon catch. 69.TS

Twins of the same sex were salmon before birth. 69.KW

The appearance of twins forecast an unusually large salmon run. 69.NK

A twin child would burst into tears if a salmon was mistreated. 69.NK

If a young girl saw a salmon jumping in the creek within a year of her puberty, all the salmon would leave the creek. 69.HA

Stone bowl of vesicular lava may represent twin salmon heads. Twins have strong association with salmon in Indian belief. Bowl is said to have been found in cave near Pemberton. 60.13.

An evil-minded person could cause the salmon run to cease by burying the heart of a salmon in a clam shell, or in a burial ground. 42.CS

If roasted salmon eyes were kept overnight in the house, and not eaten, all the salmon would disappear from the sea. 69.KW

Salmon were responsible for the birth of twins and many of these people could assume salmon form at will.

Dogfish. Limited edition silk-screen print by Bill Reid. Haida.

Using a stone or metal knife to cut fish in the First Salmon Ceremony would cause thunderstorms or some other disaster, so a shell knife had to be used. 68.TS

Like people, salmon must enjoy eating the sweet inner bark of the hemlock in spring; so balls of it were rolled up, stuck with feathers, and sent floating down the river to the fish.

Salmon hanging up on the drying racks would play among themselves when no one was watching. 42.CS

When the dog salmon returned to their village in the sea, having been up the Fraser River, they brought back songs they had learned from the people along the way, and spent most of their time singing these songs. 70.CS

Only old women past the age of childbirth were allowed to work on making or repairing salmon nets.

A piece of Devil's Club *(Oplopanax horridus)* was wrapped around the halibut hook before the bait was tied on, as a good luck charm. 74.HA

When a halibut was caught, it was laid on its back in the canoe, head towards the fisherman; otherwise he would have no more bites. 67.KW

Flicker feathers were often tied to fish hooks to bring good luck. 62.HA

The Sun Dew *(Drosera* spp.) was a good-luck plant used by a fisherman. He would tie it on the end of his net to ensure a good catch, and if he did this without anyone knowing about it, the catch would be even greater. 74.HA

To comment on the great number of fish being caught was considered unlucky. 32.CS

When a codfish was caught that was too small, it was set free and told to send its big brother. 40.CS

A lunar eclipse was caused by a codfish swallowing the moon. 72.NK

●It was considered ominous to catch a salmon having a twisted mouth, and it was therefore necessary to have it exorcised by a ritualist who then returned it to the water. 32.CS
●If herring failed to spawn, a male and a female herring were tied together and twins led them, on a string, into a bay where they were released. 40.CS
●The sturgeon was often referred to as "Sister" while being fished (70.CS) and the halibut as "Old Woman," among other names. 67.KW.
●Similarly the red snapper was never mentioned by name during the fishing, but rather was referred to as "High Class Person". 40.CS
●When a lamprey was cooked, the head, still on its stick, was thrown. If it travelled far the thrower would have a long life, but if it fell short then a short life was predicted. 42.CS

Portrait of Zeeke, said to be the oldest Makah woman about the turn of the century. She died at 109 years. 17.MK

As in cultures all over the world, many and varied were the "dos and don'ts" surrounding the Indians' staple food. Most taboos are based on a belief or a necessity, and persist because of conditioning and habit even when they seem incongruous. A severe custom was that of the Bella Coola people who made the throwing of refuse into a stream during the salmon run punishable by death. (71.BC) If this ruling stemmed from the attitude of showing great respect for so revered a personage as the salmon, the underlying aim might well have been safeguarding clear water for the migration and spawning of this life-giving resource.

Other prohibitions regarding the river were enforced during the salmon run. Freshly split planks could not be floated down the river, and a new canoe had to wait ten days before being launched. The reason for this is not documented, but I find it interesting that research scientists today believe that naturally occurring wood extractives of cedar (from which the planks were made) are toxic to fish, as they are to other forms of life.

There would also seem to be good reasoning behind a taboo directed towards the women and children of the Katzie Band of the Coast Salish: during the sockeye run, women must not make any mats because Sockeye Salmon Women, in the land of the Salmon People far out in the ocean, did not make mats. To do so might offend the fish who could inflict a sickness on the mat-making women. Also, since the Sockeye Children had put away their play things to leap into the water and change into fish to go up the river, so the children of the village must put away their favourite play things until the run ended. 70.CS

No doubt mat-making among a group of women

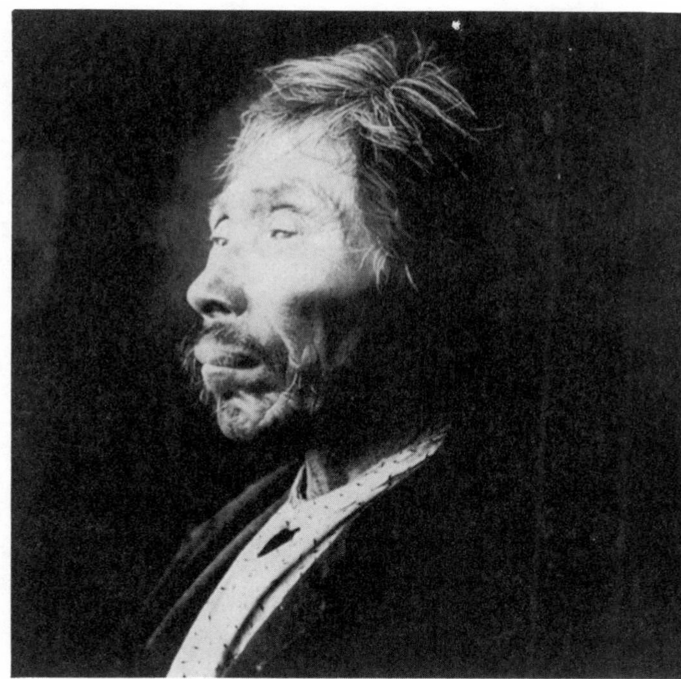

Portrait of Makah fisherman, circa 1900. 17.MK

was also a time for idle chatter and gossip, and since the men would be constantly busy with the task of catching the salmon, I suspect that such taboos were to ensure that the maximum amount of time of both women and children was spent in butchering, cleaning, smoking and preserving the catch.

A variety of taboos and customs were observed in the catching, cutting, handling, serving and eating of fish, and again most of these evolved around the hallowed salmon.

- If a fisherman caught two salmon on a single thrust of his two-pronged harpoon, he must not show any excitement or jubilation, but remain quiet; otherwise all the salmon already drying on the racks would get down and return to the sea.
- The first catch of salmon was never sold for fear that the hearts might be destroyed or fed to the dogs, for this would seriously affect the run. 69.CS
- Children were not allowed to play around with the salmon before they were cleaned; to do so would offend the fish, who would cause the child to become ill and pant the way a salmon does when it is dying. 42.CS
- The intestines of a salmon caught by spearing had to be broken off at the anal fin, not cut off, or else the spear would break when next in use. Similarly, a salmon caught by hook had the intestines cut off at the anal fin, not broken; otherwise the fishing lines would break. 69.KW
- A pregnant woman was not to split salmon in half or she would give birth to twins. 65.KW
- Those who had recent contact with puberty, birth or death (that is, the ritually impure) might not handle or eat fresh salmon. It would offend the fish and the run would cease. 68.TS
- When twins were born at a fish camp, the parents were sent back to the village and prohibited from eating any kind of fish. 69.MK
- Salmon might not be taken up the beach from the canoe in a basket; they had to be carried up one in each hand. 72.NK
- Blowing on hot, freshly cooked eulachon to cool it was taboo; this would bring windstorms. 73.TS
- Drinking water with a meal of eulachon was forbidden; to do so would bring rain and spoil the oil rendering. 73.TS

The reader may be tempted to laugh at the primitive thinking of people who would observe such taboos, finding them unfounded and absurd, but consider the belief of my friend. Serving tea to a casual group of friends, she was insistent that no woman other than herself pour from the same tea pot, for then she would become pregnant again.

Songs

Fond of music, rhythm and dancing, the Indian peoples had songs for both their everyday and ceremonial lives. Many songs, some supernaturally inspired, were the personal property of chiefs, families or individuals and they alone held the right to sing them. There were also songs of a more general nature, and both often referred to experiences of life which, quite naturally, included fishing.

This lullaby for a boy was concerned with spear fishing:

"I, the slave woman,
am glad in my heart,
I will spear a whole salmon for you,
I am glad in my heart . . .
I will snare what you are going to eat . . .
I, the slave woman,
am glad in my heart
I will spear a whole salmon for you . . .
Our three spear poles will be used [all] at once
to catch salmon.
You will fill yourself with meat, O my sister.
Why are you looking for meat?
It is only the salmon eggs that really fill you.
Yes, I got filled with salmon eggs." 82.TS

The first part of another lullaby for a boy looked forward to the time when the child would become a man:

Mother:
"Dear boy, dear boy,
dear little boy . . . "
Reply from the child:
"Sit up at night, my sister,

Steelhead. Silk-screen print by Roy Vickers, courtesy of the artist. TS

Sit up with me at night,
O my sister to make me grow,
til I become a man.
Then I will go to the creek of my forefathers
Where I will catch the large spring salmon.
Then I will fish at Echo Cliffs,
That is where I will gather the backbones
or fish spines for Thunder-Woman . . . ." 82.TS

Young boys casting for trout sang a song that was a kind of "dare" to the fish:

"Come along, trout,

I want to triumph,
I want to triumph
Over you biggest trout.
I fish for trout,
I fish for trout.
Swallow [the bait] right down
To your very tail,
To your very tail,
Why, you cannot even break one of our hairs"* 80.BC

Typical of the frolicsome chants of youth, the following was sung by boys splashing in the water trying to drive minnows ashore:

"Who is your father?
Who is your father?
Rotten stomach is your father,
Rotten stomach is your father." 80.BC

A beautiful and ancient song is that of a chief, sung at a potlatch before the distribution of gifts:

"I will sing the song of the sky.
This is the song of the tired—
the salmon panting as they swim up the swift current.
I walk around where the water runs into whirlpools.
They talk quickly, as if they are in a hurry.
The sky is turning over. They call me." 82.TS

*Refers to braided human hair used in fishing lines.

Chief's ceremonial vestment has beads and buttons in decorative halibut design on red cloth. Worn pendant down the back. 35.HA

Bibliography

Andrews, Ralph Warren. *Indian Primitive.* New York: Bonanza Books, 1960.

Barnett, Homer G. *The Coast Salish of British Columbia.* University of Oregon Studies in Anthropology, No. 4. University of Oregon, 1955.

Beresford, William. *A voyage round the world; but more particularly to the north-west coast of America:* . . . 2nd ed. London: G. Goulding, 1789.

Birch, Sir Arthur. "A letter from New Westminster." *Beaver,* Autumn (1976): 42.44.

Boas, Franz. "Ethnology of the Kwakiutl." *U.S. Bureau of American Ethnology, Annual Report* 35 (1921): 43-1481.

Boas, Franz. "The Kwakiutl of Vancouver Island." *American Museum of Natural History Memoirs* 8 (1909): 307-515.

Boas, Franz. *Primitive Art.* New York: Dover Publications, 1955.

Boas, Franz. *The Religion of the Kwakiutl Indians.* Part 2. Columbia University Contributions to Anthropology No. 10. New York: Columbia University Press, 1930.

Boas, Franz. "Tsimshian Mythology." *U.S. Bureau of American Ethnology, Annual Report* 31 (1916): 494-495.

Borden, Charles E. *Origins and Development of Early Northwest Coast Culture to about 3000 B.C.* Ottawa: National Museums of Canada, 1975.

British Columbia Provincial Museum. *Guide to anthropological collection in the Provincial Museum.* Victoria, B.C.: Printed by R. Wolfenden, 1909.

British Columbia. Department of Education. Division of Curriculum. *Coast Salish.* British Columbia Heritage Series, Volume 2, Victoria: 1952.

British Columbia. Department of Education. Division of Curriculum. *Haida.* British Columbia Heritage Series, Volume 2, Victoria: 1952.

Carl, George C. *Marine Fishes of B.C.* Victoria: British Columbia Provincial Museum, 1971.

Cook, James. *The journals of Captain James Cook on his voyages of discovery.* Edited by J. C. Beaglehole. Vol. 3 parts 1 and 2, The Voyage of the Resolution and Discovery 1776-1780. Cambridge: Published for the Hakluyt Society at the University Press, 1967.

Cook, James. *A Voyage to the Pacific Ocean* . . . 2nd ed. London: Printed by H. Huges for C. Nicol, 1785.

Drucker, Philip. *Indians of the Northwest Coast.* Garden City, N.J.: History Press, 1963.

Drucker, Philip. "The Northern and Central Nootkan Tribes." *U.S. Bureau of American Ethnology, Bulletin,* 144 (1951): 1-490.

Duff, Wilson. *Images: Stone: BC.* Saanichton, B.C.: Hancock House, 1975.

Duff, Wilson. *The Upper Stalo Indians of the Fraser Valley, British Columbia.* Anthropology in British Columbia. Memoir No. 1. Victoria: British Columbia Provincial Museum, Department of Education, 1953.

Garfield, Viola E. *The Tsimshian: Their arts and their music.* New York: J. J. Augustin, 1951.

Goddard, Pliny E. *Indians of the Northwest Coast.* New York: American Museum Press, 1945.

Gunther, Erna. "An Analysis of the First Salmon Ceremony." *American Anthropologist,* N.S., 28 (1926): 605-617.

Gunther, Erna. "A Further Analysis of the First Salmon Ceremony." *Washington University. Publications in Anthropology,* 2 (1928): 129-173.

Gunther, Erna. *Art in the Life of the Northwest Coast Indians.* Seattle: Superior, 1966.

Gunther, Erna. *Indian life on the northwest coast of North America.* Chicago: University of Chicago Press, 1972.

Haig-Brown, Roderick. *The Salmon.* Ottawa: Environment Canada, Fisheries and Marine Service, 1974.

Harner, Michael J. *Art of the Northwest Coast.* Berkeley: University of California, 1965.

Hart, John Lawson. *Pacific Fishes of Canada.* Ottawa: Fisheries Research Board of Canada, 1973.

Hawthorn, Audrey. *People of the potlatch; native arts and culture of the Pacific northwest coast.* Vancouver Art Gallery with the University of B.C., 1956.

Hawthorn, Audrey. *Art of the Kwakiutl Indians and other Northwest Coast Tribes.* Vancouver: University of British Columbia, 1967.

Hill, Beth, and Hill, Ray. *Indian Petroglyphs of the Pacific Northwest.* Saanichton: Hancock House, 1974.

Hobler, Philip M. "Archaeological Survey and Excavations in the Vicinity of Bella Coola." *B.C. Studies* No. 6-7 (1970): 77-94.

Holm, Bill, and Reid, William. *Form and Freedom.* Houston: Institute for the Arts, Rice University, 1975.

Indian Food, a cookbook of native foods from British Columbia. (sponsored by) Vancouver: Medical Services, Pacific Region, Health and Welfare Canada, 1974.

Inverarity, Robert Bruce. *Art of the Northwest Coast Indians.* Berkeley and Los Angeles: University of California Press, 1950.

Jenness, Diamond. *The Faith of a Coast Salish Indian.* Anthropology in B.C. Memoir No. 3. Victoria: British Columbia Provincial Museum, Department of Education, 1955.

Jewitt, John R. *The Adventures and Sufferings of John R. Jewitt, Captive Among the Nootka. 1803-1805. (from the Edinburgh 1824 edition).* Toronto: McClelland & Stewart, 1974.

Kennedy, Dorothy I.D., and Bouchard, Randy. "Utilization of Fishes, Beach Foods and Marine Animals by the Tl'uhus Indian People of B.C." Unpublished manuscript. Victoria: British Columbia Indian Language Project, 1974.

Kirk, Ruth. *David, Young Chief of the Quileutes, an American Indian today.* New York: Harcourt, Brace and World, 1967.

Kirk, Ruth, and Daugherty, Richard. *Hunters of the Whale; an adventure of northwest coast archaeology.* New York: Morrow, 1974.

Krause, Aurel. *The Tlingit Indians.* Translated by Erna Gunther. Seattle: University of Washington Press, 1956.

Lawrance, Scott. "Eulachon: Salvation." *Raincoast Chronicles* No. 5 (1975): 18-19.

Lawrance, Scott. "Halibut: Scenting Woman." *Raincoast Chronicles* No. 5 (1975): 31- 32.

Lord, John K. *A Naturalist in Vancouver Island and British Columbia.* London: R. Bently, 1866.

McDonald, Archibald. Journal of the Voyage from Fort Vancouver to Fraser's River and of the Establishment of Fort Langley commencing 27th June 1827 and carried up to the 17th February 1828 . . . Typescript based upon manuscript from Series C. No. 22, Bancroft Collection, University of California, Berkeley.

McIlwraith, Thomas F. *The Bella Coola Indians.* Toronto: University of Toronto Press, 1948.

Mathews, Major J.S. *Conversations with August Jack Khahtsahlano.* Unpublished manuscript. Vancouver: 1932-54.

Moser, Charles. *Reminiscences of the West Coast of Vancouver Island.* Victoria: Printed by Acme Press, 1926.

Niblack, Albert P. "The Coast Indians of Southern Alaska and Northern British Columbia." *U.S. National Museum, Annual Report,* 1888. Washington, 1890. p. 225-386.

Pomoroy, Anthony. *Stone Fish Traps of the Bella Bella.* Current Research Reports. Burnaby, B.C.: Simon Fraser University, 1976.

Scagel, Robert F. *Guide to Common Seaweeds of British Columbia.* Victoria: A. Sutton, Printer to the Queen, 1967.

Stewart, Hilary. *Artifacts of the Northwest Coast Indians.* Saanichton, B.C.: Hancock House, 1973.

Suttles, Wayne. *Katzie Ethnographic Notes.* Anthropology in B.C. Memoir No. 2. Victoria: British Columbia Provincial Museum; Department of Education, 1956.

Suttles, Wayne. *The Economic Life of the Coast Salish of Haro and Rosario Straits.* New York: Garland, 1974.

Swanton, J.R. "Haida texts and myths." U.S. Bureau of American Ethnology, Bulletin 29 (1904) 1-448.

Underhill, Ruth. *Indians of the Pacific Northwest.* Riverside, California: Sherman Institute Press, 1945.

Vancouver, George. *A voyage of discovery of the North Pacific ocean, and round the world; . . .* London, Printed for G.G. and J. Robinson (etc.) 1798.

Waterman, T.T. *Notes on the Ethnology of the Indians of Puget Sound.* New York: M.A.I., 1973.

Whatcom Museum of History and Art. *Arts of a Vanished Era.* Bellingham, Wash., 1968.

Index